X-FACTOR
LIFE & DEATH MATTERS

Writer: **PETER DAVID**

Art: **ARIEL OLIVETTI (Issue #7),
DENNIS CALERO (Issues #8-9) &
RENATO ARLEM** with **ROY ALLEN MARTINEZ
(Issues #10-12)**

Color Art: **JOSE VILLARRUBIA**

Letters: **VIRTUAL CALLIGRAPHY'S CORY PETIT**
Cover Art: **RYAN SOOK WITH JOSE VILLARRUBIA**
Assistant Editors: **MOLLY LAZER & AUBREY SITTERSON**
Editor: **ANDY SCHMIDT**

Collection Editor: **JENNIFER GRÜNWALD**
Assistant Editor: **MICHAEL SHORT**
Associate Editor: **MARK D. BEAZLEY**
Senior Editor, Special Projects: **JEFF YOUNGQUIST**
Vice President of Sales: **DAVID GABRIEL**
Production: **JERRON QUALITY COLOR**
Vice President of Creative: **TOM MARVELLI**

Editor in Chief: **JOE QUESADA**
Publisher: **DAN BUCKLEY**

PREVIOUSLY:

Although matters have settled down somewhat in Mutant Town after the events of the Decimation, The X-Factor Detective Agency is still no closer to determining the reasons behind the disempowering of ninety percent of the world's mutants.

In addition to dealing with that frustration, X-Factor was reeling over Siryn's being accosted and beaten nearly to death. While Siryn is on the mend, Guido and Jamie Madrox confronted Damian Tryp, Junior — co-owner of Singularity Investigations, and their chief suspect in Siryn's assault. The encounter ended inconclusively, although Tryp, Junior was, in fact, responsible for the assault.

Meanwhile, X-Factor learned some of Layla Miller's background, including that she is an orphan, and took her in on a semi-permanent and somewhat unofficial basis. What they don't know is that the "facts" they've learned are at odds with what she's told the X-Men, or that Layla was deeply involved in the Decimation. Rictor, however, remains suspicious of the newly nicknamed "Butterfly" and is keeping a wary eye on her.

X-FACTOR: LIFE AND DEATH MATTERS. Contains material originally published in magazine form as X-FACTOR #7-12. First printing 2007. ISBN# 0-7851-2623-6. Published by MARVEL PUBLISH INC., a subsidiary of MARVEL ENTERTAINMENT, INC. OFFICE OF PUBLICATION: 417 5th Avenue, New York, NY 10016. Copyright © 2006 and 2007 Marvel Characters, Inc. All rights reserved. $1 per copy in the U.S. and $32.00 in Canada (GST #R127032852); Canadian Agreement #40668537. All characters featured in this issue and the distinctive names and likenesses thereof, and all re indicia are trademarks of Marvel Characters, Inc. No similarity between any of the names, characters, persons, and/or institutions in this magazine with those of any living or dead person or institut intended, and any such similarity which may exist is purely coincidental. **Printed in the U.S.A.** ALAN FINE, President & CEO Of Marvel Toys and Marvel Publishing, Inc.; DAVID BOGART, VP Of Publis Operations; DAN CARR, Executive Director of Publishing Technology; JUSTIN F. GABRIE, Managing Editor; STAN LEE, Chairman Emeritus. For information regarding advertising in Marvel Comics

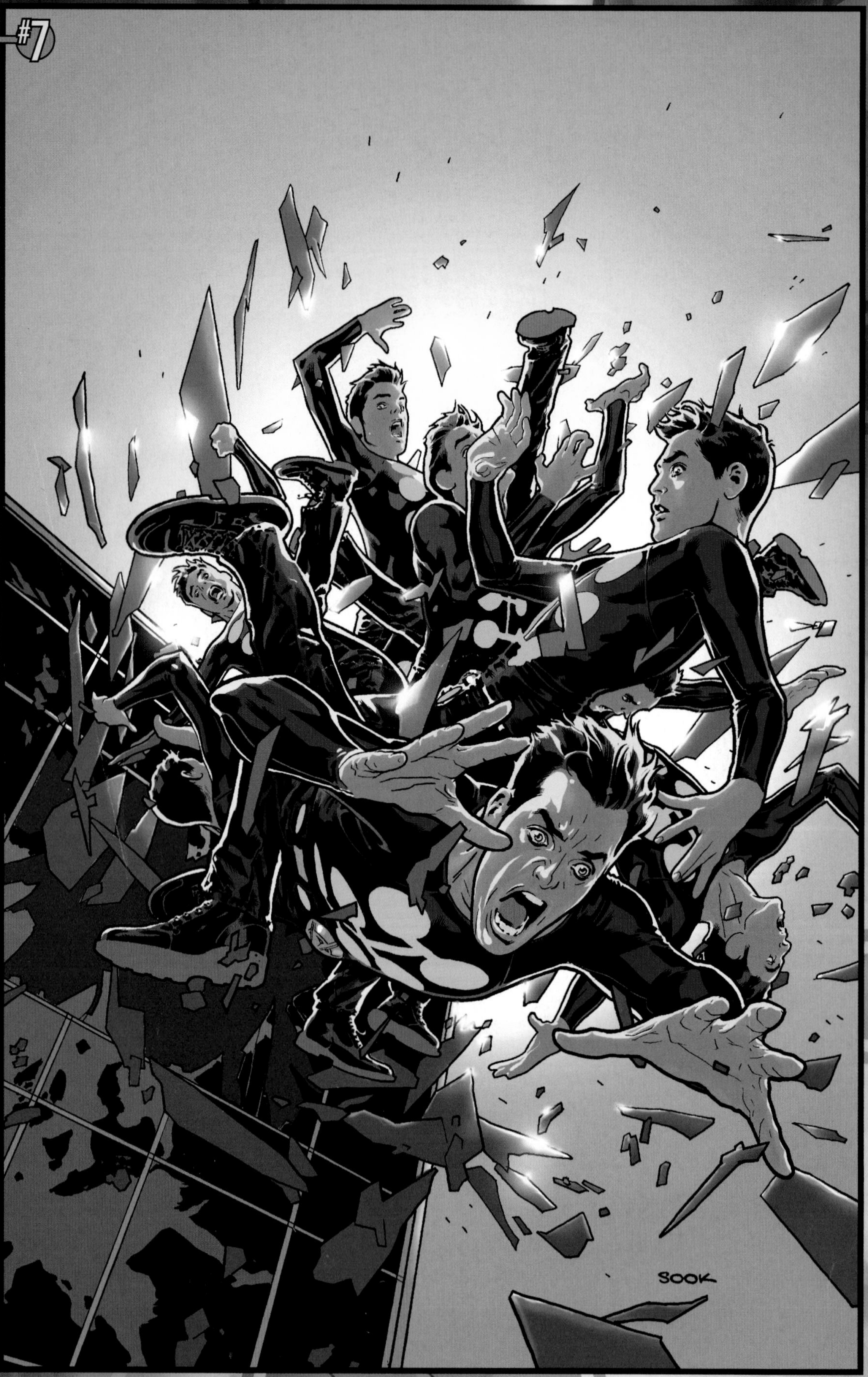
#7
SOOK

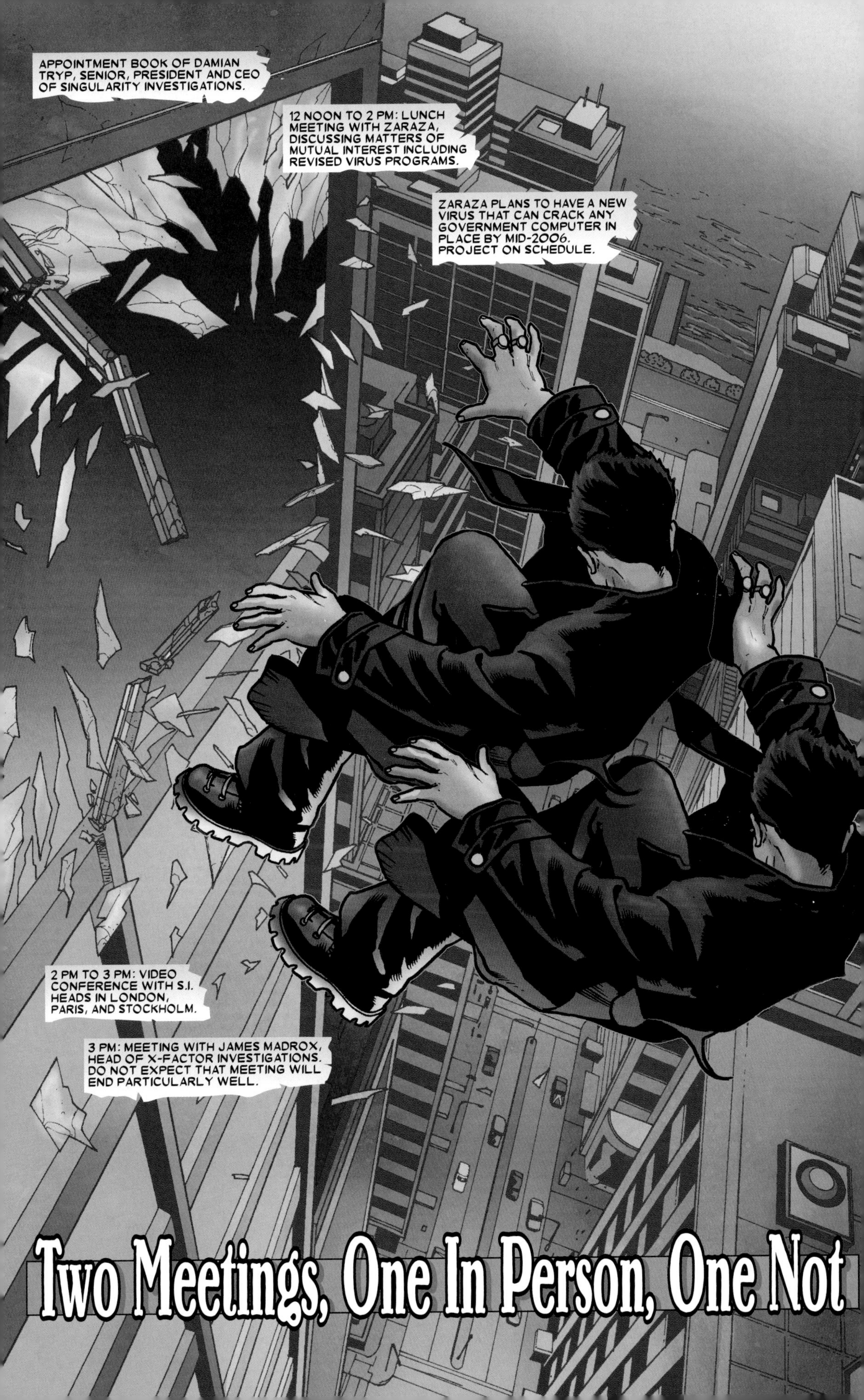
APPOINTMENT BOOK OF DAMIAN TRYP, SENIOR, PRESIDENT AND CEO OF SINGULARITY INVESTIGATIONS.
12 NOON TO 2 PM: LUNCH MEETING WITH ZARAZA, DISCUSSING MATTERS OF MUTUAL INTEREST INCLUDING REVISED VIRUS PROGRAMS.
ZARAZA PLANS TO HAVE A NEW VIRUS THAT CAN CRACK ANY GOVERNMENT COMPUTER IN PLACE BY MID-2006. PROJECT ON SCHEDULE.
2 PM TO 3 PM: VIDEO CONFERENCE WITH S.I. HEADS IN LONDON, PARIS, AND STOCKHOLM.
3 PM: MEETING WITH JAMES MADROX, HEAD OF X-FACTOR INVESTIGATIONS. DO NOT EXPECT THAT MEETING WILL END PARTICULARLY WELL.
Two Meetings, One In Person, One Not

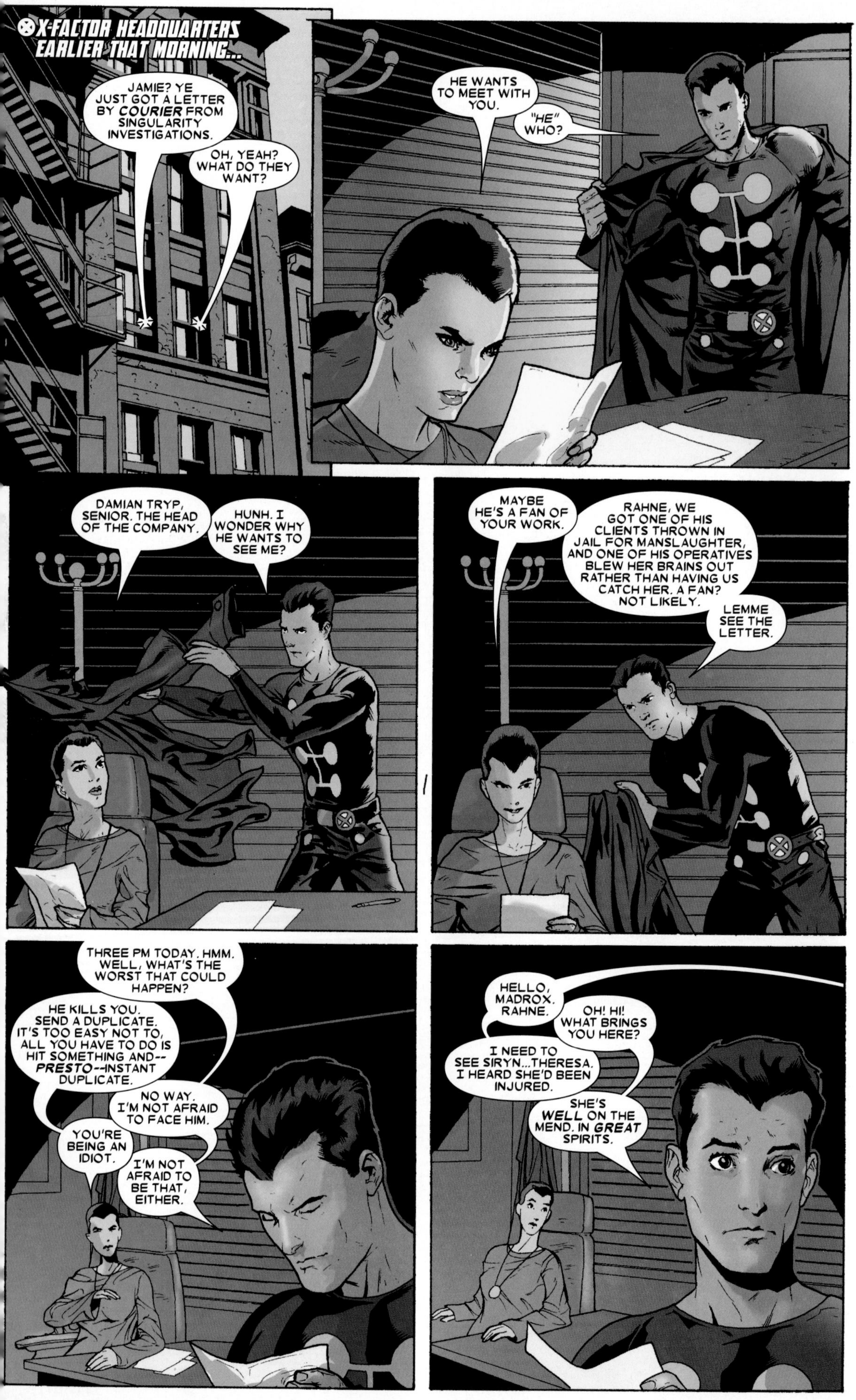
X-FACTOR HEADQUARTERS EARLIER THAT MORNING...
JAMIE? YE JUST GOT A LETTER BY COURIER FROM SINGULARITY INVESTIGATIONS.
OH, YEAH? WHAT DO THEY WANT?
HE WANTS TO MEET WITH YOU.
"HE" WHO?
DAMIAN TRYP, SENIOR. THE HEAD OF THE COMPANY.
HUNH. I WONDER WHY HE WANTS TO SEE ME?
MAYBE HE'S A FAN OF YOUR WORK.
RAHNE, WE GOT ONE OF HIS CLIENTS THROWN IN JAIL FOR MANSLAUGHTER, AND ONE OF HIS OPERATIVES BLEW HER BRAINS OUT RATHER THAN HAVING US CATCH HER. A FAN? NOT LIKELY.
LEMME SEE THE LETTER.
THREE PM TODAY. HMM. WELL, WHAT'S THE WORST THAT COULD HAPPEN?
HE KILLS YOU. SEND A DUPLICATE. IT'S TOO EASY NOT TO, ALL YOU HAVE TO DO IS HIT SOMETHING AND--PRESTO--INSTANT DUPLICATE.
NO WAY. I'M NOT AFRAID TO FACE HIM.
YOU'RE BEING AN IDIOT.
I'M NOT AFRAID TO BE THAT, EITHER.
HELLO, MADROX. RAHNE.
OH! HI! WHAT BRINGS YOU HERE?
I NEED TO SEE SIRYN...THERESA. I HEARD SHE'D BEEN INJURED.
SHE'S WELL ON THE MEND. IN GREAT SPIRITS.

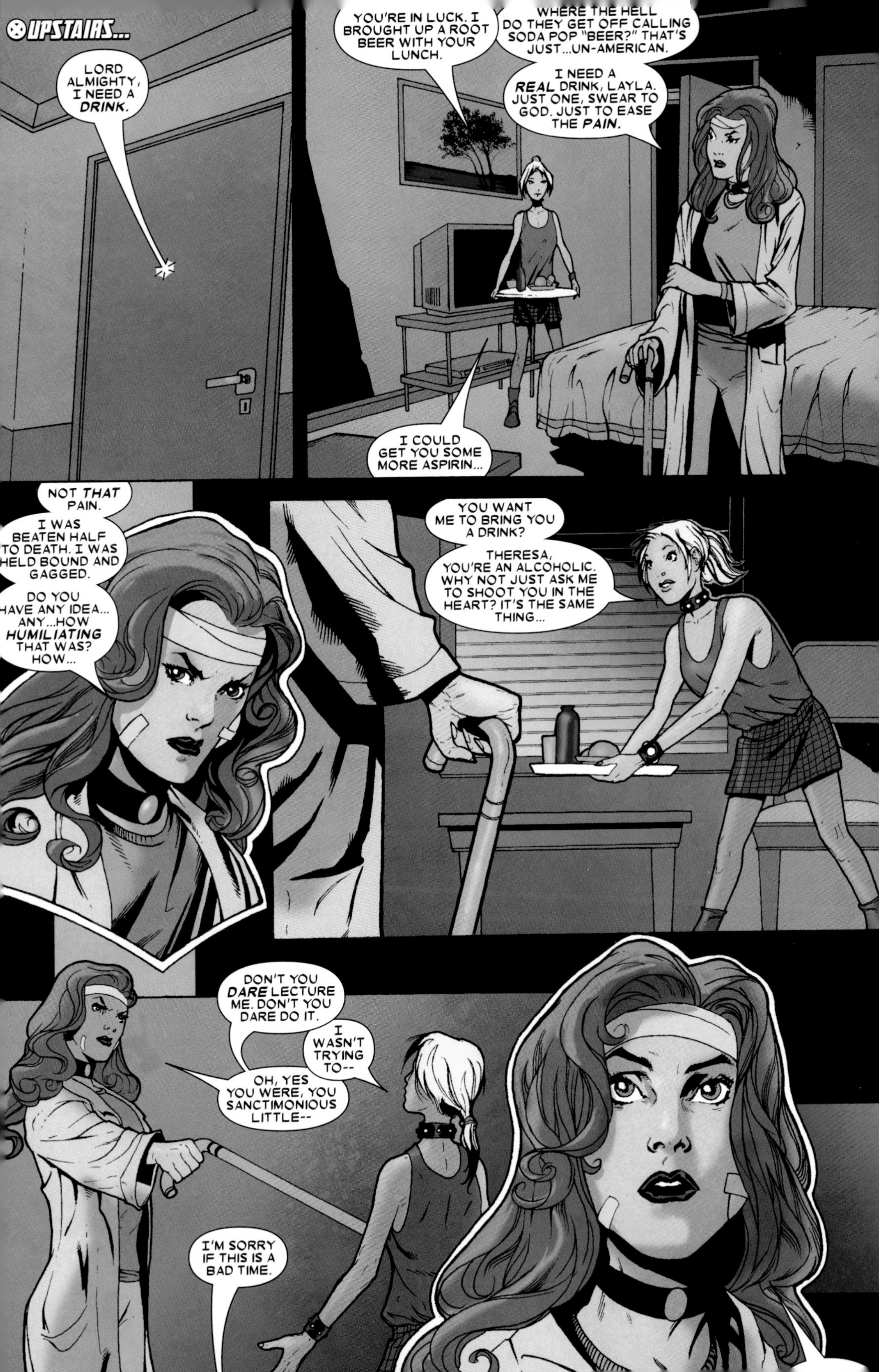

UPSTAIRS...
LORD ALMIGHTY, I NEED A DRINK.
YOU'RE IN LUCK. I BROUGHT UP A ROOT BEER WITH YOUR LUNCH.
WHERE THE HELL DO THEY GET OFF CALLING SODA POP "BEER?" THAT'S JUST...UN-AMERICAN.
I NEED A REAL DRINK, LAYLA. JUST ONE, SWEAR TO GOD. JUST TO EASE THE PAIN.
I COULD GET YOU SOME MORE ASPIRIN...
NOT THAT PAIN.
I WAS BEATEN HALF TO DEATH. I WAS HELD BOUND AND GAGGED.
DO YOU HAVE ANY IDEA... ANY...HOW HUMILIATING THAT WAS? HOW...
YOU WANT ME TO BRING YOU A DRINK?
THERESA, YOU'RE AN ALCOHOLIC. WHY NOT JUST ASK ME TO SHOOT YOU IN THE HEART? IT'S THE SAME THING...
DON'T YOU DARE LECTURE ME. DON'T YOU DARE DO IT.
I WASN'T TRYING TO--
OH, YES YOU WERE, YOU SANCTIMONIOUS LITTLE--
I'M SORRY IF THIS IS A BAD TIME.

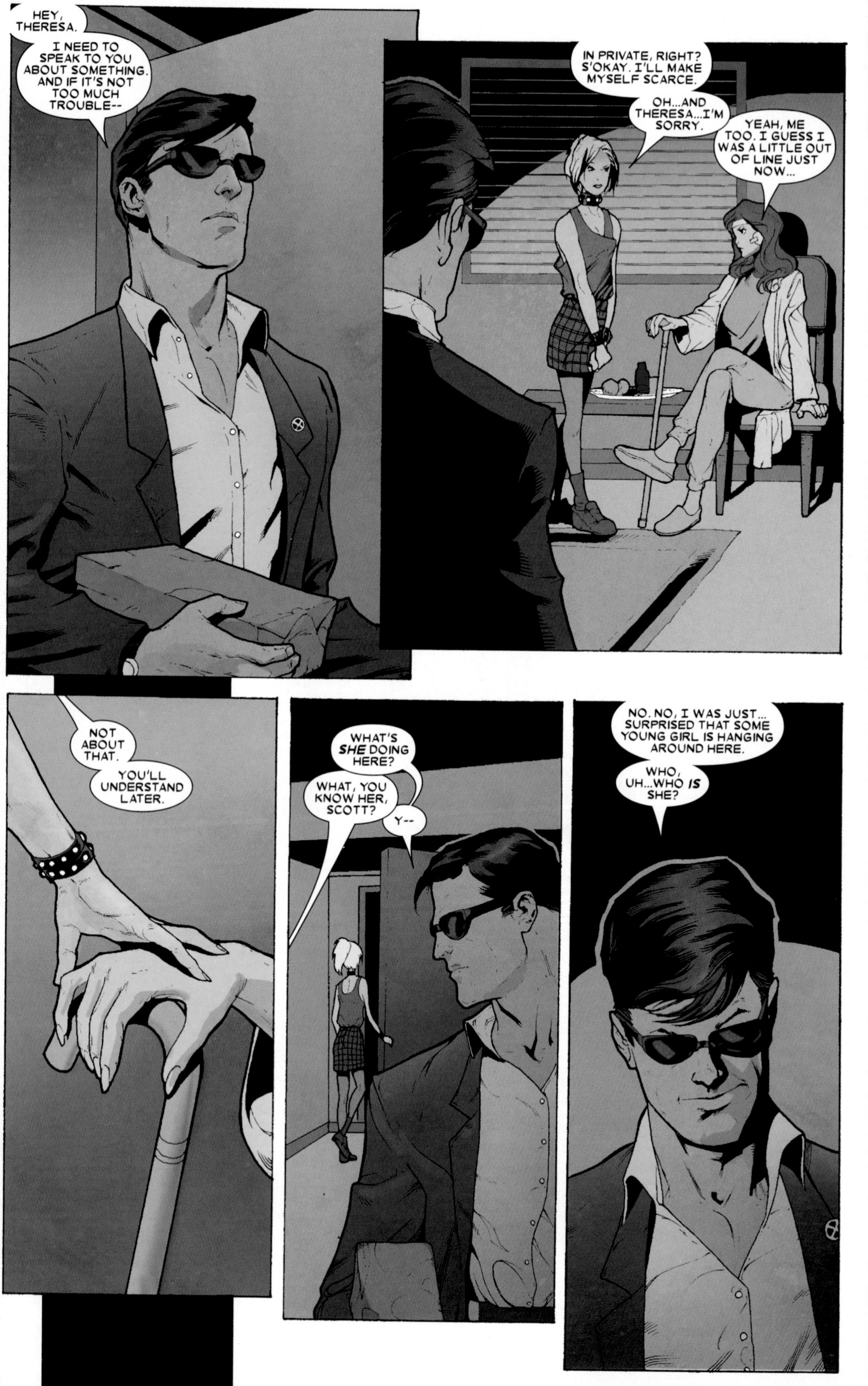
HEY, THERESA.
I NEED TO SPEAK TO YOU ABOUT SOMETHING. AND IF IT'S NOT TOO MUCH TROUBLE--
IN PRIVATE, RIGHT? S'OKAY. I'LL MAKE MYSELF SCARCE.
OH...AND THERESA...I'M SORRY.
YEAH, ME TOO. I GUESS I WAS A LITTLE OUT OF LINE JUST NOW...
NOT ABOUT THAT.
YOU'LL UNDERSTAND LATER.
WHAT'S *SHE* DOING HERE?
WHAT, YOU KNOW HER, SCOTT?
Y--
NO. NO, I WAS JUST... SURPRISED THAT SOME YOUNG GIRL IS HANGING AROUND HERE.
WHO, UH...WHO *IS* SHE?

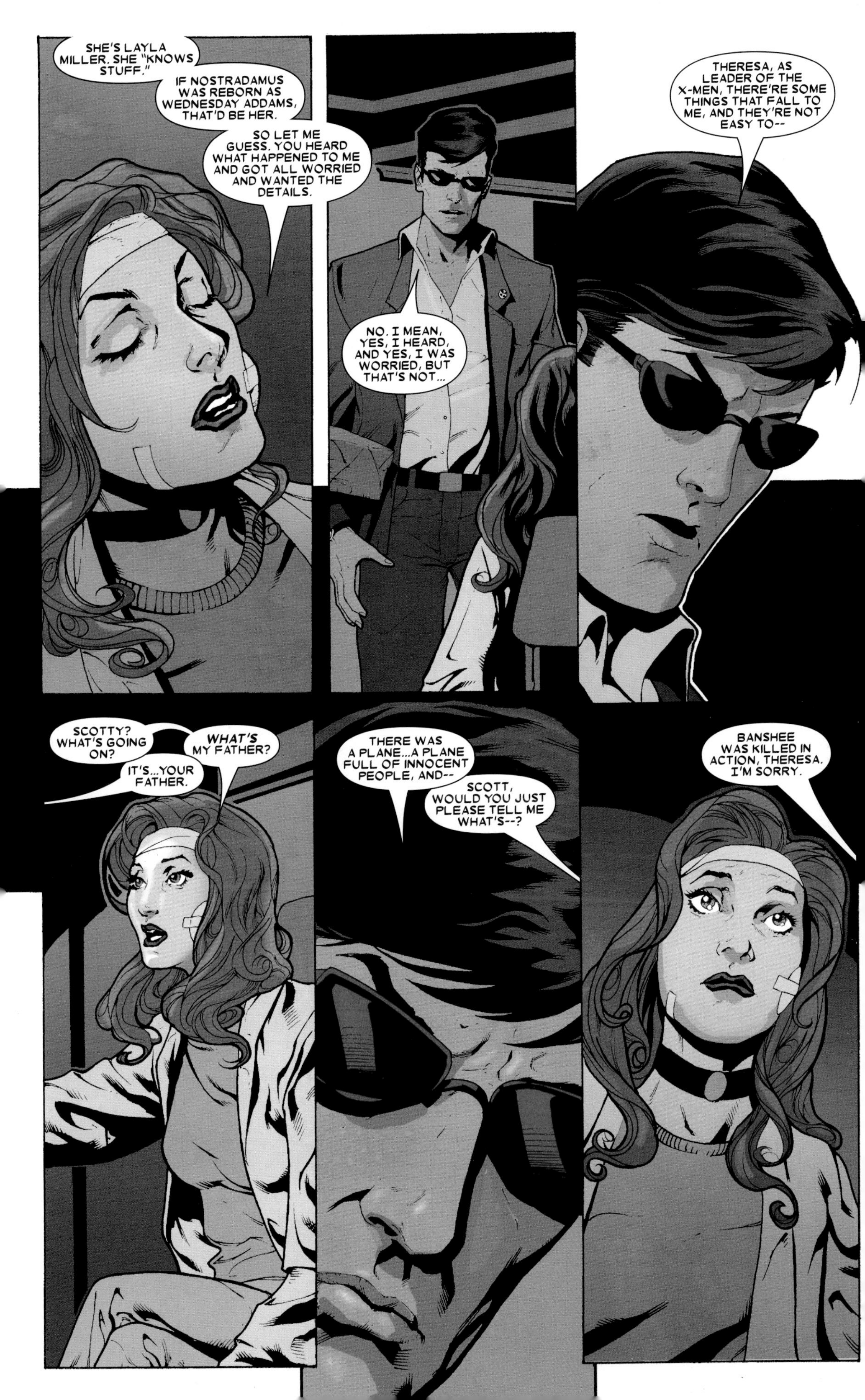
SHE'S LAYLA MILLER. SHE "KNOWS STUFF."
IF NOSTRADAMUS WAS REBORN AS WEDNESDAY ADDAMS, THAT'D BE HER.
SO LET ME GUESS. YOU HEARD WHAT HAPPENED TO ME AND GOT ALL WORRIED AND WANTED THE DETAILS.
NO. I MEAN, YES, I HEARD, AND YES, I WAS WORRIED, BUT THAT'S NOT...
THERESA, AS LEADER OF THE X-MEN, THERE'RE SOME THINGS THAT FALL TO ME, AND THEY'RE NOT EASY TO--
SCOTTY? WHAT'S GOING ON?
IT'S...YOUR FATHER.
WHAT'S MY FATHER?
THERE WAS A PLANE...A PLANE FULL OF INNOCENT PEOPLE, AND--
SCOTT, WOULD YOU JUST PLEASE TELL ME WHAT'S--?
BANSHEE WAS KILLED IN ACTION, THERESA. I'M SORRY.

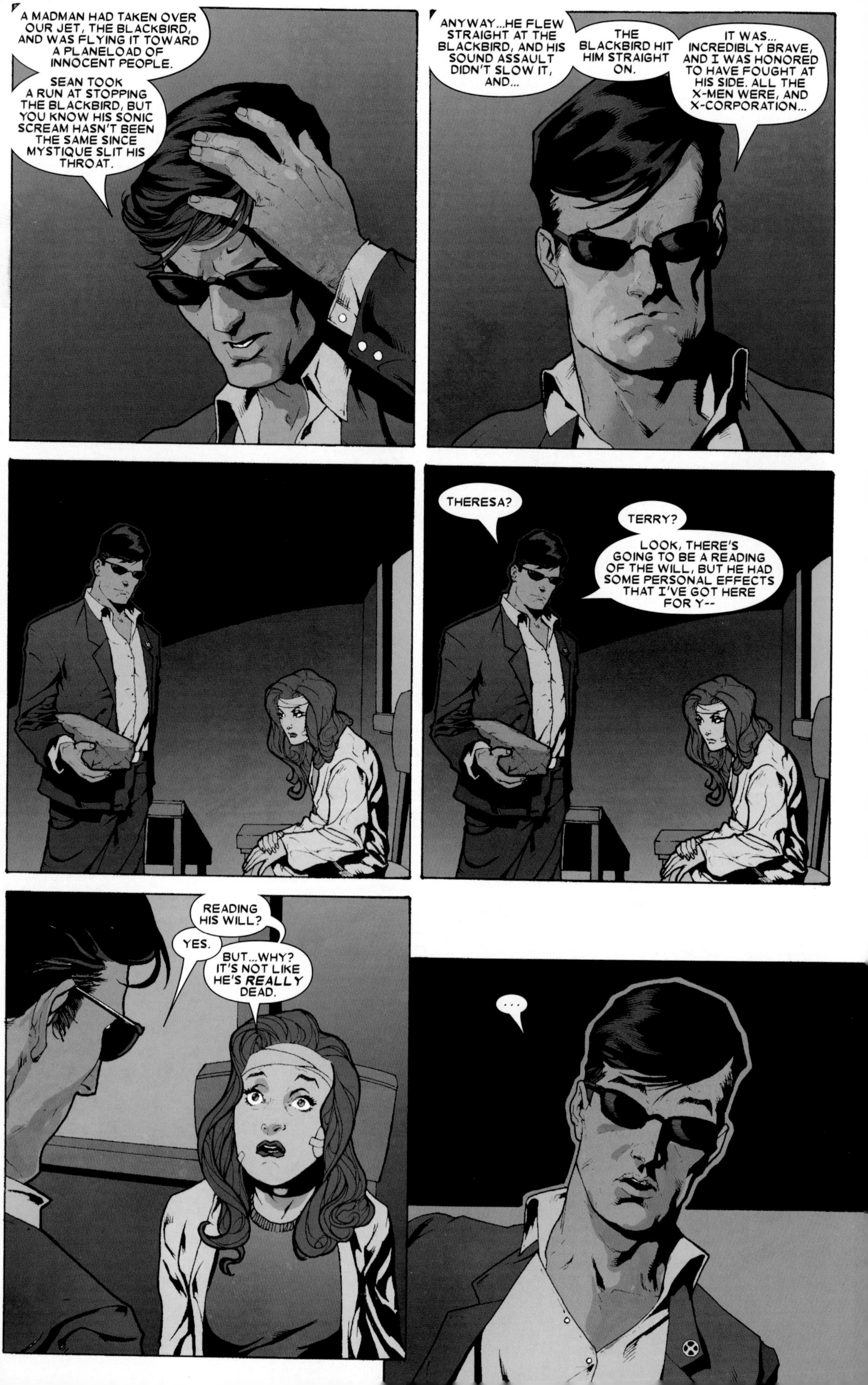
A MADMAN HAD TAKEN OVER OUR JET, THE BLACKBIRD, AND WAS FLYING IT TOWARD A PLANELOAD OF INNOCENT PEOPLE.
SEAN TOOK A RUN AT STOPPING THE BLACKBIRD, BUT YOU KNOW HIS SONIC SCREAM HASN'T BEEN THE SAME SINCE MYSTIQUE SLIT HIS THROAT.
ANYWAY...HE FLEW STRAIGHT AT THE BLACKBIRD, AND HIS SOUND ASSAULT DIDN'T SLOW IT, AND...
THE BLACKBIRD HIT HIM STRAIGHT ON.
IT WAS... INCREDIBLY BRAVE, AND I WAS HONORED TO HAVE FOUGHT AT HIS SIDE. ALL THE X-MEN WERE, AND X-CORPORATION...
THERESA?
TERRY?
LOOK, THERE'S GOING TO BE A READING OF THE WILL, BUT HE HAD SOME PERSONAL EFFECTS THAT I'VE GOT HERE FOR Y--
READING HIS WILL?
YES.
BUT...WHY? IT'S NOT LIKE HE'S *REALLY* DEAD.
...

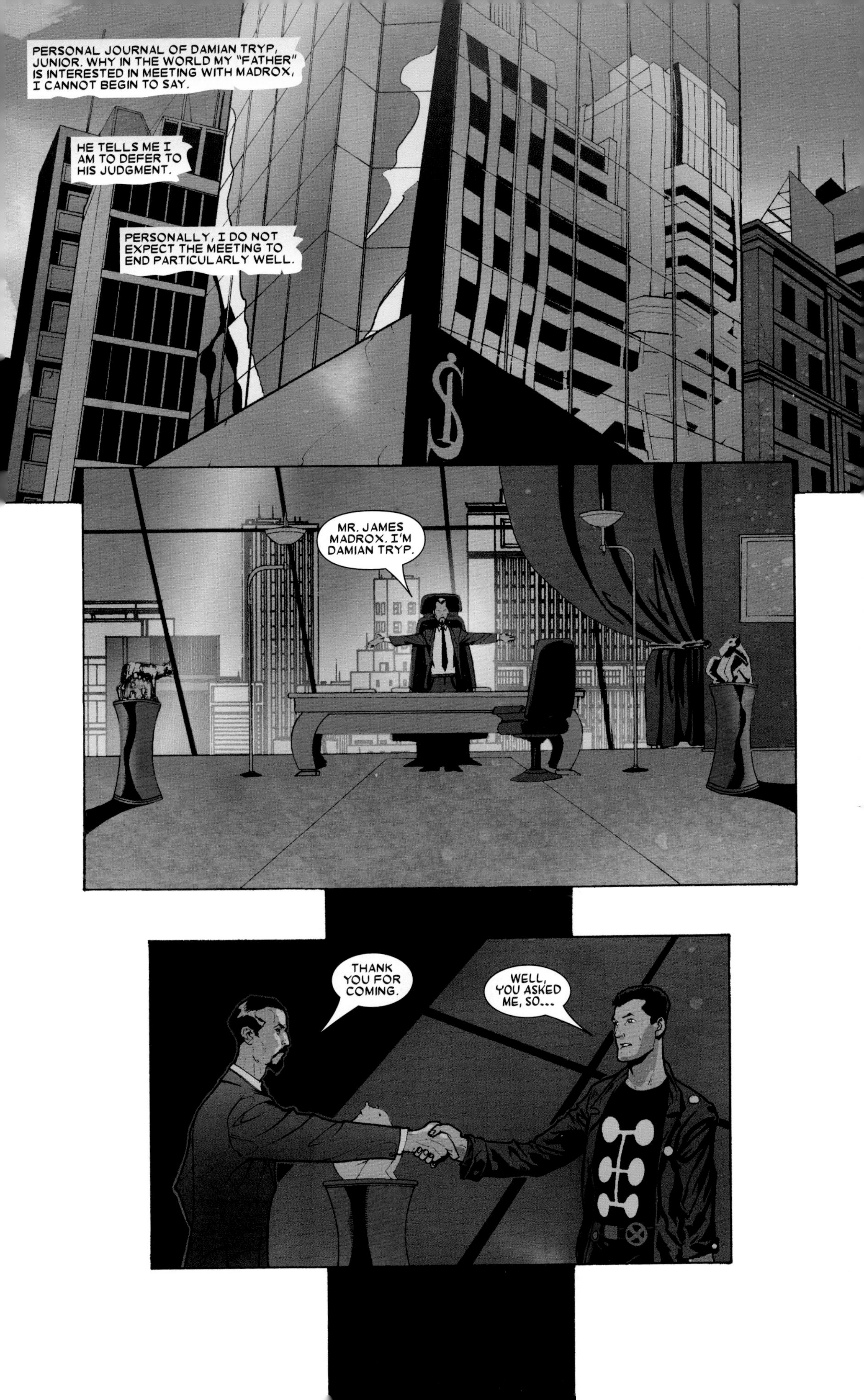
PERSONAL JOURNAL OF DAMIAN TRYP, JUNIOR. WHY IN THE WORLD MY "FATHER" IS INTERESTED IN MEETING WITH MADROX, I CANNOT BEGIN TO SAY.
HE TELLS ME I AM TO DEFER TO HIS JUDGMENT.
PERSONALLY, I DO NOT EXPECT THE MEETING TO END PARTICULARLY WELL.
MR. JAMES MADROX. I'M DAMIAN TRYP.
THANK YOU FOR COMING.
WELL, YOU ASKED ME, SO...

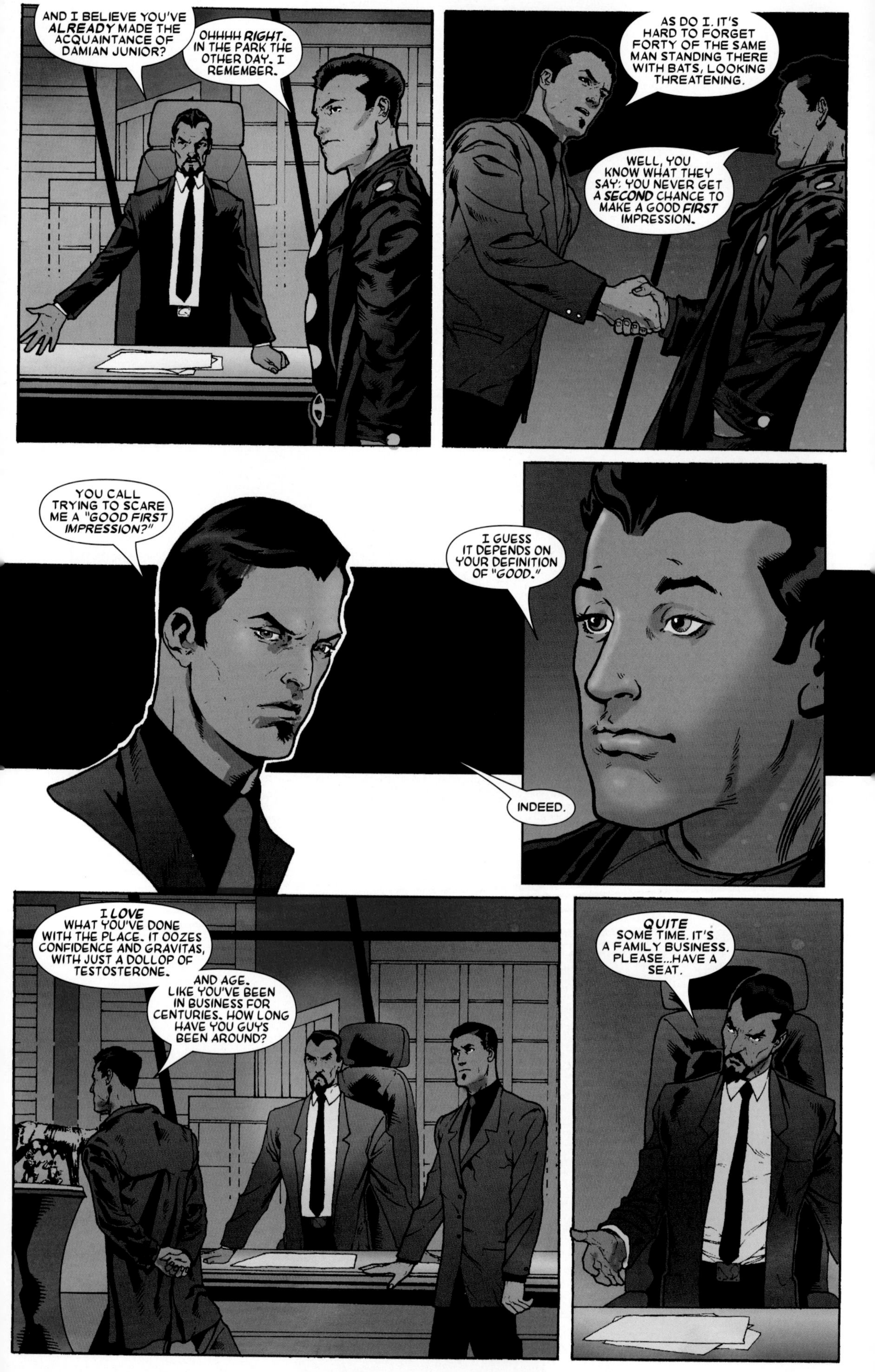

AND I BELIEVE YOU'VE ALREADY MADE THE ACQUAINTANCE OF DAMIAN JUNIOR?
OHHHH RIGHT. IN THE PARK THE OTHER DAY. I REMEMBER.
AS DO I. IT'S HARD TO FORGET FORTY OF THE SAME MAN STANDING THERE WITH BATS, LOOKING THREATENING.
WELL, YOU KNOW WHAT THEY SAY: YOU NEVER GET A SECOND CHANCE TO MAKE A GOOD FIRST IMPRESSION.
YOU CALL TRYING TO SCARE ME A "GOOD FIRST IMPRESSION?"
I GUESS IT DEPENDS ON YOUR DEFINITION OF "GOOD."
INDEED.
I LOVE WHAT YOU'VE DONE WITH THE PLACE. IT OOZES CONFIDENCE AND GRAVITAS, WITH JUST A DOLLOP OF TESTOSTERONE.
AND AGE. LIKE YOU'VE BEEN IN BUSINESS FOR CENTURIES. HOW LONG HAVE YOU GUYS BEEN AROUND?
QUITE SOME TIME. IT'S A FAMILY BUSINESS. PLEASE...HAVE A SEAT.

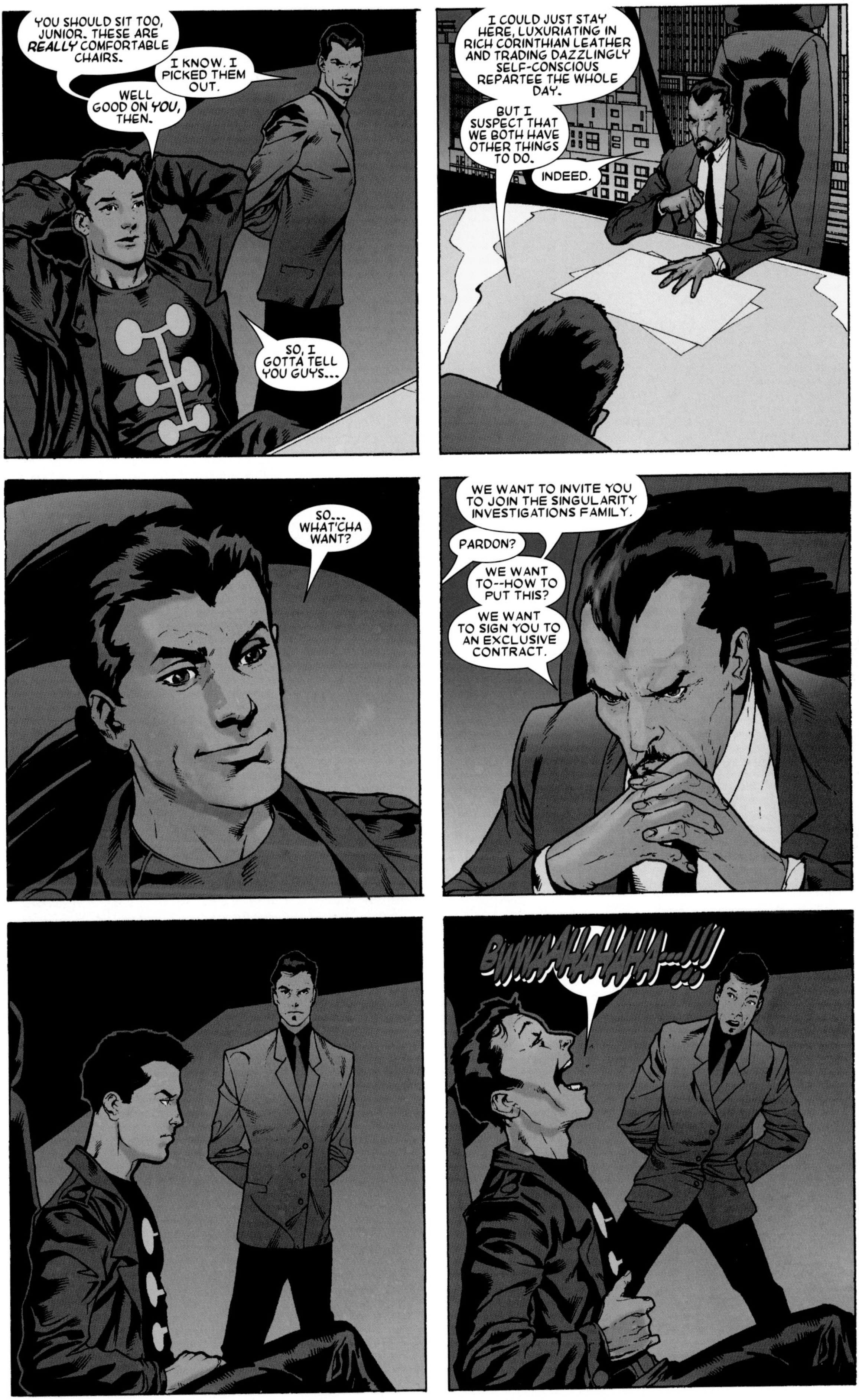
YOU SHOULD SIT TOO, JUNIOR. THESE ARE *REALLY* COMFORTABLE CHAIRS.
I KNOW. I PICKED THEM OUT.
WELL GOOD ON *YOU*, THEN.
SO, I GOTTA TELL YOU GUYS...
I COULD JUST STAY HERE, LUXURIATING IN RICH CORINTHIAN LEATHER AND TRADING DAZZLINGLY SELF-CONSCIOUS REPARTEE THE WHOLE DAY.
BUT I SUSPECT THAT WE BOTH HAVE OTHER THINGS TO DO.
INDEED.
SO... WHAT'CHA WANT?
WE WANT TO INVITE YOU TO JOIN THE SINGULARITY INVESTIGATIONS FAMILY.
PARDON?
WE WANT TO--HOW TO PUT THIS?
WE WANT TO SIGN YOU TO AN EXCLUSIVE CONTRACT.
BWWAHAHAHAHA...!!!

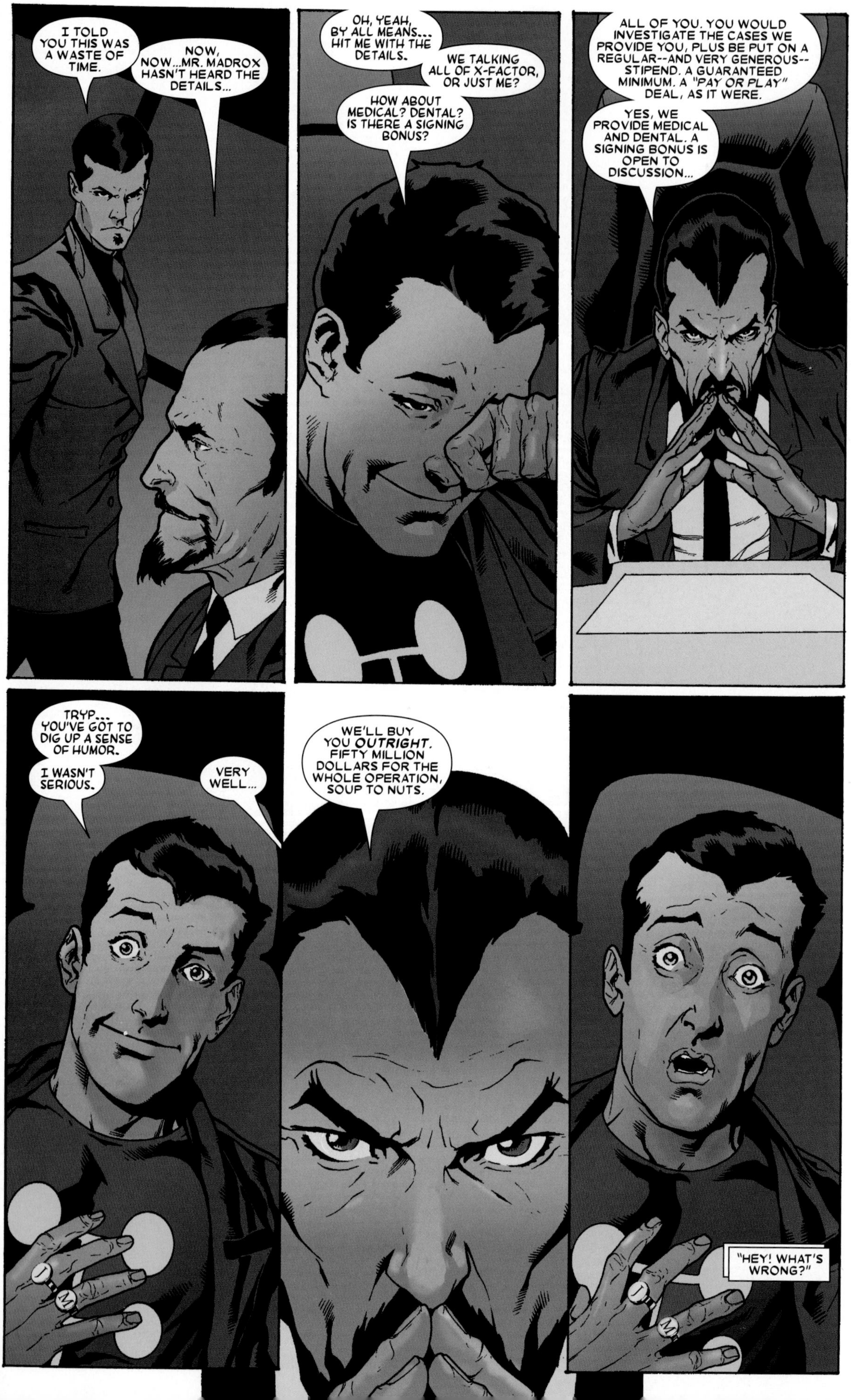
I TOLD YOU THIS WAS A WASTE OF TIME.
NOW, NOW...MR. MADROX HASN'T HEARD THE DETAILS...
OH, YEAH, BY ALL MEANS... HIT ME WITH THE DETAILS.
WE TALKING ALL OF X-FACTOR, OR JUST ME?
HOW ABOUT MEDICAL? DENTAL? IS THERE A SIGNING BONUS?
ALL OF YOU. YOU WOULD INVESTIGATE THE CASES WE PROVIDE YOU, PLUS BE PUT ON A REGULAR--AND VERY GENEROUS--STIPEND. A GUARANTEED MINIMUM. A "PAY OR PLAY" DEAL, AS IT WERE.
YES, WE PROVIDE MEDICAL AND DENTAL. A SIGNING BONUS IS OPEN TO DISCUSSION...
TRYP... YOU'VE GOT TO DIG UP A SENSE OF HUMOR.
I WASN'T SERIOUS.
VERY WELL...
WE'LL BUY YOU OUTRIGHT. FIFTY MILLION DOLLARS FOR THE WHOLE OPERATION, SOUP TO NUTS.
"HEY! WHAT'S WRONG?"

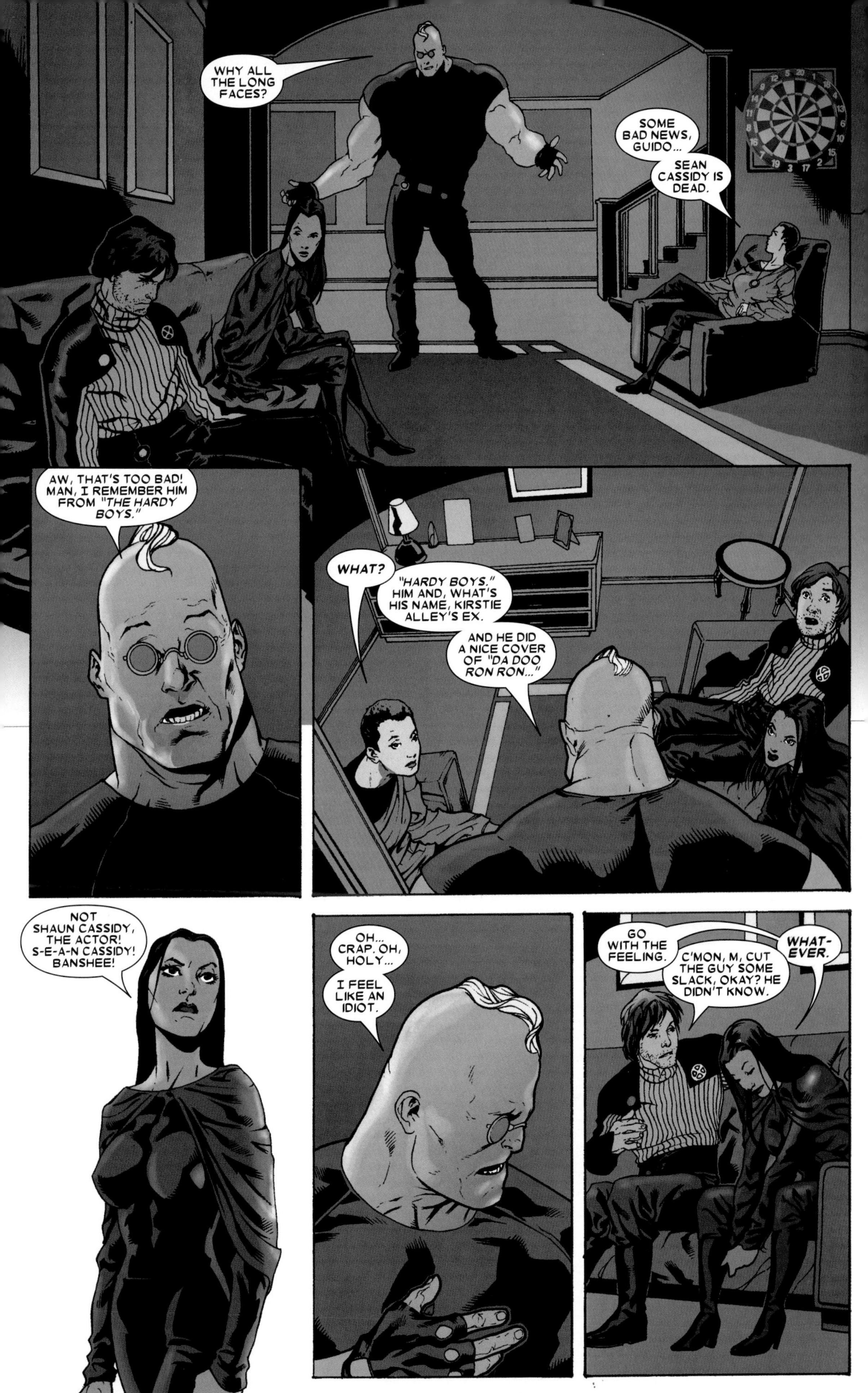

WHY ALL THE LONG FACES?
SOME BAD NEWS, GUIDO...
SEAN CASSIDY IS DEAD.
AW, THAT'S TOO BAD! MAN, I REMEMBER HIM FROM "THE HARDY BOYS."
WHAT?
"HARDY BOYS." HIM AND, WHAT'S HIS NAME, KIRSTIE ALLEY'S EX.
AND HE DID A NICE COVER OF "DA DOO RON RON..."
NOT SHAUN CASSIDY, THE ACTOR! S-E-A-N CASSIDY! BANSHEE!
OH... CRAP. OH, HOLY...
I FEEL LIKE AN IDIOT.
GO WITH THE FEELING.
C'MON, M, CUT THE GUY SOME SLACK, OKAY? HE DIDN'T KNOW.
WHAT-EVER.

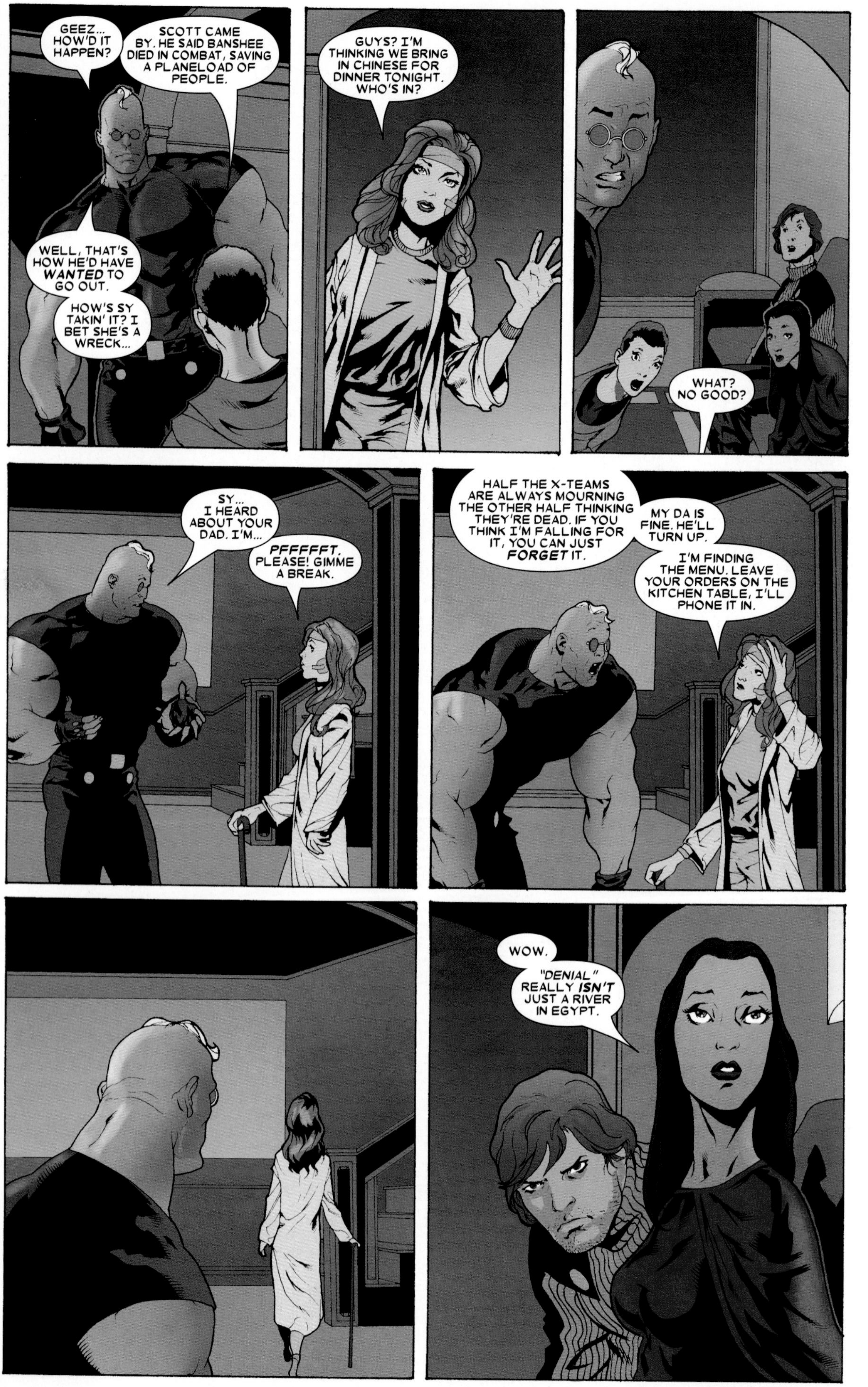
GEEZ... HOW'D IT HAPPEN?
SCOTT CAME BY. HE SAID BANSHEE DIED IN COMBAT, SAVING A PLANELOAD OF PEOPLE.
WELL, THAT'S HOW HE'D HAVE *WANTED* TO GO OUT.
HOW'S SY TAKIN' IT? I BET SHE'S A WRECK...
GUYS? I'M THINKING WE BRING IN CHINESE FOR DINNER TONIGHT. WHO'S IN?
WHAT? NO GOOD?
SY... I HEARD ABOUT YOUR DAD. I'M...
PFFFFFT. PLEASE! GIMME A BREAK.
HALF THE X-TEAMS ARE ALWAYS MOURNING THE OTHER HALF THINKING THEY'RE DEAD. IF YOU THINK I'M FALLING FOR IT, YOU CAN JUST *FORGET* IT.
MY DA IS FINE. HE'LL TURN UP.
I'M FINDING THE MENU. LEAVE YOUR ORDERS ON THE KITCHEN TABLE, I'LL PHONE IT IN.
WOW.
"*DENIAL*" REALLY *ISN'T* JUST A RIVER IN EGYPT.

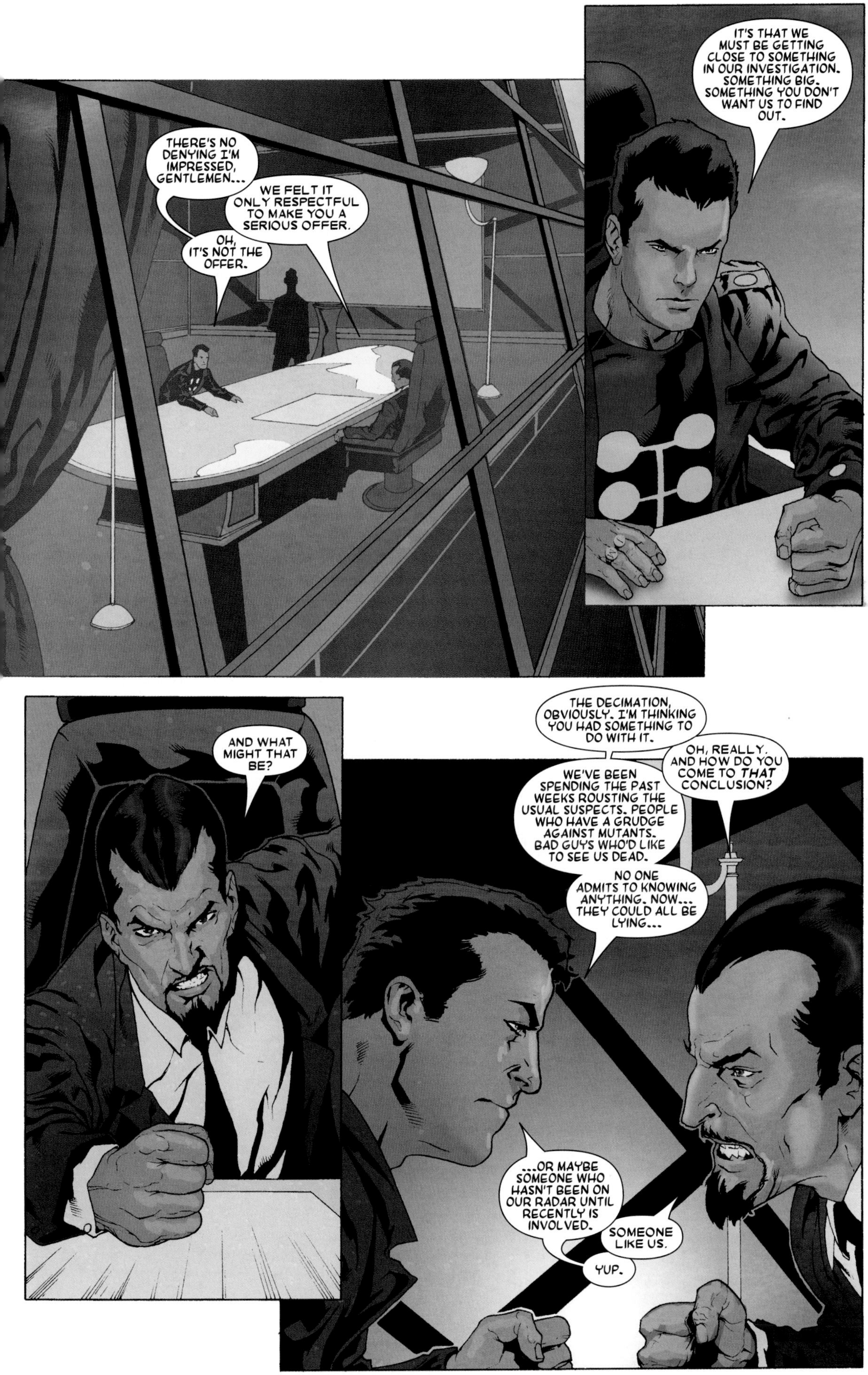
THERE'S NO DENYING I'M IMPRESSED, GENTLEMEN...
WE FELT IT ONLY RESPECTFUL TO MAKE YOU A SERIOUS OFFER.
OH, IT'S NOT THE OFFER.
IT'S THAT WE MUST BE GETTING CLOSE TO SOMETHING IN OUR INVESTIGATION. SOMETHING BIG. SOMETHING YOU DON'T WANT US TO FIND OUT.
AND WHAT MIGHT THAT BE?
THE DECIMATION, OBVIOUSLY. I'M THINKING YOU HAD SOMETHING TO DO WITH IT.
OH, REALLY. AND HOW DO YOU COME TO THAT CONCLUSION?
WE'VE BEEN SPENDING THE PAST WEEKS ROUSTING THE USUAL SUSPECTS. PEOPLE WHO HAVE A GRUDGE AGAINST MUTANTS. BAD GUYS WHO'D LIKE TO SEE US DEAD.
NO ONE ADMITS TO KNOWING ANYTHING. NOW... THEY COULD ALL BE LYING...
...OR MAYBE SOMEONE WHO HASN'T BEEN ON OUR RADAR UNTIL RECENTLY IS INVOLVED.
SOMEONE LIKE US.
YUP.

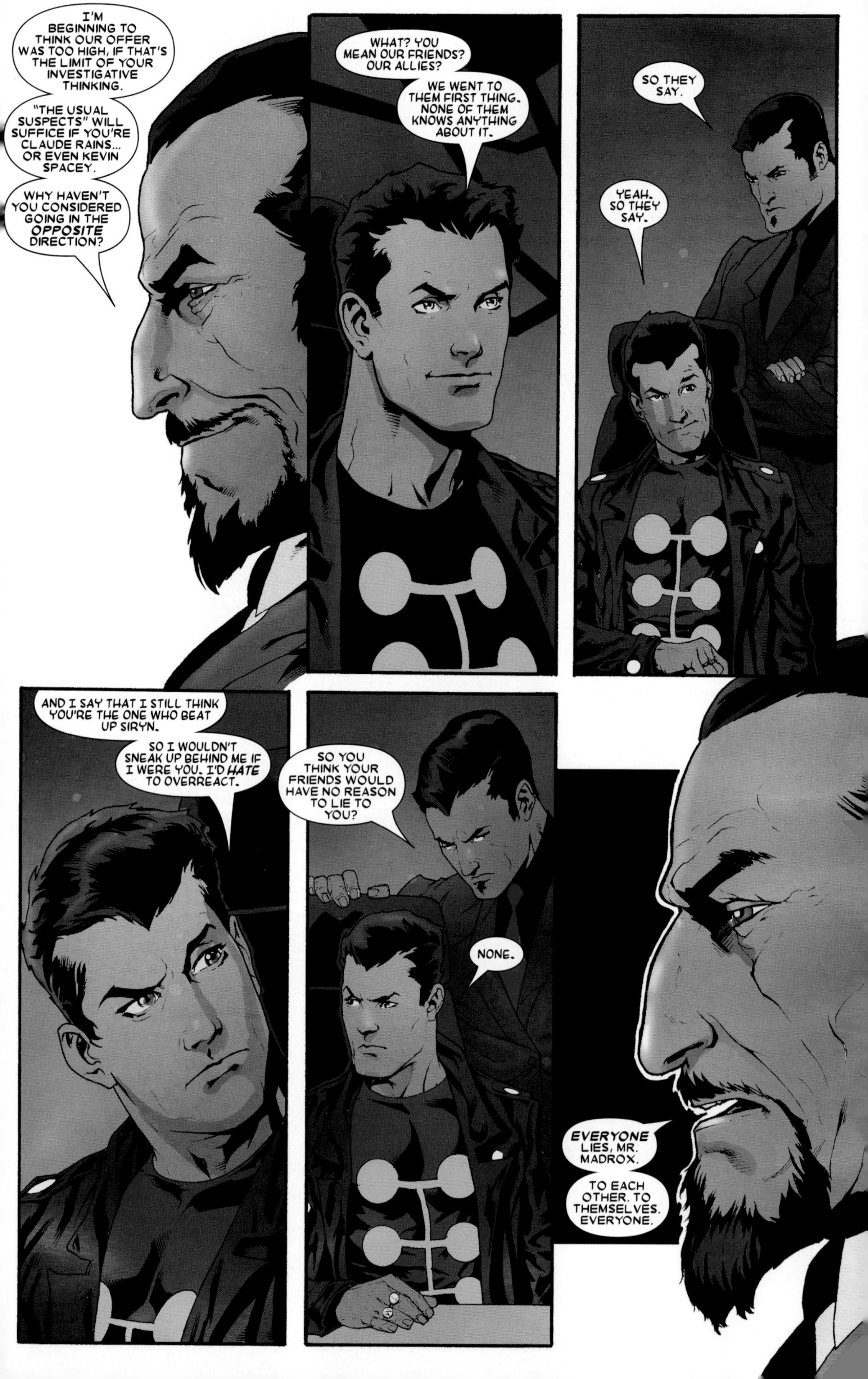
I'M BEGINNING TO THINK OUR OFFER WAS TOO HIGH, IF THAT'S THE LIMIT OF YOUR INVESTIGATIVE THINKING.
"THE USUAL SUSPECTS" WILL SUFFICE IF YOU'RE CLAUDE RAINS... OR EVEN KEVIN SPACEY.
WHY HAVEN'T YOU CONSIDERED GOING IN THE *OPPOSITE* DIRECTION?
WHAT? YOU MEAN OUR FRIENDS? OUR ALLIES?
WE WENT TO THEM FIRST THING. NONE OF THEM KNOWS ANYTHING ABOUT IT.
SO THEY SAY.
YEAH. SO THEY SAY.
AND I SAY THAT I STILL THINK YOU'RE THE ONE WHO BEAT UP SIRYN.
SO I WOULDN'T SNEAK UP BEHIND ME IF I WERE YOU. I'D *HATE* TO OVERREACT.
SO YOU THINK YOUR FRIENDS WOULD HAVE NO REASON TO LIE TO YOU?
NONE.
EVERYONE LIES, MR. MADROX.
TO EACH OTHER. TO THEMSELVES. EVERYONE.

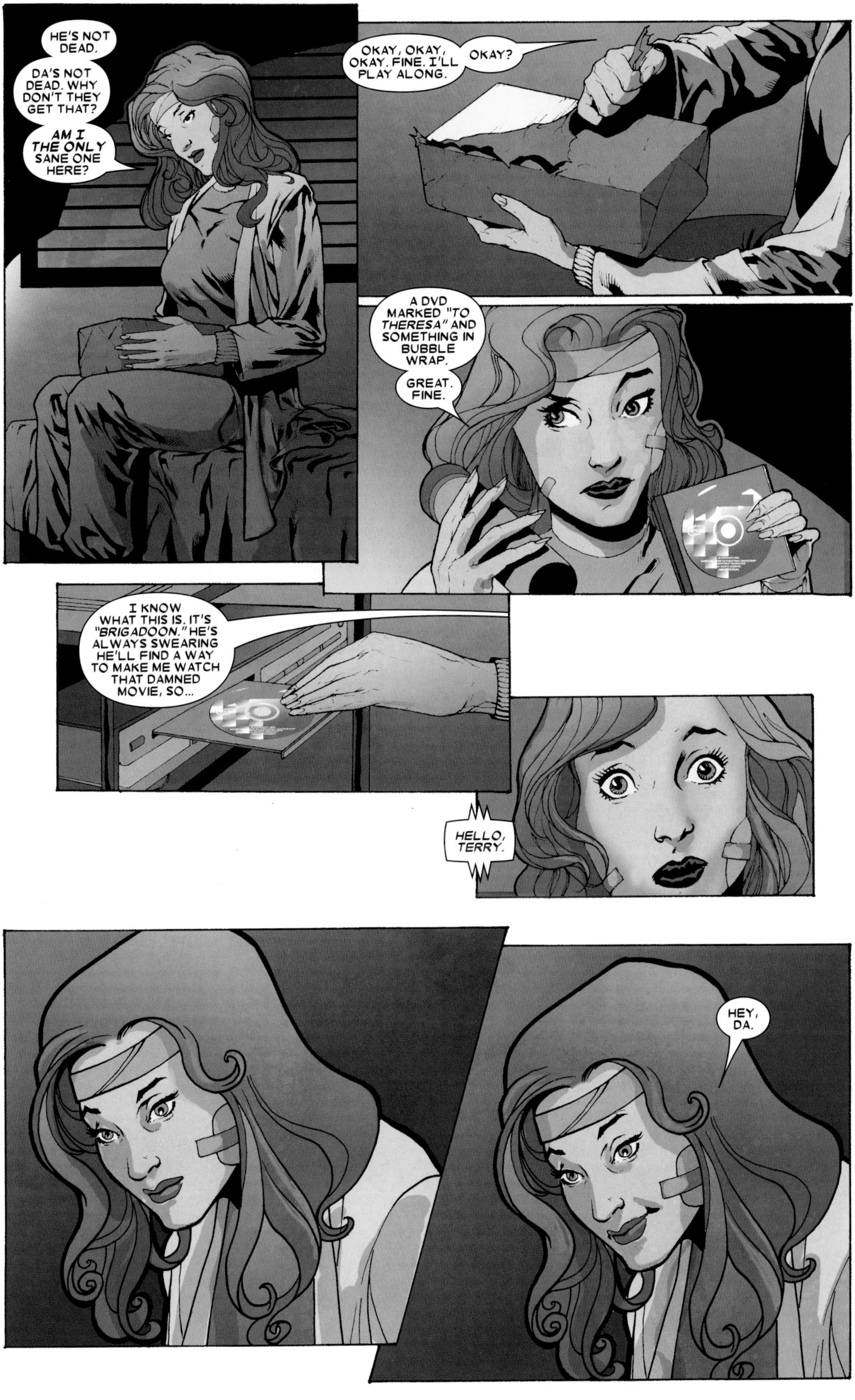
HE'S NOT DEAD.
DA'S NOT DEAD. WHY DON'T THEY GET THAT?
AM I THE ONLY SANE ONE HERE?
OKAY, OKAY, OKAY. FINE. I'LL PLAY ALONG.
OKAY?
A DVD MARKED "TO THERESA" AND SOMETHING IN BUBBLE WRAP.
GREAT. FINE.
I KNOW WHAT THIS IS. IT'S "BRIGADOON." HE'S ALWAYS SWEARING HE'LL FIND A WAY TO MAKE ME WATCH THAT DAMNED MOVIE, SO...
HELLO, TERRY.
HEY, DA.

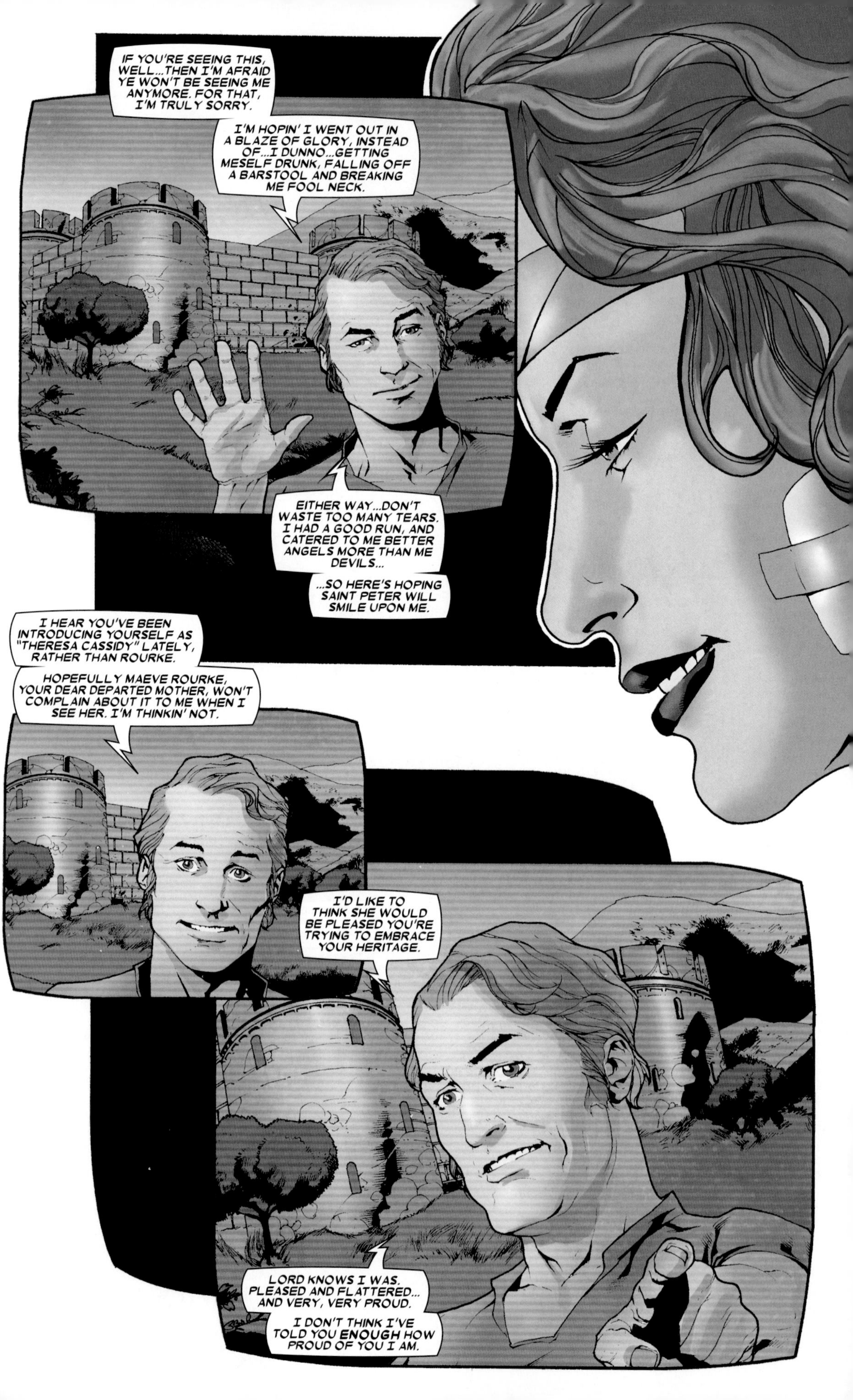
IF YOU'RE SEEING THIS, WELL...THEN I'M AFRAID YE WON'T BE SEEING ME ANYMORE. FOR THAT, I'M TRULY SORRY.
I'M HOPIN' I WENT OUT IN A BLAZE OF GLORY, INSTEAD OF...I DUNNO...GETTING MESELF DRUNK, FALLING OFF A BARSTOOL AND BREAKING ME FOOL NECK.
EITHER WAY...DON'T WASTE TOO MANY TEARS. I HAD A GOOD RUN, AND CATERED TO ME BETTER ANGELS MORE THAN ME DEVILS...
...SO HERE'S HOPING SAINT PETER WILL SMILE UPON ME.
I HEAR YOU'VE BEEN INTRODUCING YOURSELF AS "THERESA CASSIDY" LATELY, RATHER THAN ROURKE.
HOPEFULLY MAEVE ROURKE, YOUR DEAR DEPARTED MOTHER, WON'T COMPLAIN ABOUT IT TO ME WHEN I SEE HER. I'M THINKIN' NOT.
I'D LIKE TO THINK SHE WOULD BE PLEASED YOU'RE TRYING TO EMBRACE YOUR HERITAGE.
LORD KNOWS I WAS. PLEASED AND FLATTERED... AND VERY, VERY PROUD.
I DON'T THINK I'VE TOLD YOU ENOUGH HOW PROUD OF YOU I AM.

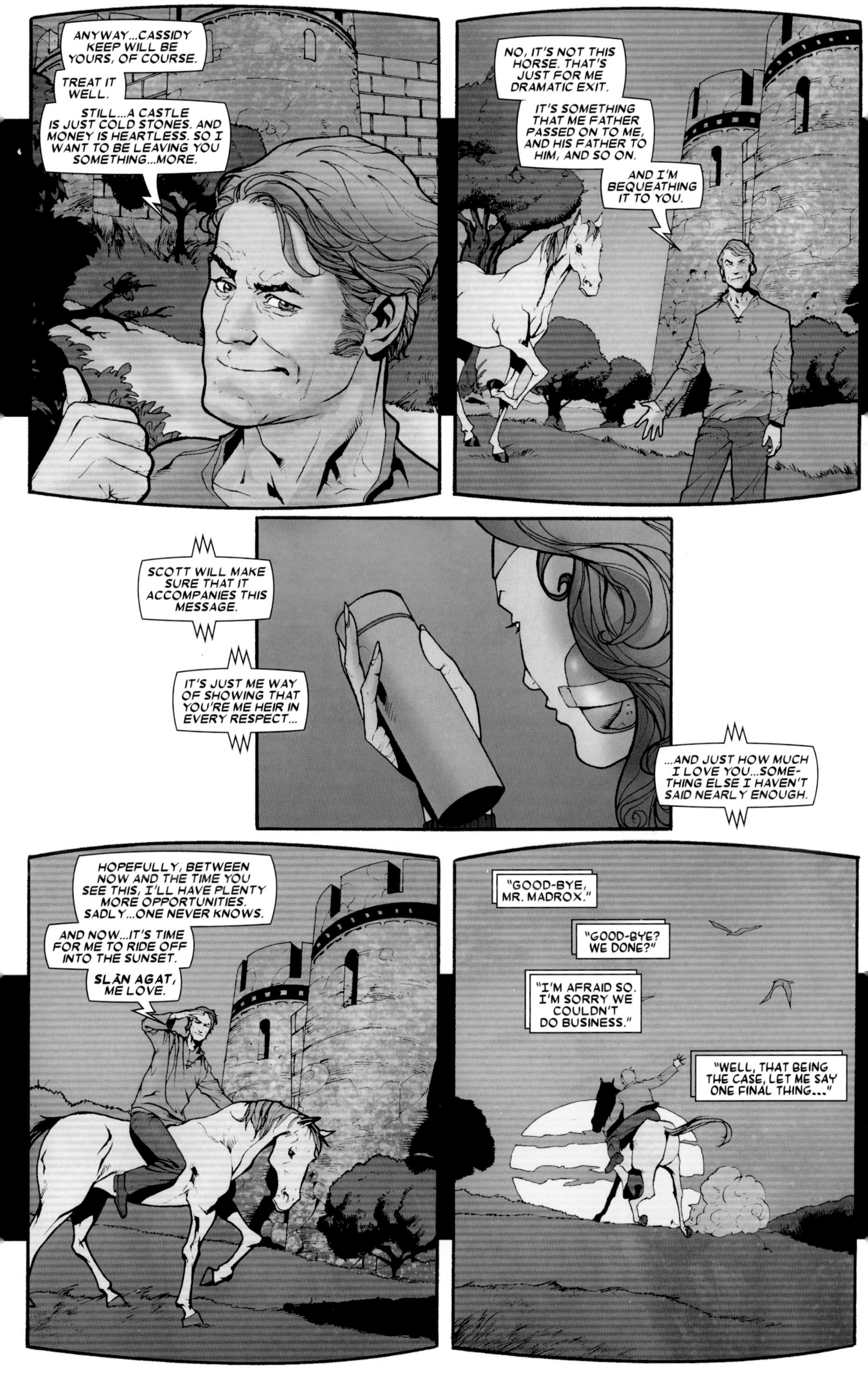
ANYWAY...CASSIDY KEEP WILL BE YOURS, OF COURSE.
TREAT IT WELL.
STILL...A CASTLE IS JUST COLD STONES. AND MONEY IS HEARTLESS. SO I WANT TO BE LEAVING YOU SOMETHING...MORE.
NO, IT'S NOT THIS HORSE. THAT'S JUST FOR ME DRAMATIC EXIT.
IT'S SOMETHING THAT ME FATHER PASSED ON TO ME, AND HIS FATHER TO HIM, AND SO ON.
AND I'M BEQUEATHING IT TO YOU.
SCOTT WILL MAKE SURE THAT IT ACCOMPANIES THIS MESSAGE.
IT'S JUST ME WAY OF SHOWING THAT YOU'RE ME HEIR IN EVERY RESPECT...
...AND JUST HOW MUCH I LOVE YOU...SOME-THING ELSE I HAVEN'T SAID NEARLY ENOUGH.
HOPEFULLY, BETWEEN NOW AND THE TIME YOU SEE THIS, I'LL HAVE PLENTY MORE OPPORTUNITIES. SADLY...ONE NEVER KNOWS.
AND NOW...IT'S TIME FOR ME TO RIDE OFF INTO THE SUNSET.
SLÁN AGAT, ME LOVE.
"GOOD-BYE, MR. MADROX."
"GOOD-BYE? WE DONE?"
"I'M AFRAID SO. I'M SORRY WE COULDN'T DO BUSINESS."
"WELL, THAT BEING THE CASE, LET ME SAY ONE FINAL THING..."

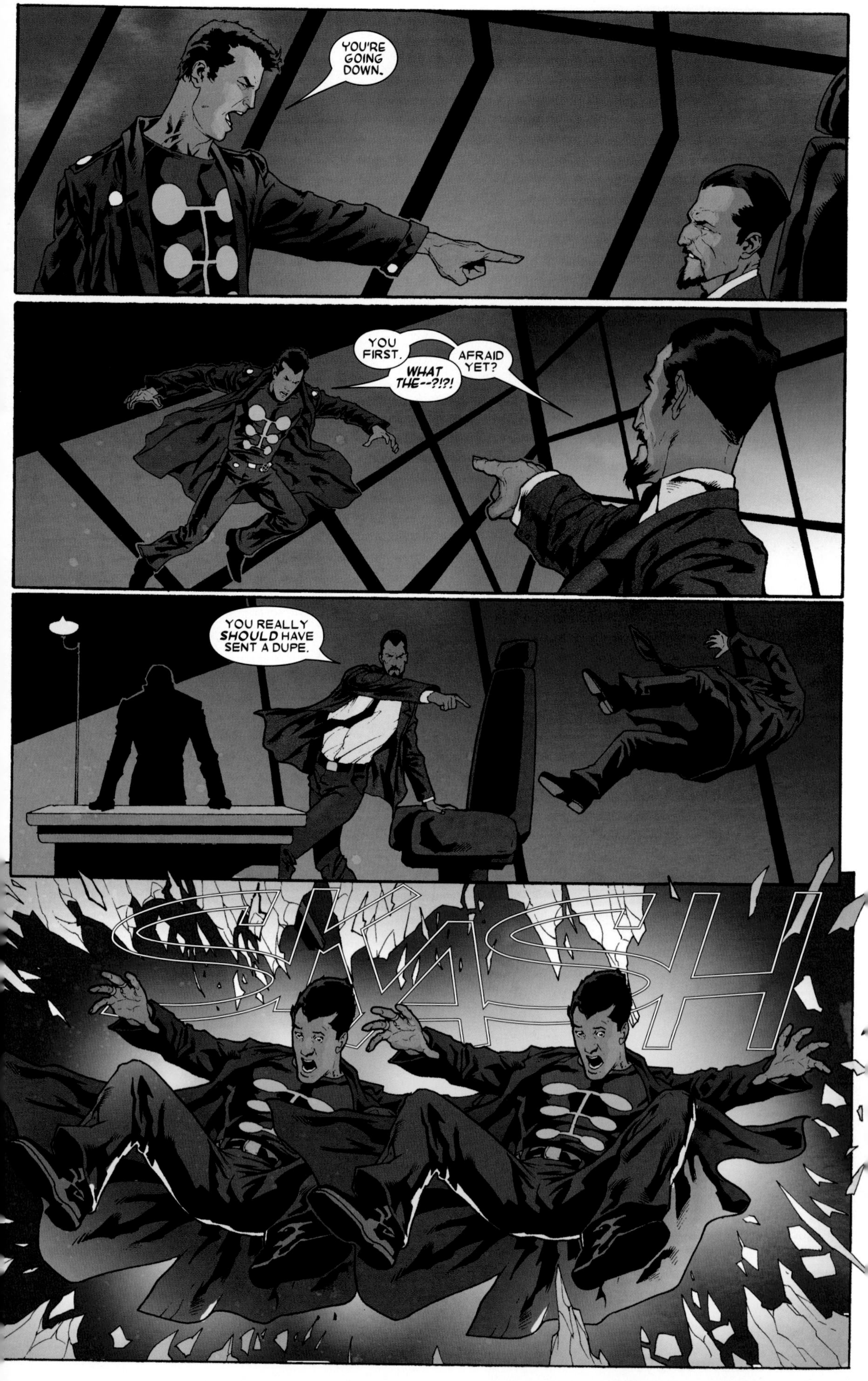
YOU'RE GOING DOWN.
YOU FIRST.
WHAT THE--?!?!
AFRAID YET?
YOU REALLY SHOULD HAVE SENT A DUPE.
SMASH

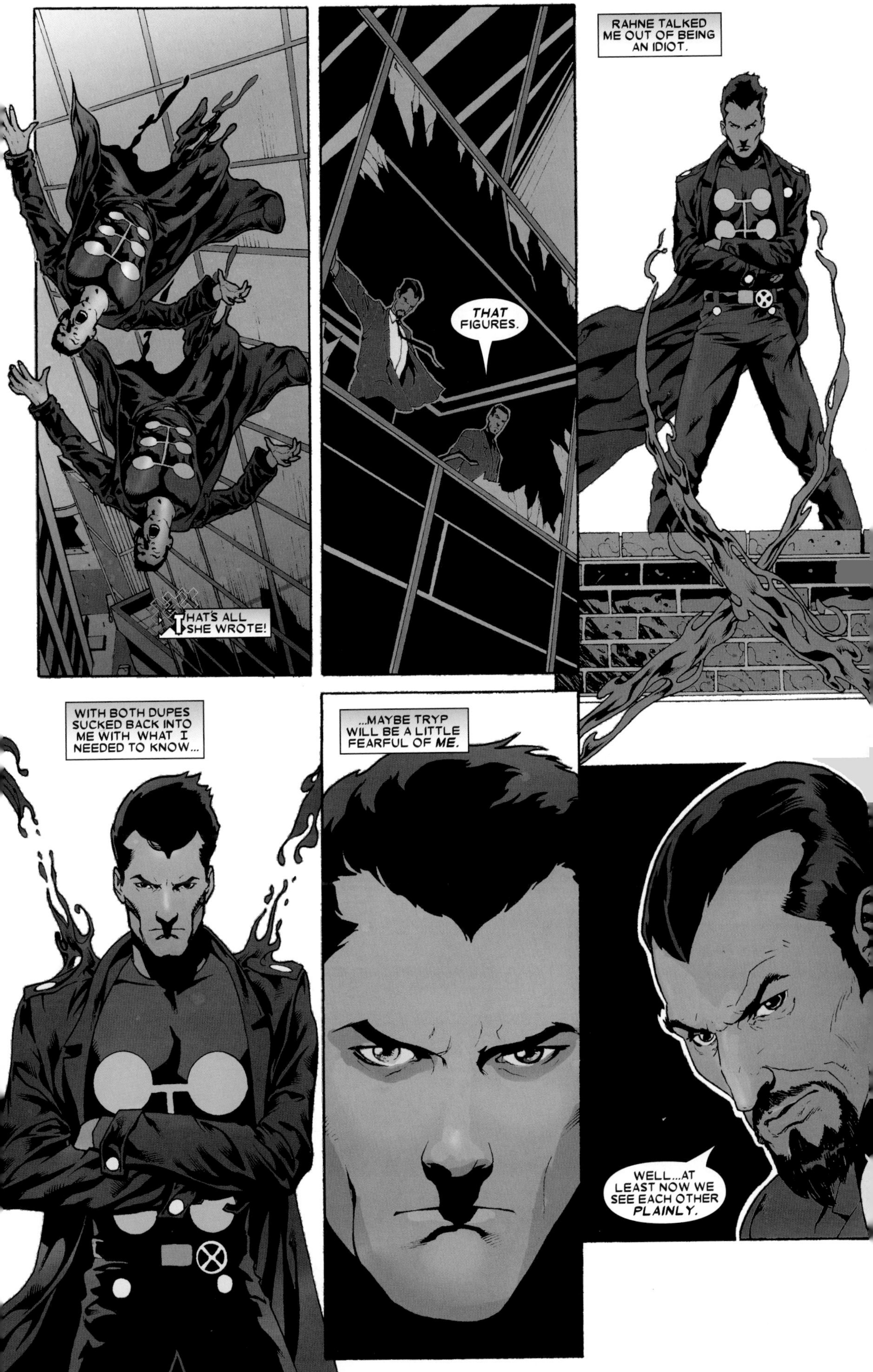
THAT'S ALL SHE WROTE!
THAT FIGURES.
RAHNE TALKED ME OUT OF BEING AN IDIOT.
WITH BOTH DUPES SUCKED BACK INTO ME WITH WHAT I NEEDED TO KNOW...
...MAYBE TRYP WILL BE A LITTLE FEARFUL OF ME.
WELL...AT LEAST NOW WE SEE EACH OTHER PLAINLY.

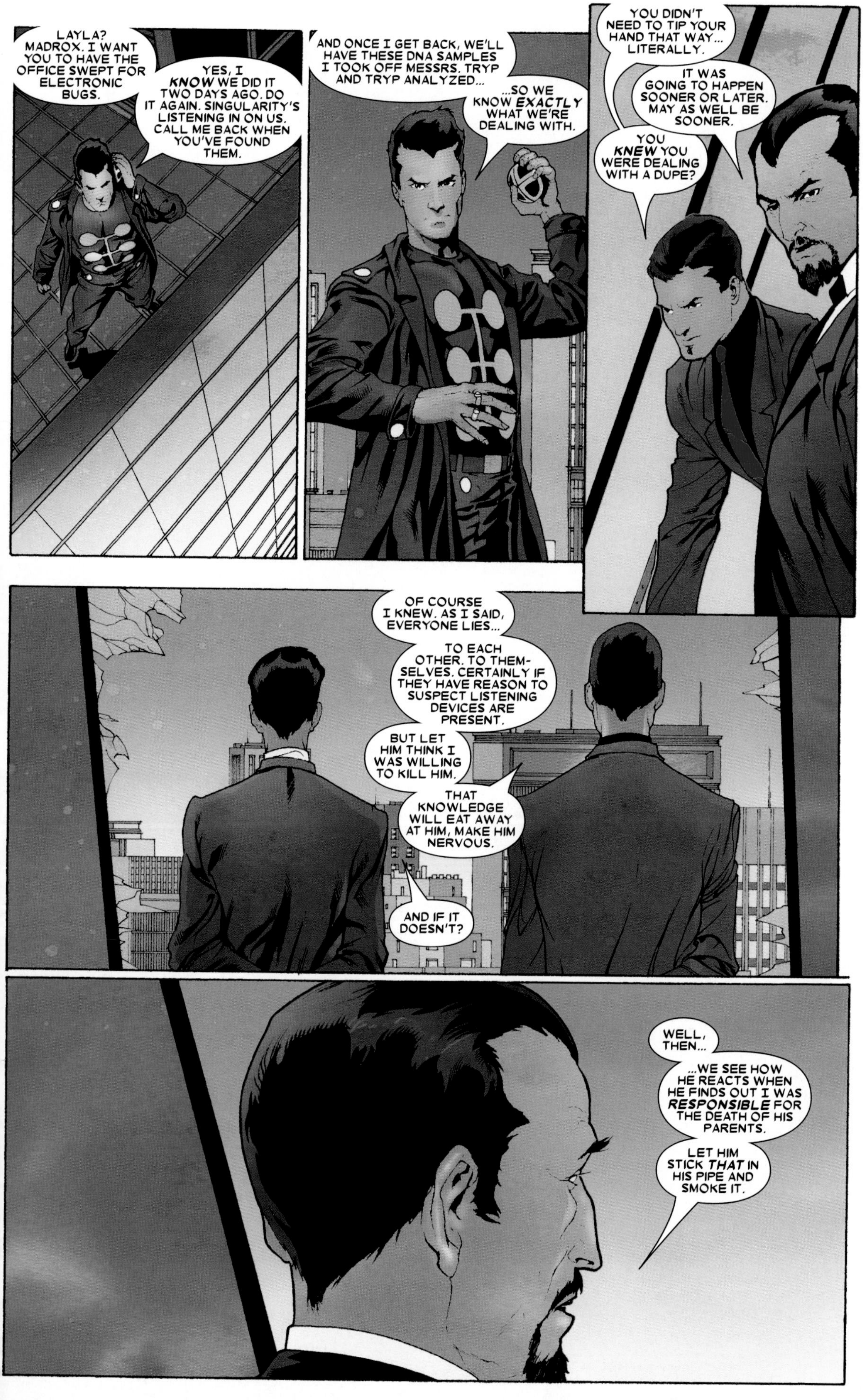
LAYLA? MADROX. I WANT YOU TO HAVE THE OFFICE SWEPT FOR ELECTRONIC BUGS.
YES, I KNOW WE DID IT TWO DAYS AGO. DO IT AGAIN. SINGULARITY'S LISTENING IN ON US. CALL ME BACK WHEN YOU'VE FOUND THEM.
AND ONCE I GET BACK, WE'LL HAVE THESE DNA SAMPLES I TOOK OFF MESSRS. TRYP AND TRYP ANALYZED...
...SO WE KNOW EXACTLY WHAT WE'RE DEALING WITH.
YOU DIDN'T NEED TO TIP YOUR HAND THAT WAY... LITERALLY.
IT WAS GOING TO HAPPEN SOONER OR LATER. MAY AS WELL BE SOONER.
YOU KNEW YOU WERE DEALING WITH A DUPE?
OF COURSE I KNEW. AS I SAID, EVERYONE LIES...
TO EACH OTHER. TO THEM-SELVES. CERTAINLY IF THEY HAVE REASON TO SUSPECT LISTENING DEVICES ARE PRESENT.
BUT LET HIM THINK I WAS WILLING TO KILL HIM.
THAT KNOWLEDGE WILL EAT AWAY AT HIM, MAKE HIM NERVOUS.
AND IF IT DOESN'T?
WELL, THEN...
...WE SEE HOW HE REACTS WHEN HE FINDS OUT I WAS RESPONSIBLE FOR THE DEATH OF HIS PARENTS.
LET HIM STICK THAT IN HIS PIPE AND SMOKE IT.

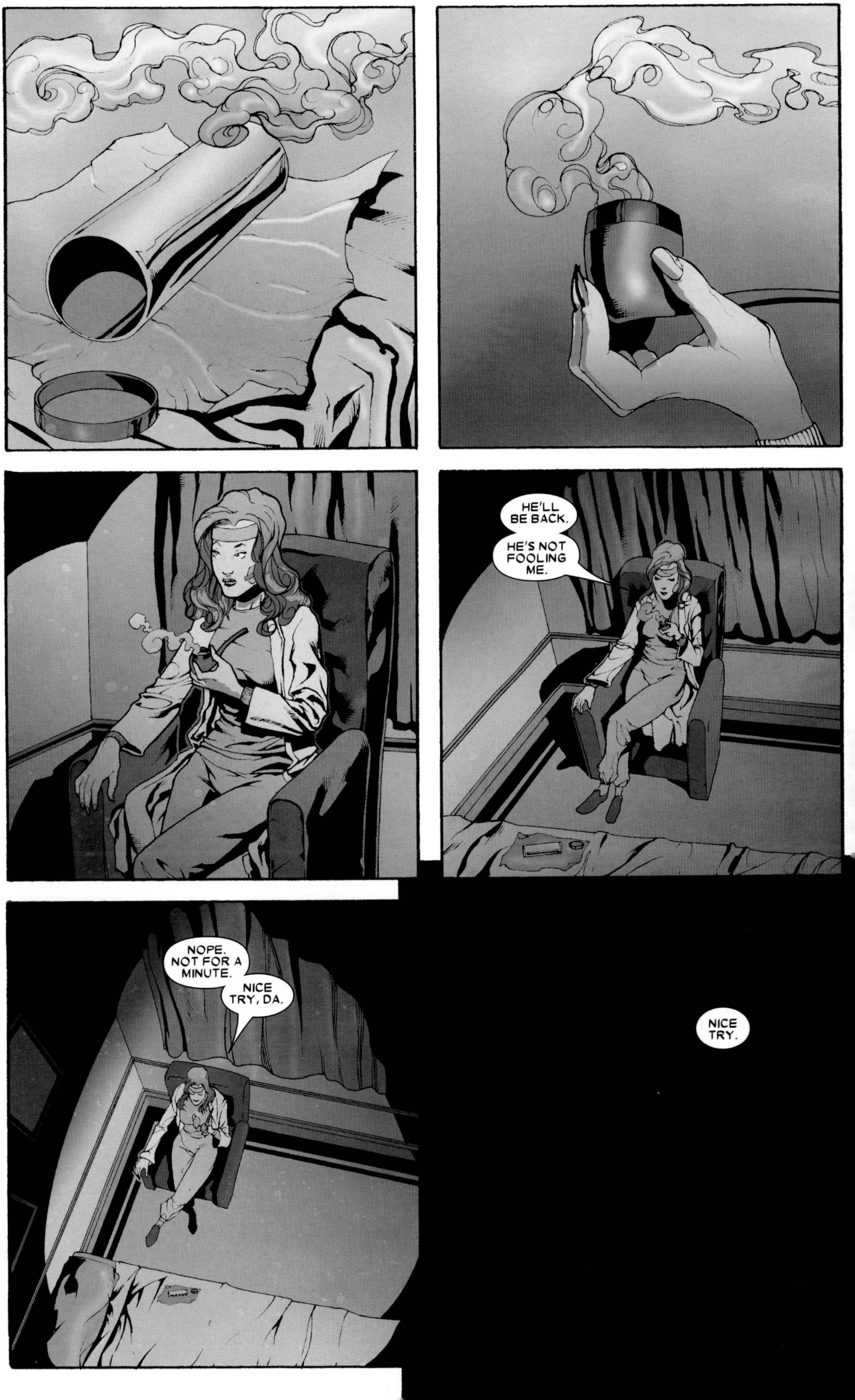
HE'LL BE BACK.
HE'S NOT FOOLING ME.
NOPE. NOT FOR A MINUTE.
NICE TRY, DA.
NICE TRY.

#8 Variant by Dennis Calero

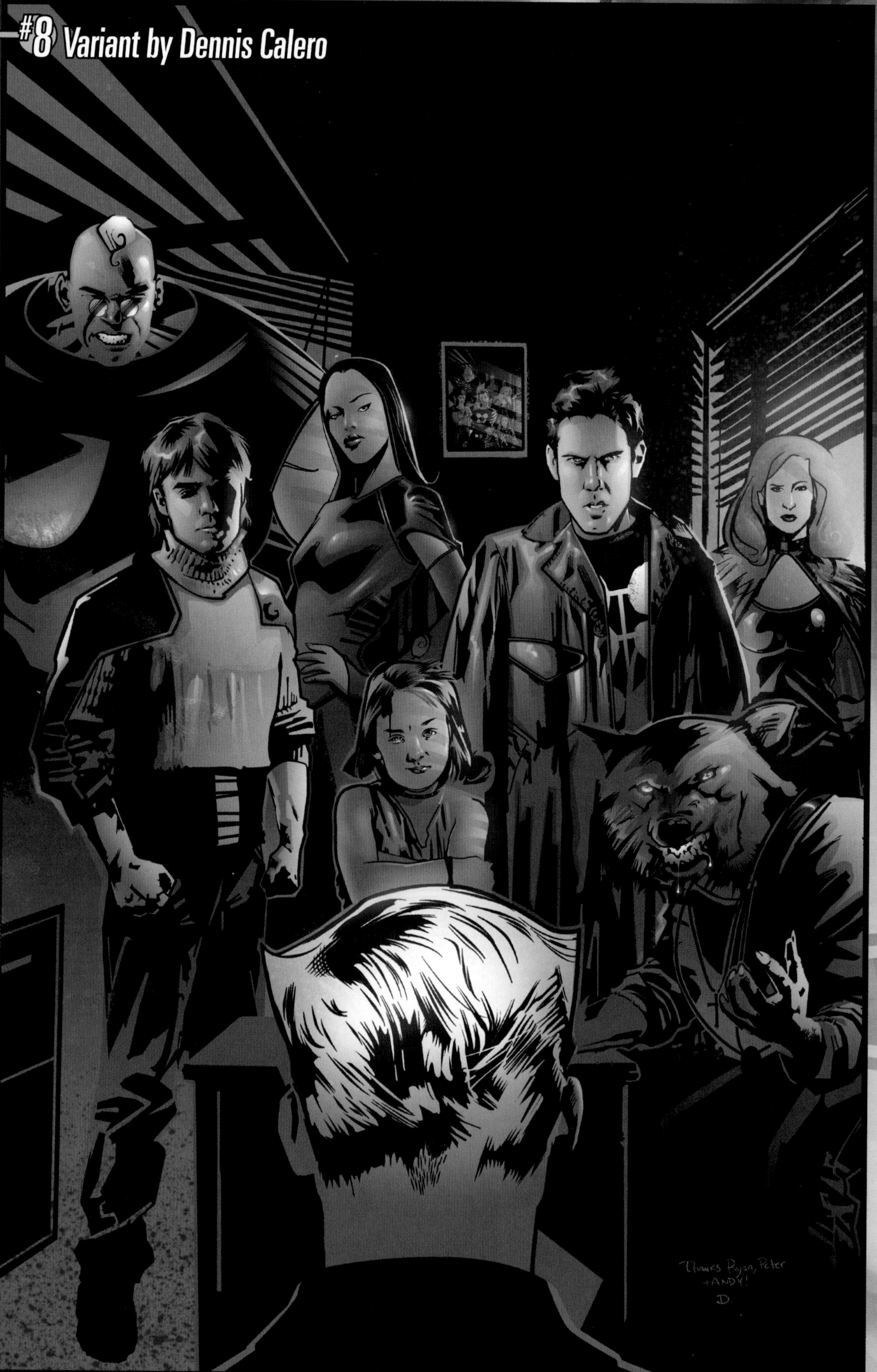
Thanks Ryan, Peter
+ANDY!
D

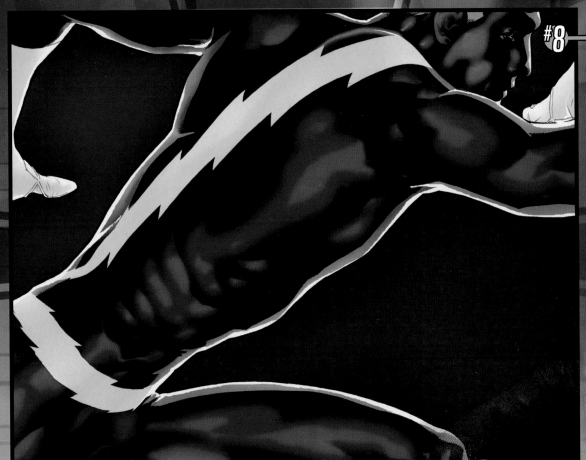

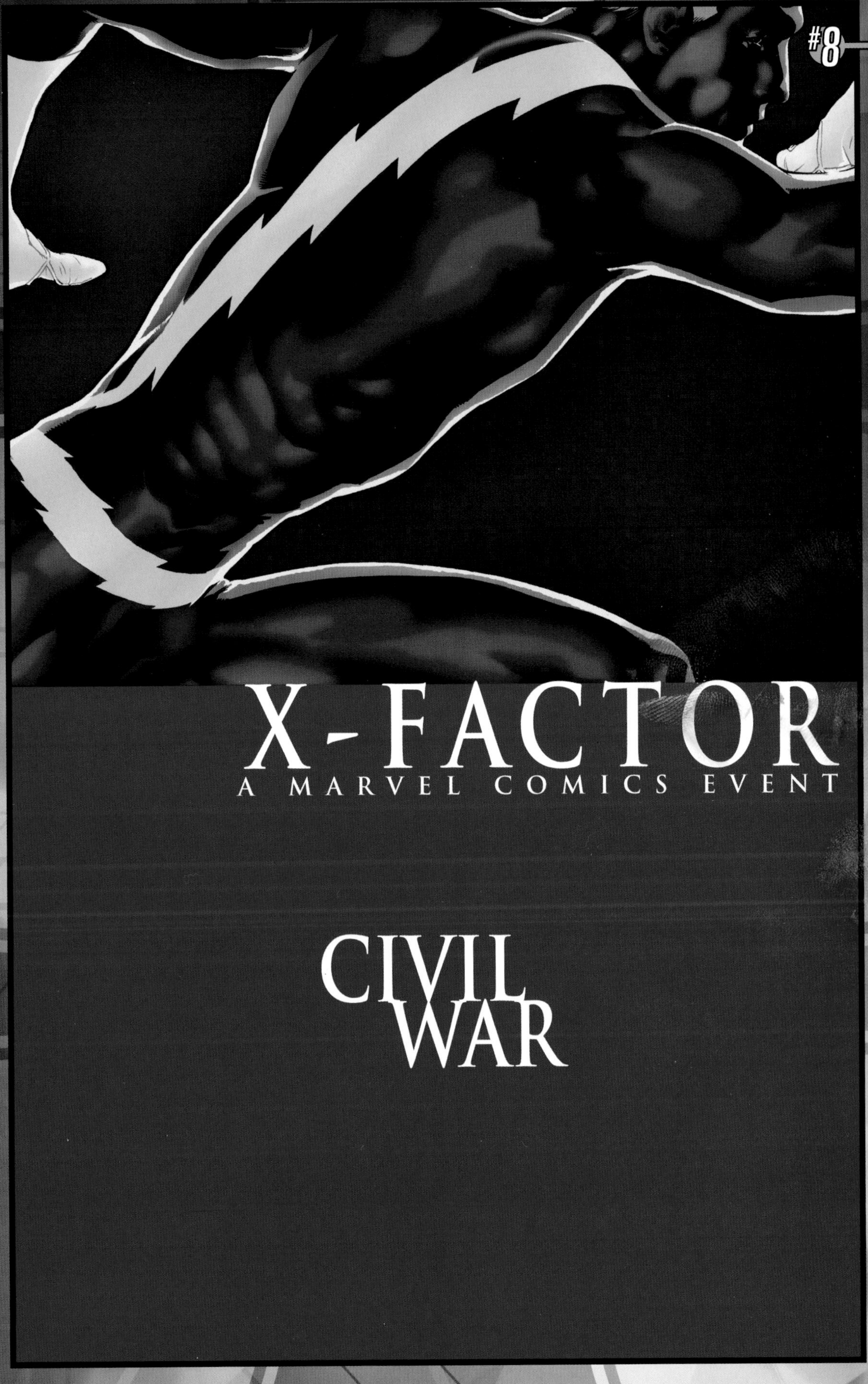

8

X-FACTOR

A MARVEL COMICS EVENT

CIVIL WAR

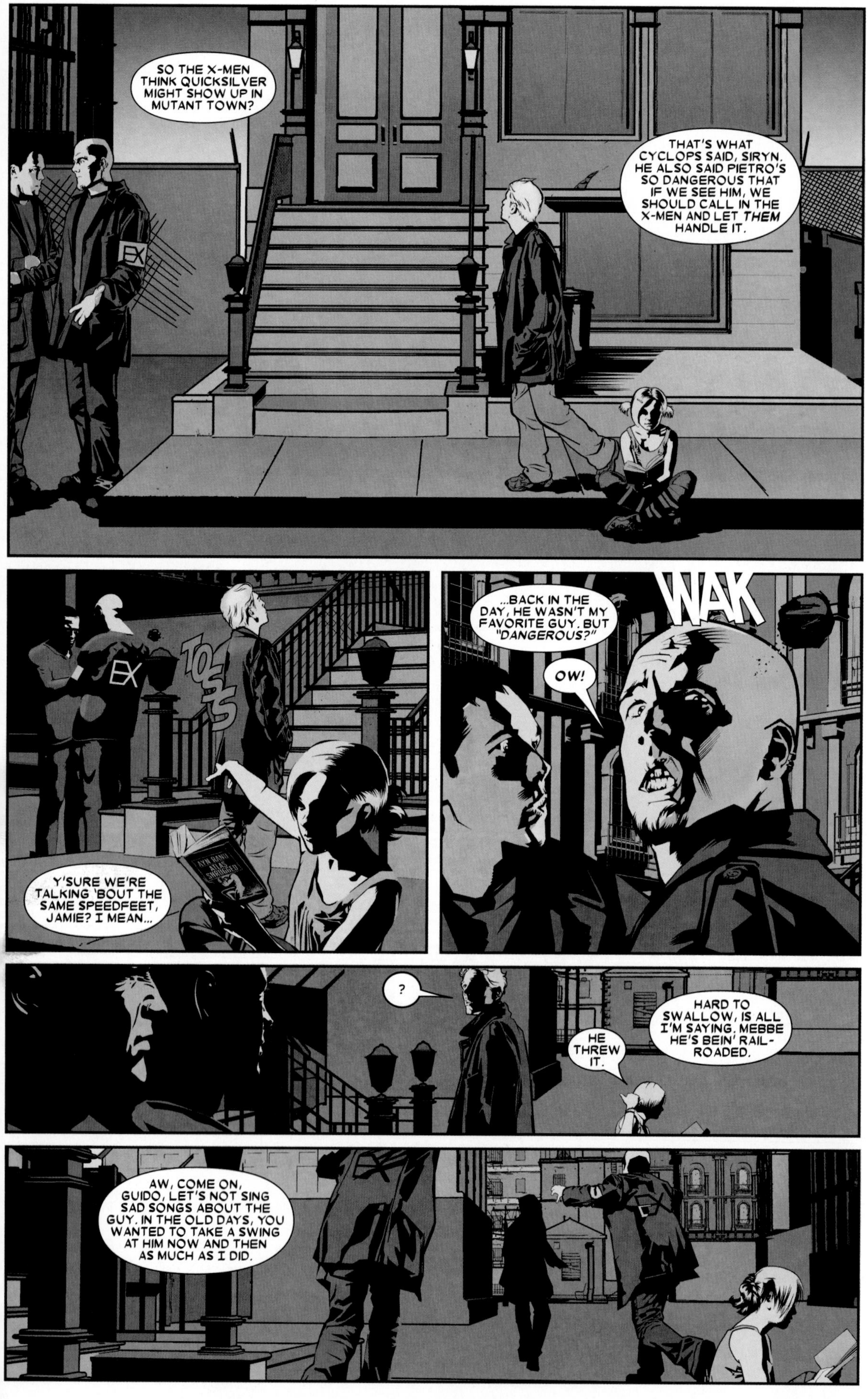

SO THE X-MEN THINK QUICKSILVER MIGHT SHOW UP IN MUTANT TOWN?
THAT'S WHAT CYCLOPS SAID, SIRYN. HE ALSO SAID PIETRO'S SO DANGEROUS THAT IF WE SEE HIM, WE SHOULD CALL IN THE X-MEN AND LET THEM HANDLE IT.
TOSS
Y'SURE WE'RE TALKING 'BOUT THE SAME SPEEDFEET, JAMIE? I MEAN...
AYN RAND ATLAS SHRUGGED
...BACK IN THE DAY, HE WASN'T MY FAVORITE GUY. BUT "DANGEROUS?"
WAK
OW!
?
HE THREW IT.
HARD TO SWALLOW, IS ALL I'M SAYING. MEBBE HE'S BEIN' RAIL-ROADED.
AW, COME ON, GUIDO, LET'S NOT SING SAD SONGS ABOUT THE GUY. IN THE OLD DAYS, YOU WANTED TO TAKE A SWING AT HIM NOW AND THEN AS MUCH AS I DID.

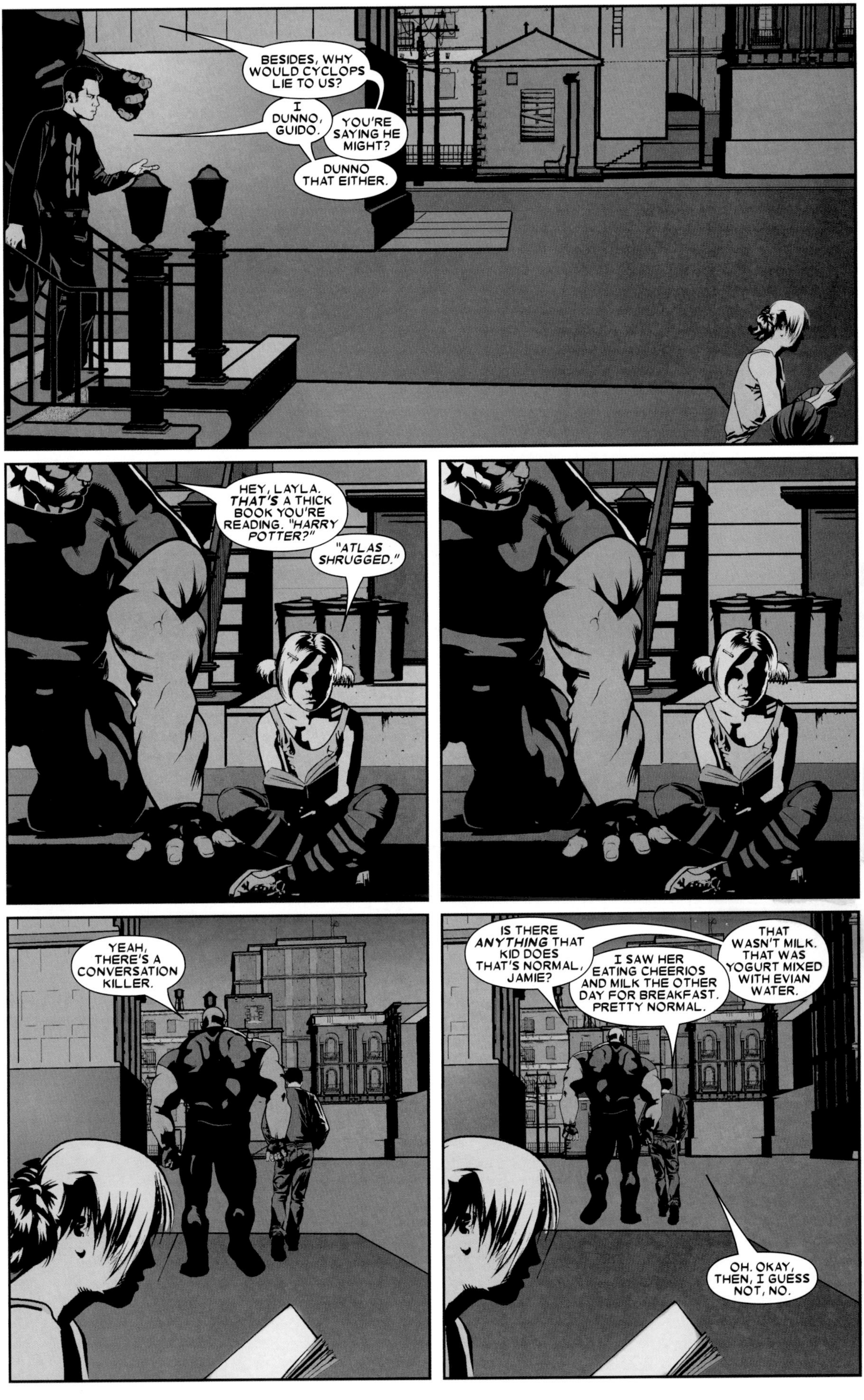
BESIDES, WHY WOULD CYCLOPS LIE TO US?
I DUNNO, GUIDO.
YOU'RE SAYING HE MIGHT?
DUNNO THAT EITHER.
HEY, LAYLA. *THAT'S* A THICK BOOK YOU'RE READING. "HARRY POTTER?"
"ATLAS SHRUGGED."
YEAH, THERE'S A CONVERSATION KILLER.
IS THERE *ANYTHING* THAT KID DOES THAT'S NORMAL, JAMIE?
I SAW HER EATING CHEERIOS AND MILK THE OTHER DAY FOR BREAKFAST. PRETTY NORMAL.
THAT WASN'T MILK. THAT WAS YOGURT MIXED WITH EVIAN WATER.
OH. OKAY, THEN, I GUESS NOT, NO.

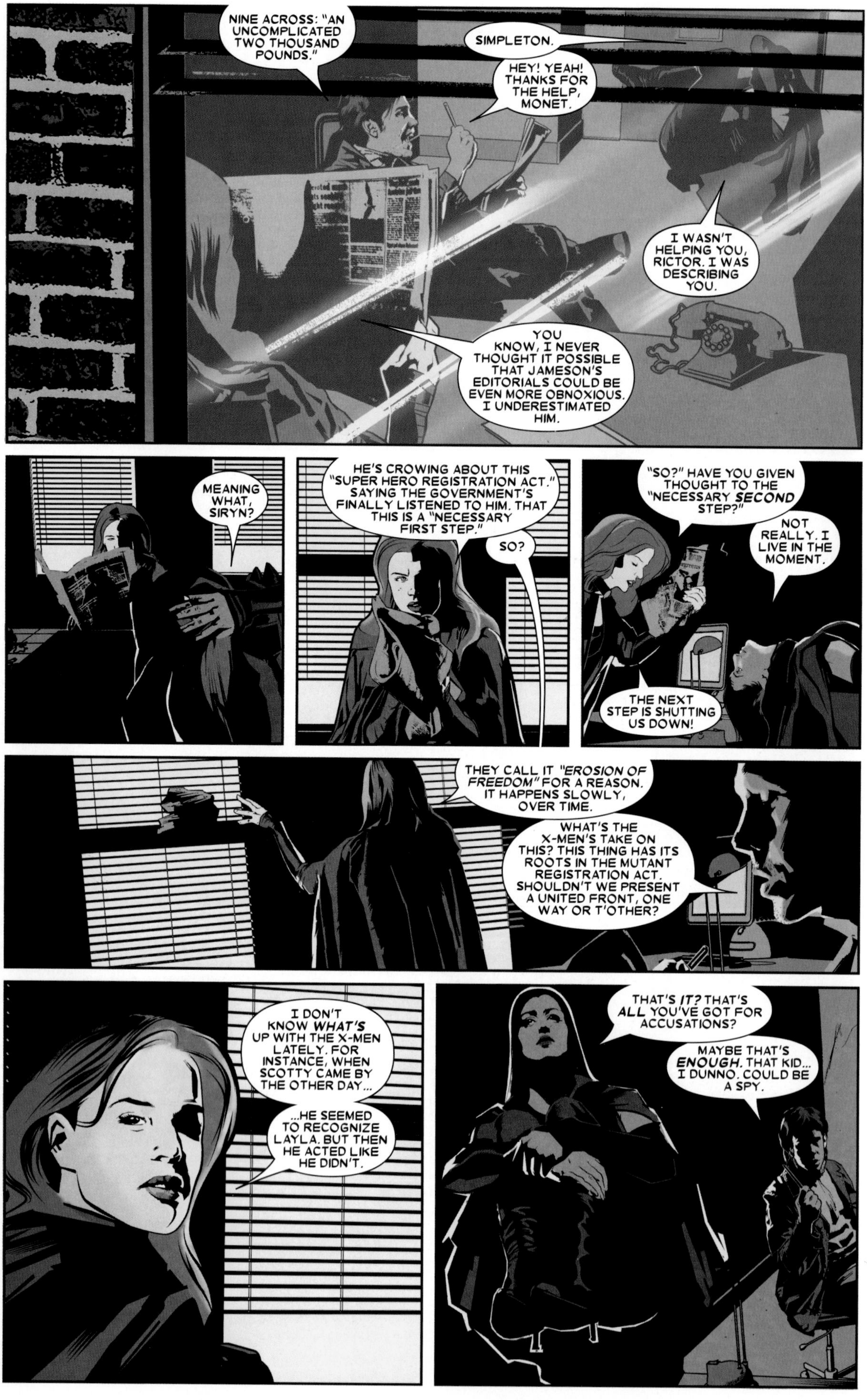
NINE ACROSS: "AN UNCOMPLICATED TWO THOUSAND POUNDS."
SIMPLETON.
HEY! YEAH! THANKS FOR THE HELP, MONET.
I WASN'T HELPING YOU, RICTOR. I WAS DESCRIBING YOU.
YOU KNOW, I NEVER THOUGHT IT POSSIBLE THAT JAMESON'S EDITORIALS COULD BE EVEN MORE OBNOXIOUS. I UNDERESTIMATED HIM.
MEANING WHAT, SIRYN?
HE'S CROWING ABOUT THIS "SUPER HERO REGISTRATION ACT." SAYING THE GOVERNMENT'S FINALLY LISTENED TO HIM. THAT THIS IS A "NECESSARY FIRST STEP."
SO?
"SO?" HAVE YOU GIVEN THOUGHT TO THE "NECESSARY SECOND STEP?"
NOT REALLY. I LIVE IN THE MOMENT.
THE NEXT STEP IS SHUTTING US DOWN!
THEY CALL IT "EROSION OF FREEDOM" FOR A REASON. IT HAPPENS SLOWLY, OVER TIME.
WHAT'S THE X-MEN'S TAKE ON THIS? THIS THING HAS ITS ROOTS IN THE MUTANT REGISTRATION ACT. SHOULDN'T WE PRESENT A UNITED FRONT, ONE WAY OR T'OTHER?
I DON'T KNOW WHAT'S UP WITH THE X-MEN LATELY. FOR INSTANCE, WHEN SCOTTY CAME BY THE OTHER DAY...
...HE SEEMED TO RECOGNIZE LAYLA. BUT THEN HE ACTED LIKE HE DIDN'T.
THAT'S IT? THAT'S ALL YOU'VE GOT FOR ACCUSATIONS?
MAYBE THAT'S ENOUGH. THAT KID... I DUNNO. COULD BE A SPY.

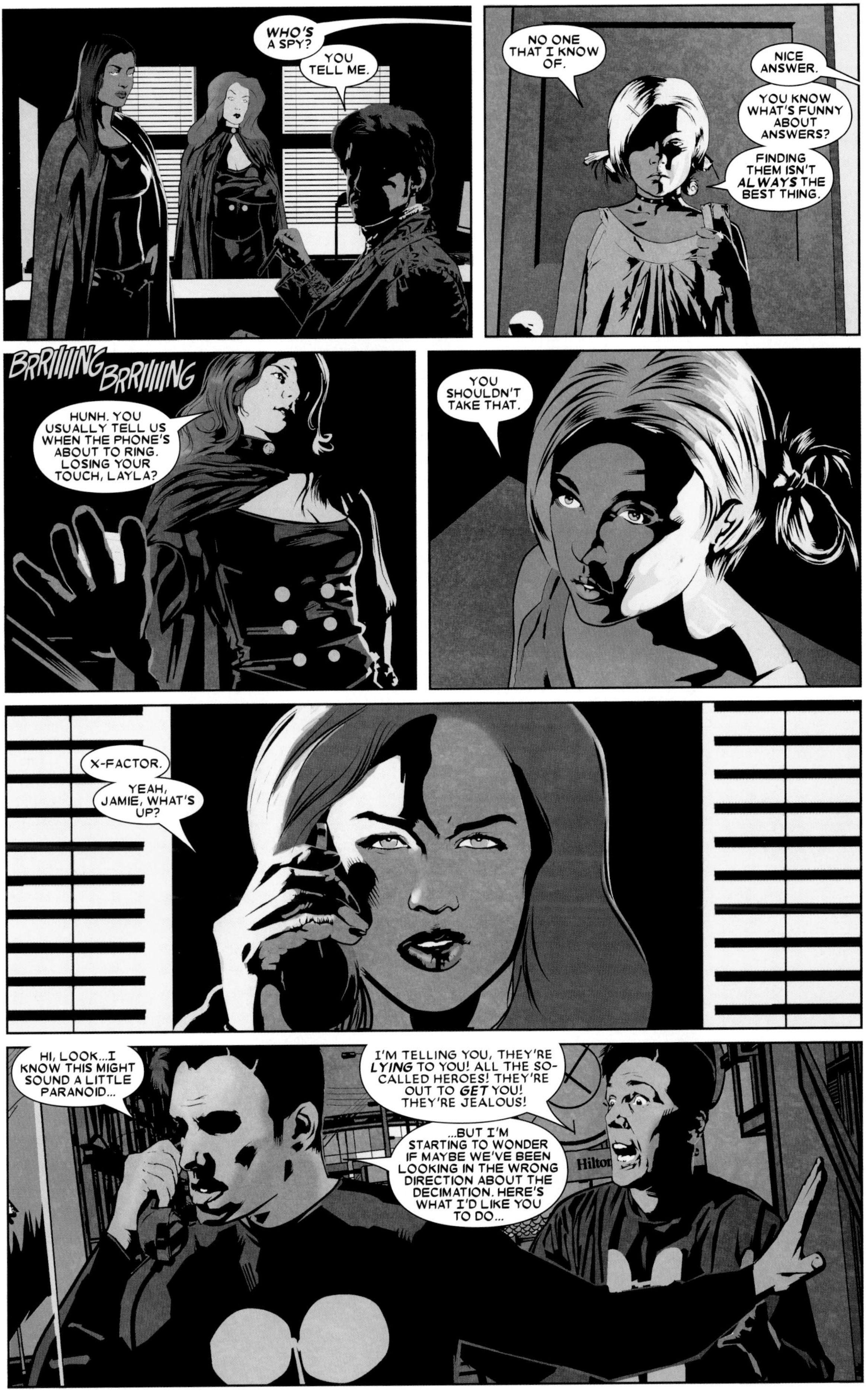
WHO'S A SPY?
YOU TELL ME.
NO ONE THAT I KNOW OF.
NICE ANSWER.
YOU KNOW WHAT'S FUNNY ABOUT ANSWERS?
FINDING THEM ISN'T ALWAYS THE BEST THING.
BRRIIIING BRRIIIING
HUNH. YOU USUALLY TELL US WHEN THE PHONE'S ABOUT TO RING. LOSING YOUR TOUCH, LAYLA?
YOU SHOULDN'T TAKE THAT.
X-FACTOR.
YEAH, JAMIE, WHAT'S UP?
HI, LOOK...I KNOW THIS MIGHT SOUND A LITTLE PARANOID...
I'M TELLING YOU, THEY'RE LYING TO YOU! ALL THE SO-CALLED HEROES! THEY'RE OUT TO GET YOU! THEY'RE JEALOUS!
...BUT I'M STARTING TO WONDER IF MAYBE WE'VE BEEN LOOKING IN THE WRONG DIRECTION ABOUT THE DECIMATION. HERE'S WHAT I'D LIKE YOU TO DO...
Hilton

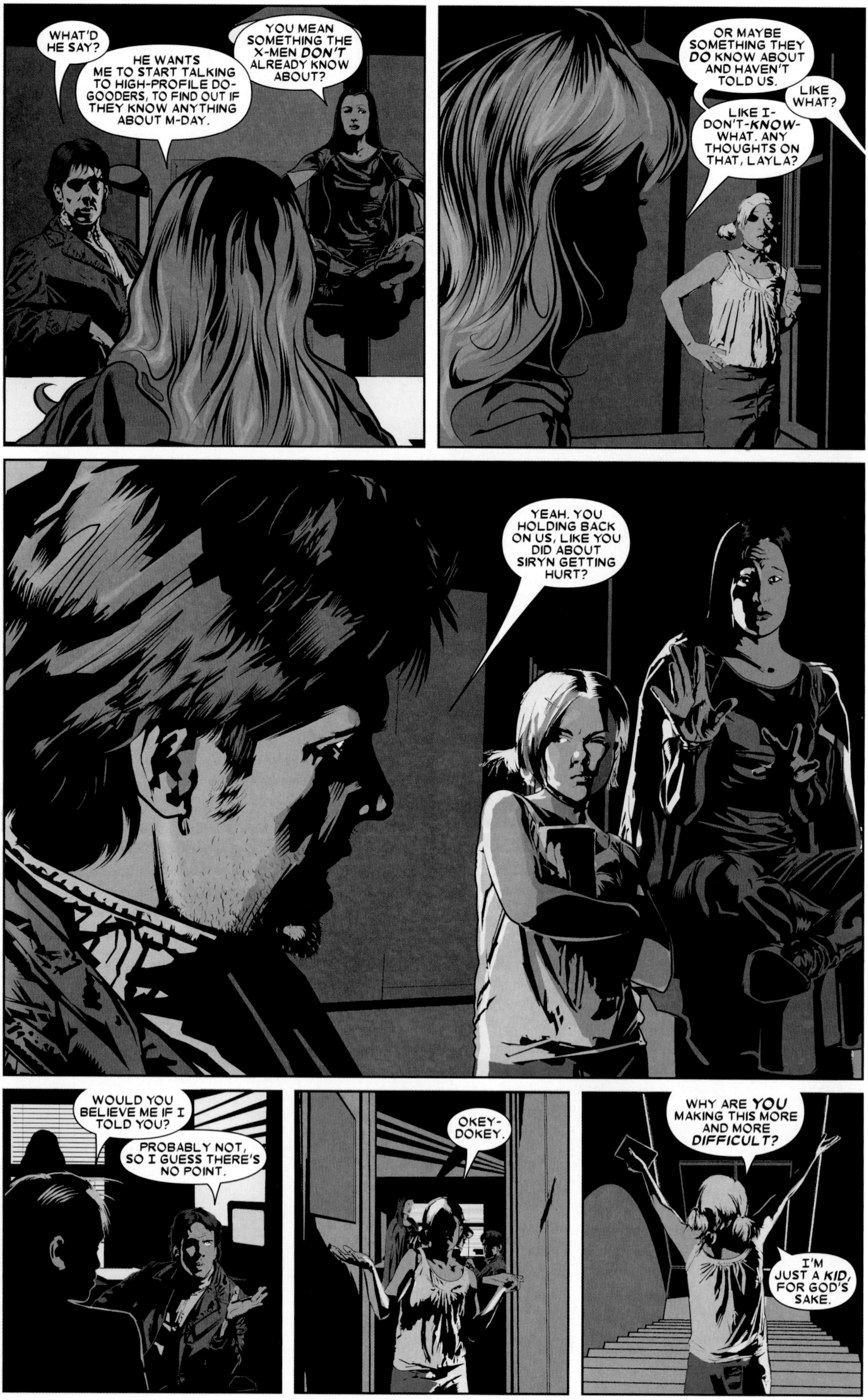
WHAT'D HE SAY?
HE WANTS ME TO START TALKING TO HIGH-PROFILE DO-GOODERS, TO FIND OUT IF THEY KNOW ANYTHING ABOUT M-DAY.
YOU MEAN SOMETHING THE X-MEN DON'T ALREADY KNOW ABOUT?
OR MAYBE SOMETHING THEY DO KNOW ABOUT AND HAVEN'T TOLD US.
LIKE WHAT?
LIKE I-DON'T-KNOW-WHAT. ANY THOUGHTS ON THAT, LAYLA?
YEAH. YOU HOLDING BACK ON US, LIKE YOU DID ABOUT SIRYN GETTING HURT?
WOULD YOU BELIEVE ME IF I TOLD YOU?
PROBABLY NOT, SO I GUESS THERE'S NO POINT.
OKEY-DOKEY.
WHY ARE YOU MAKING THIS MORE AND MORE DIFFICULT?
I'M JUST A KID, FOR GOD'S SAKE.

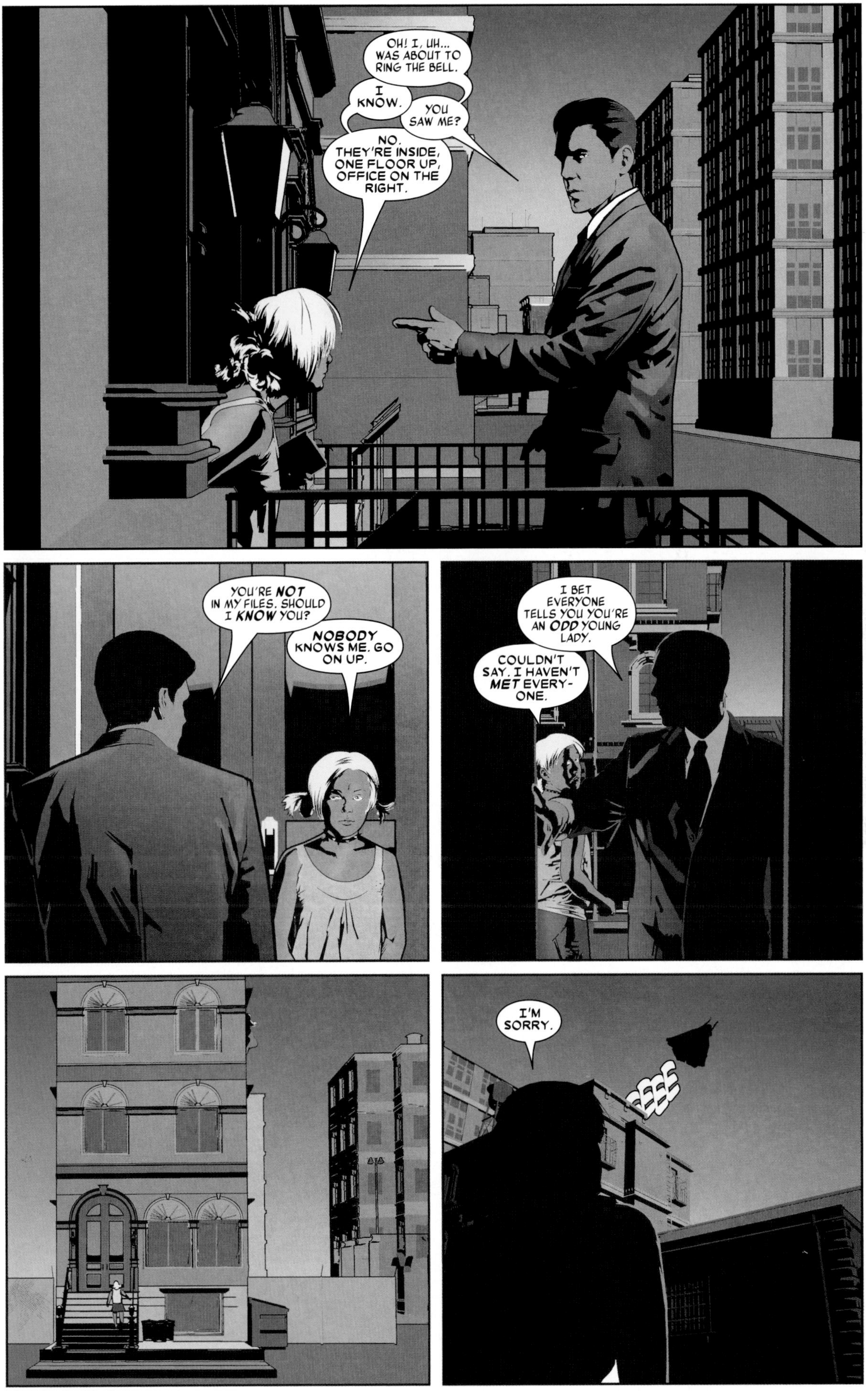
OH! I, UH... WAS ABOUT TO RING THE BELL.
I KNOW.
YOU SAW ME?
NO. THEY'RE INSIDE, ONE FLOOR UP, OFFICE ON THE RIGHT.
YOU'RE **NOT** IN MY FILES. SHOULD I **KNOW** YOU?
NOBODY KNOWS ME. GO ON UP.
I BET EVERYONE TELLS YOU YOU'RE AN **ODD** YOUNG LADY.
COULDN'T SAY. I HAVEN'T **MET** EVERY-ONE.
I'M SORRY.
EEEE

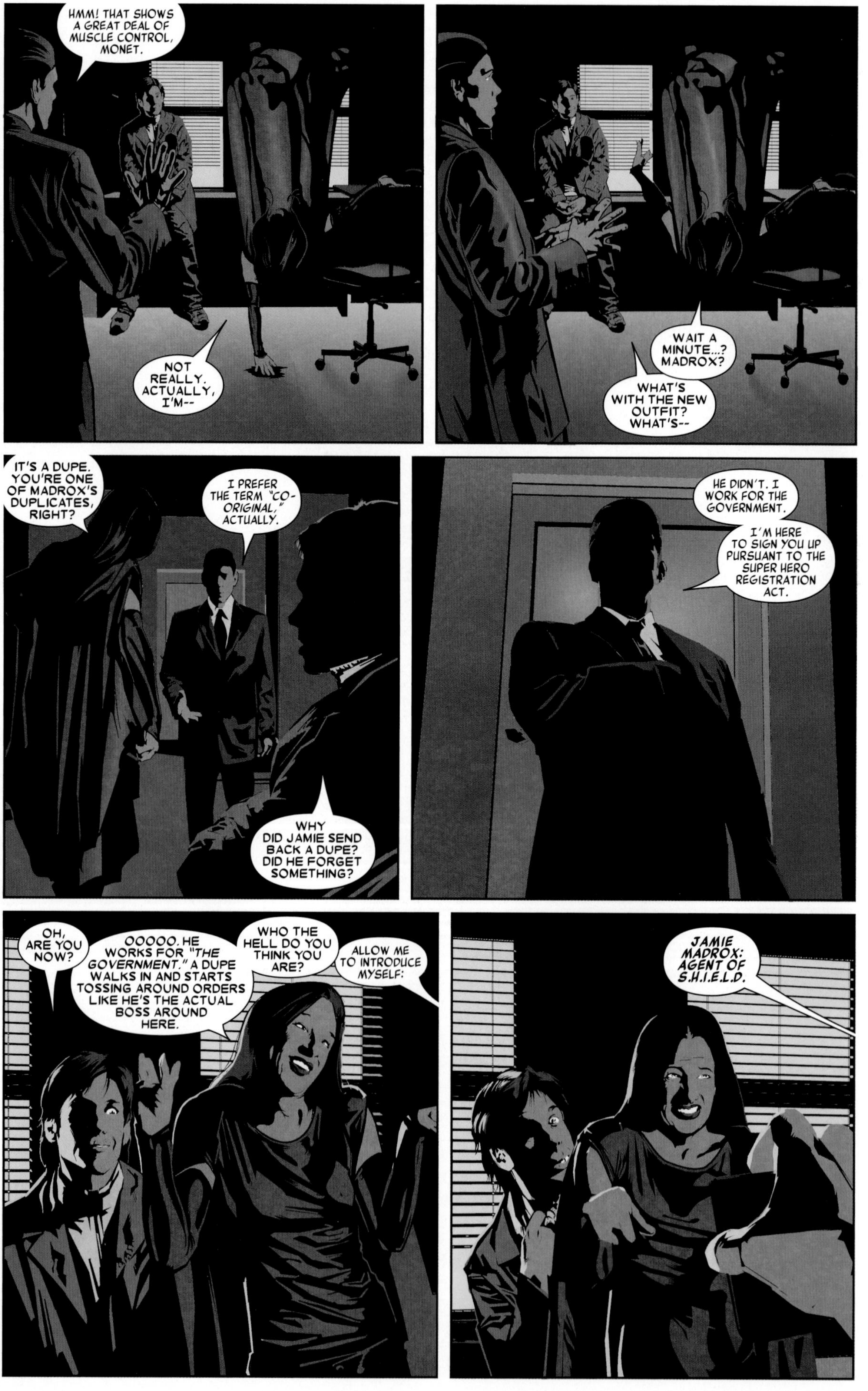
HMM! THAT SHOWS A GREAT DEAL OF MUSCLE CONTROL, MONET.
NOT REALLY. ACTUALLY, I'M--
WAIT A MINUTE...? MADROX?
WHAT'S WITH THE NEW OUTFIT? WHAT'S--
IT'S A DUPE. YOU'RE ONE OF MADROX'S DUPLICATES, RIGHT?
I PREFER THE TERM "CO-ORIGINAL," ACTUALLY.
WHY DID JAMIE SEND BACK A DUPE? DID HE FORGET SOMETHING?
HE DIDN'T. I WORK FOR THE GOVERNMENT.
I'M HERE TO SIGN YOU UP PURSUANT TO THE SUPER HERO REGISTRATION ACT.
OH, ARE YOU NOW?
OOOOO. HE WORKS FOR "THE GOVERNMENT." A DUPE WALKS IN AND STARTS TOSSING AROUND ORDERS LIKE HE'S THE ACTUAL BOSS AROUND HERE.
WHO THE HELL DO YOU THINK YOU ARE?
ALLOW ME TO INTRODUCE MYSELF:
JAMIE MADROX: AGENT OF S.H.I.E.L.D.

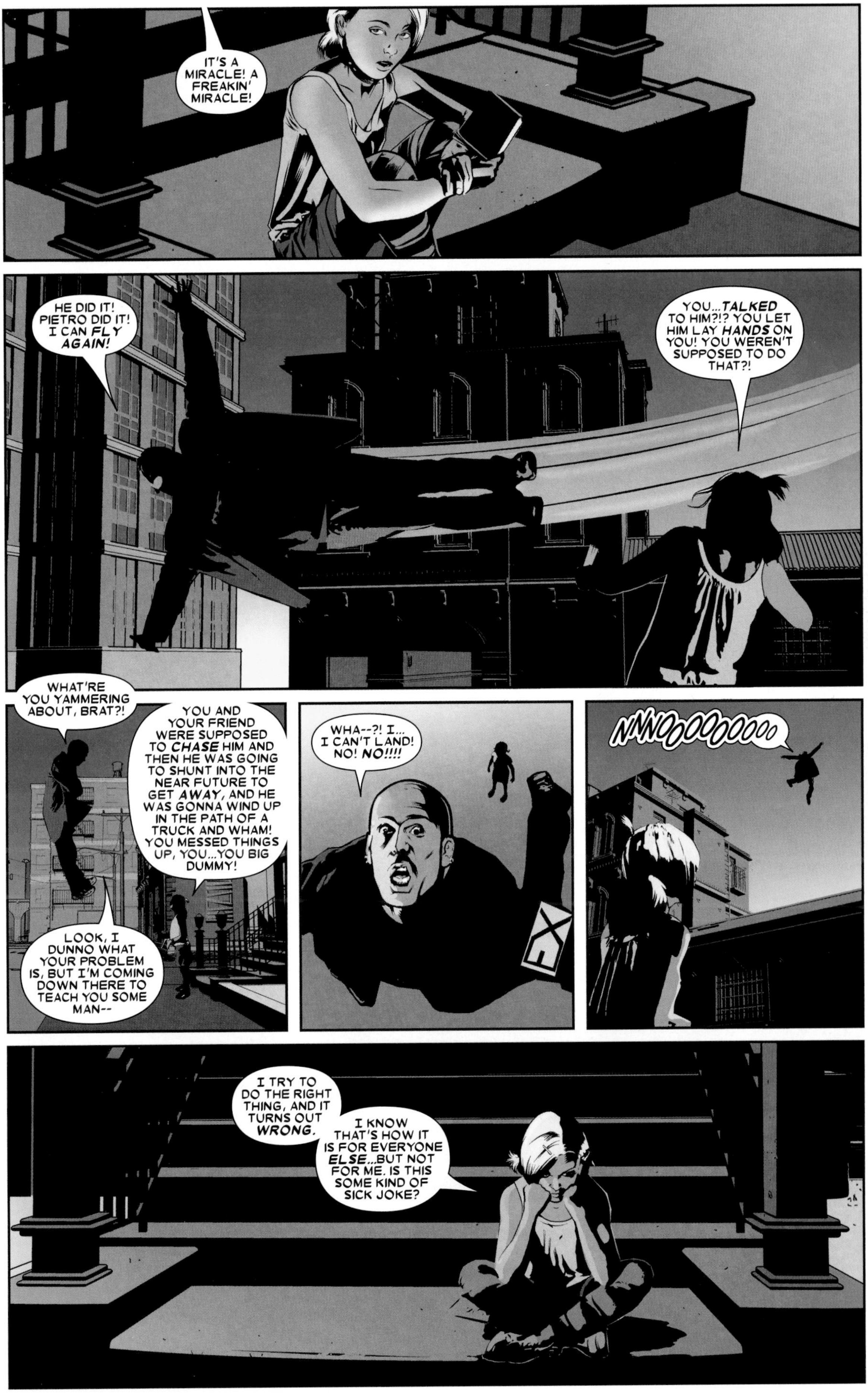
IT'S A MIRACLE! A FREAKIN' MIRACLE!
HE DID IT! PIETRO DID IT! I CAN FLY AGAIN!
YOU...TALKED TO HIM?!? YOU LET HIM LAY HANDS ON YOU! YOU WEREN'T SUPPOSED TO DO THAT?!
WHAT'RE YOU YAMMERING ABOUT, BRAT?!
YOU AND YOUR FRIEND WERE SUPPOSED TO CHASE HIM AND THEN HE WAS GOING TO SHUNT INTO THE NEAR FUTURE TO GET AWAY, AND HE WAS GONNA WIND UP IN THE PATH OF A TRUCK AND WHAM! YOU MESSED THINGS UP, YOU...YOU BIG DUMMY!
LOOK, I DUNNO WHAT YOUR PROBLEM IS, BUT I'M COMING DOWN THERE TO TEACH YOU SOME MAN--
WHA--?! I... I CAN'T LAND! NO! NO!!!!
NNNOOOOOOOOOO
I TRY TO DO THE RIGHT THING, AND IT TURNS OUT WRONG.
I KNOW THAT'S HOW IT IS FOR EVERYONE ELSE...BUT NOT FOR ME. IS THIS SOME KIND OF SICK JOKE?

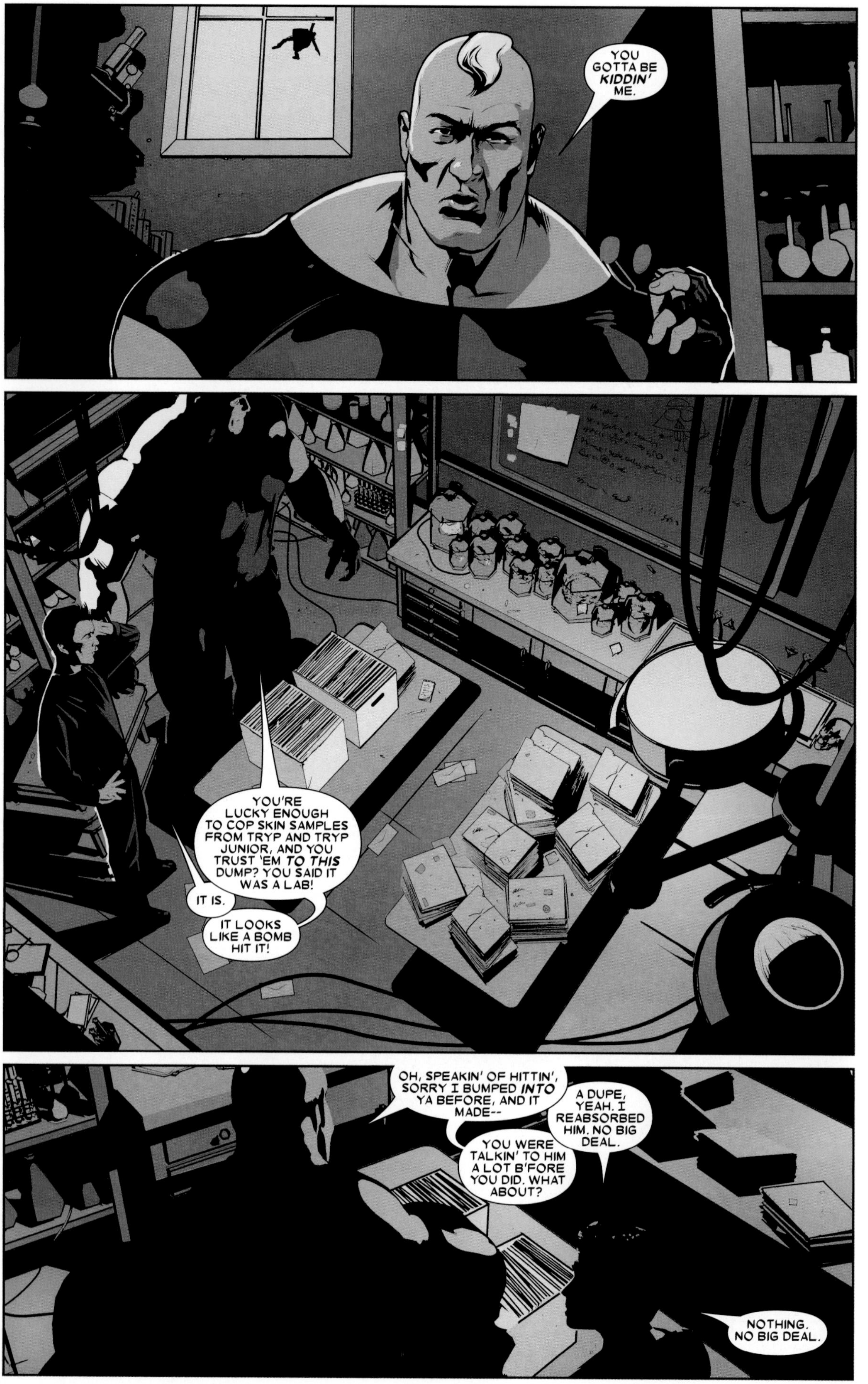
YOU GOTTA BE KIDDIN' ME.
YOU'RE LUCKY ENOUGH TO COP SKIN SAMPLES FROM TRYP AND TRYP JUNIOR, AND YOU TRUST 'EM TO THIS DUMP? YOU SAID IT WAS A LAB!
IT IS.
IT LOOKS LIKE A BOMB HIT IT!
OH, SPEAKIN' OF HITTIN', SORRY I BUMPED INTO YA BEFORE, AND IT MADE--
A DUPE, YEAH. I REABSORBED HIM. NO BIG DEAL.
YOU WERE TALKIN' TO HIM A LOT B'FORE YOU DID. WHAT ABOUT?
NOTHING. NO BIG DEAL.

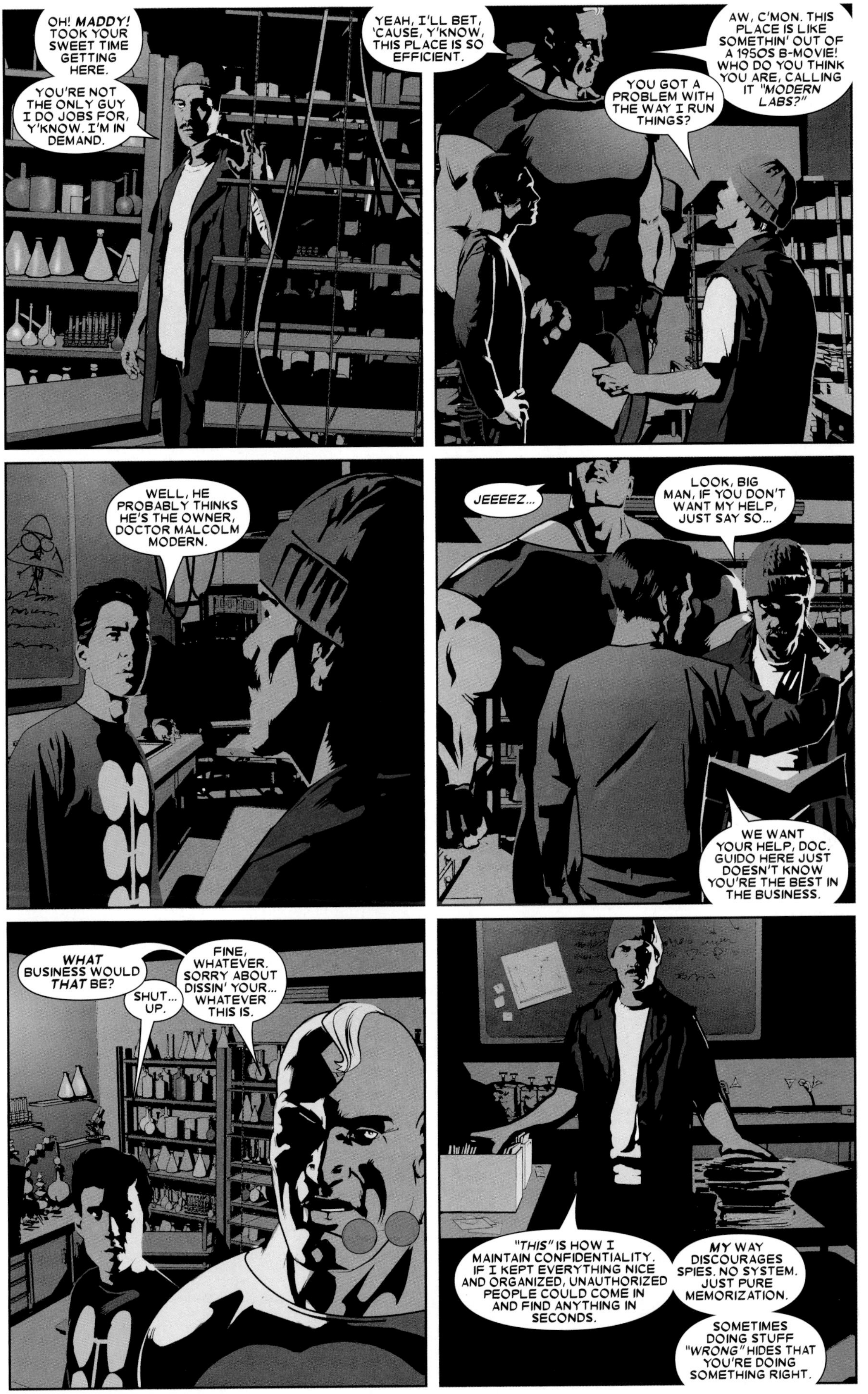
OH! MADDY! TOOK YOUR SWEET TIME GETTING HERE.
YOU'RE NOT THE ONLY GUY I DO JOBS FOR, Y'KNOW. I'M IN DEMAND.
YEAH, I'LL BET, 'CAUSE, Y'KNOW, THIS PLACE IS SO EFFICIENT.
AW, C'MON. THIS PLACE IS LIKE SOMETHIN' OUT OF A 1950S B-MOVIE! WHO DO YOU THINK YOU ARE, CALLING IT "MODERN LABS?"
YOU GOT A PROBLEM WITH THE WAY I RUN THINGS?
WELL, HE PROBABLY THINKS HE'S THE OWNER, DOCTOR MALCOLM MODERN.
JEEEEZ...
LOOK, BIG MAN, IF YOU DON'T WANT MY HELP, JUST SAY SO...
WE WANT YOUR HELP, DOC. GUIDO HERE JUST DOESN'T KNOW YOU'RE THE BEST IN THE BUSINESS.
WHAT BUSINESS WOULD THAT BE?
SHUT... UP.
FINE, WHATEVER. SORRY ABOUT DISSIN' YOUR... WHATEVER THIS IS.
"THIS" IS HOW I MAINTAIN CONFIDENTIALITY. IF I KEPT EVERYTHING NICE AND ORGANIZED, UNAUTHORIZED PEOPLE COULD COME IN AND FIND ANYTHING IN SECONDS.
MY WAY DISCOURAGES SPIES. NO SYSTEM. JUST PURE MEMORIZATION.
SOMETIMES DOING STUFF "WRONG" HIDES THAT YOU'RE DOING SOMETHING RIGHT.

HERE WE GO.

THE FOLDER'S MARKED "WEIRD."

THAT'S 'CAUSE WHAT I FOUND WAS WEIRD. THIS SAMPLE YOU BROUGHT IN...IT'S LIKE NOTHING I'VE EVER SEEN.

MEANING WHAT?

MEANING IF THERE'S ANYTHING LIKE IT, I HAVEN'T SEEN IT.

THERE'S SOME TOTALLY NEW DNA MARKERS IN HERE. COMPLETELY UNCHARTED.

YOU'RE SAYING HE'S... WHAT? ALIEN?

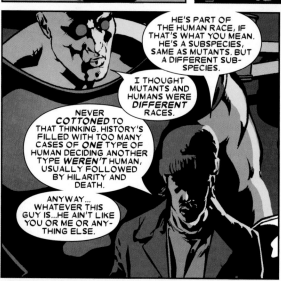

HE'S PART OF THE HUMAN RACE, IF THAT'S WHAT YOU MEAN. HE'S A SUBSPECIES, SAME AS MUTANTS. BUT A DIFFERENT SUB-SPECIES.

I THOUGHT MUTANTS AND HUMANS WERE DIFFERENT RACES.

NEVER COTTONED TO THAT THINKING. HISTORY'S FILLED WITH TOO MANY CASES OF ONE TYPE OF HUMAN DECIDING ANOTHER TYPE WEREN'T HUMAN, USUALLY FOLLOWED BY HILARITY AND DEATH.

ANYWAY... WHATEVER THIS GUY IS...HE AIN'T LIKE YOU OR ME OR ANY-THING ELSE.

OKAY... THAT'S TRYP. WHAT ABOUT THE OTHER GUY?

WHAT OTHER GUY?

HIS SON. JUNIOR.

MADDY, I DUNNO WHAT THE HELL YOU'RE TALKIN' ABOUT.

THE TWO SAMPLES YOU GAVE ME...I JUST FIGURED YOU WERE PLAYING IT SAFE.

SAFE? I DON'T--?

THE TWO SAMPLES ARE EXACT DNA MATCHES. THEY'RE THE SAME GUY.

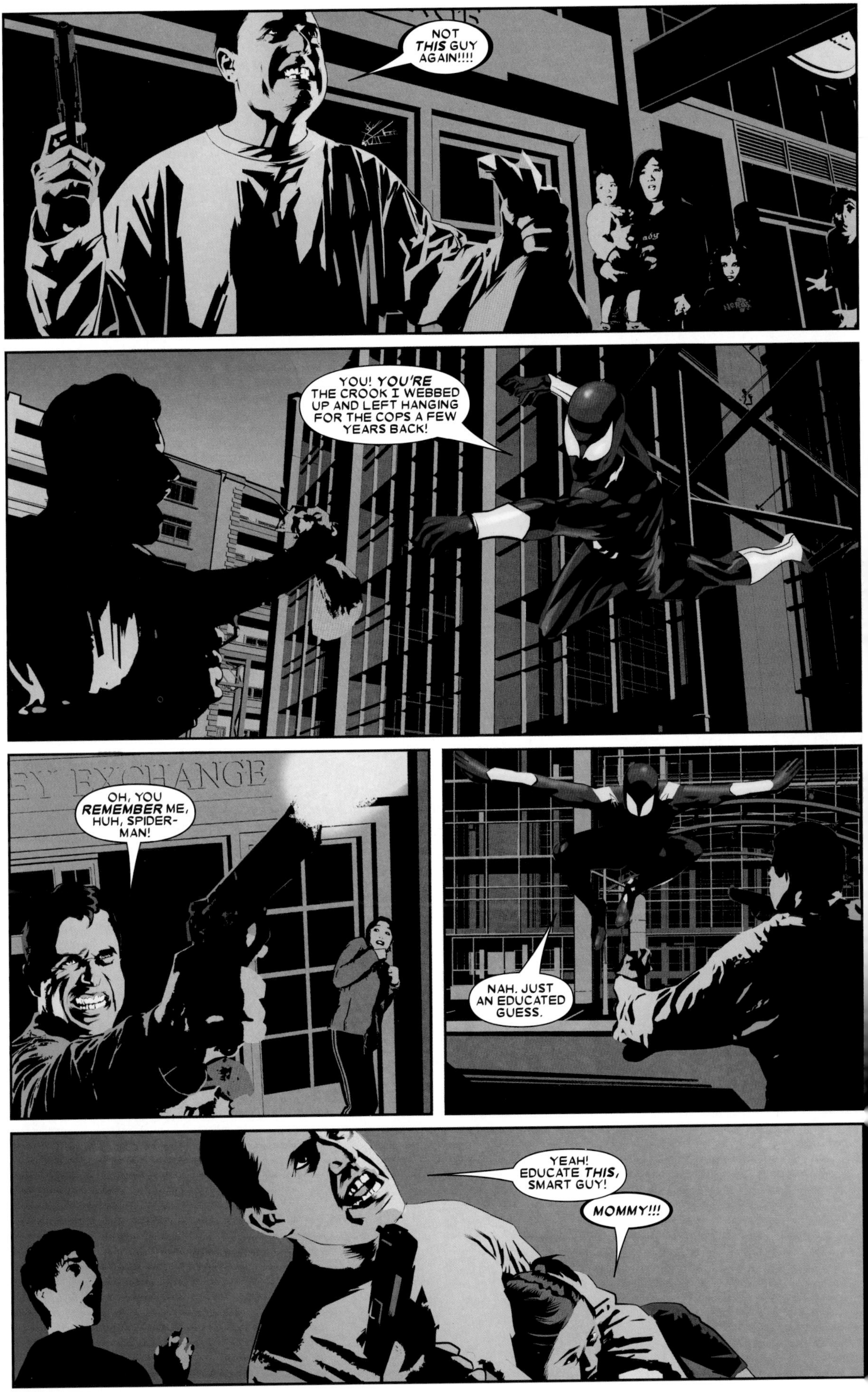
NOT *THIS* GUY AGAIN!!!!
YOU! *YOU'RE* THE CROOK I WEBBED UP AND LEFT HANGING FOR THE COPS A FEW YEARS BACK!
EY EXCHANGE
OH, YOU *REMEMBER* ME, HUH, SPIDER-MAN!
NAH. JUST AN EDUCATED GUESS.
YEAH! EDUCATE *THIS*, SMART GUY!
MOMMY!!!

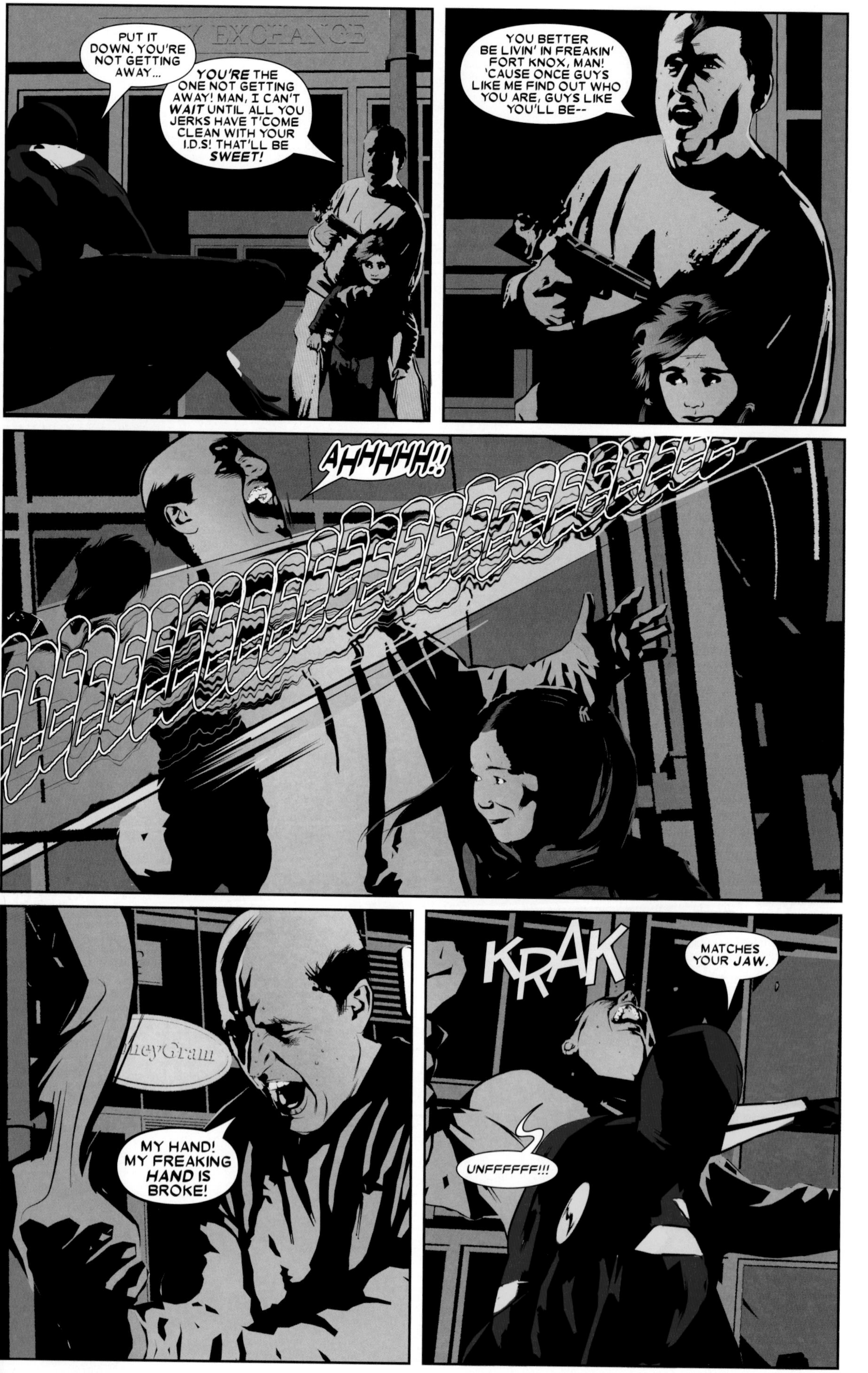
Y EXCHANGE
PUT IT DOWN. YOU'RE NOT GETTING AWAY...
YOU'RE THE ONE NOT GETTING AWAY! MAN, I CAN'T WAIT UNTIL ALL YOU JERKS HAVE T'COME CLEAN WITH YOUR I.D.S! THAT'LL BE SWEET!
YOU BETTER BE LIVIN' IN FREAKIN' FORT KNOX, MAN! 'CAUSE ONCE GUYS LIKE ME FIND OUT WHO YOU ARE, GUYS LIKE YOU'LL BE--
AHHHHH!!
EEEEEEEEEEEEEEEEEEEEEEEEEEEEEEEEEEEEEEEEEEEEE
ileyGram
MY HAND! MY FREAKING HAND IS BROKE!
KRAK
MATCHES YOUR JAW.
UNFFFFFF!!!

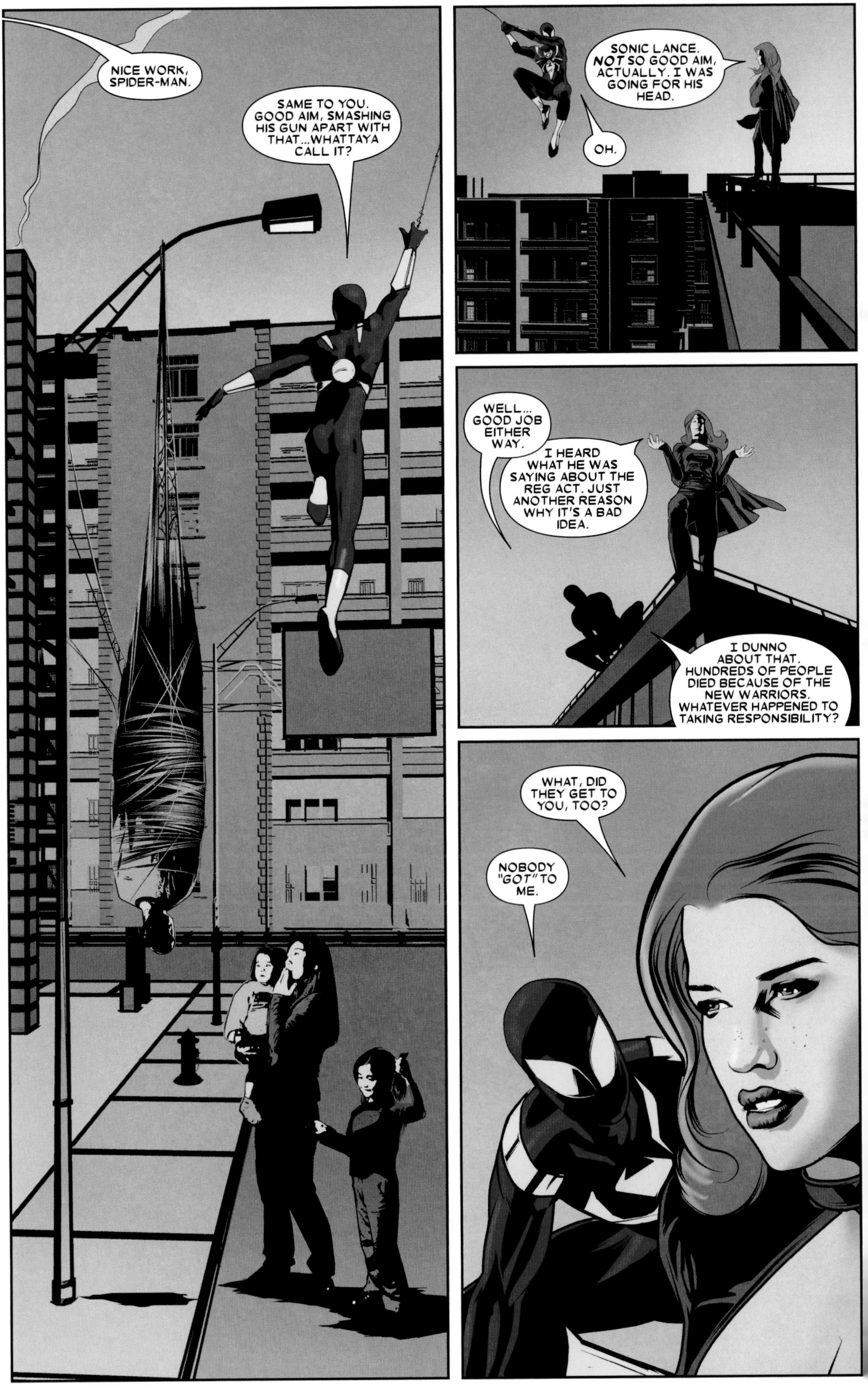

NICE WORK, SPIDER-MAN.
SAME TO YOU. GOOD AIM, SMASHING HIS GUN APART WITH THAT...WHATTAYA CALL IT?
SONIC LANCE. NOT SO GOOD AIM, ACTUALLY. I WAS GOING FOR HIS HEAD.
OH.
WELL... GOOD JOB EITHER WAY.
I HEARD WHAT HE WAS SAYING ABOUT THE REG ACT. JUST ANOTHER REASON WHY IT'S A BAD IDEA.
I DUNNO ABOUT THAT. HUNDREDS OF PEOPLE DIED BECAUSE OF THE NEW WARRIORS. WHATEVER HAPPENED TO TAKING RESPONSIBILITY?
WHAT, DID THEY GET TO YOU, TOO?
NOBODY "GOT" TO ME.

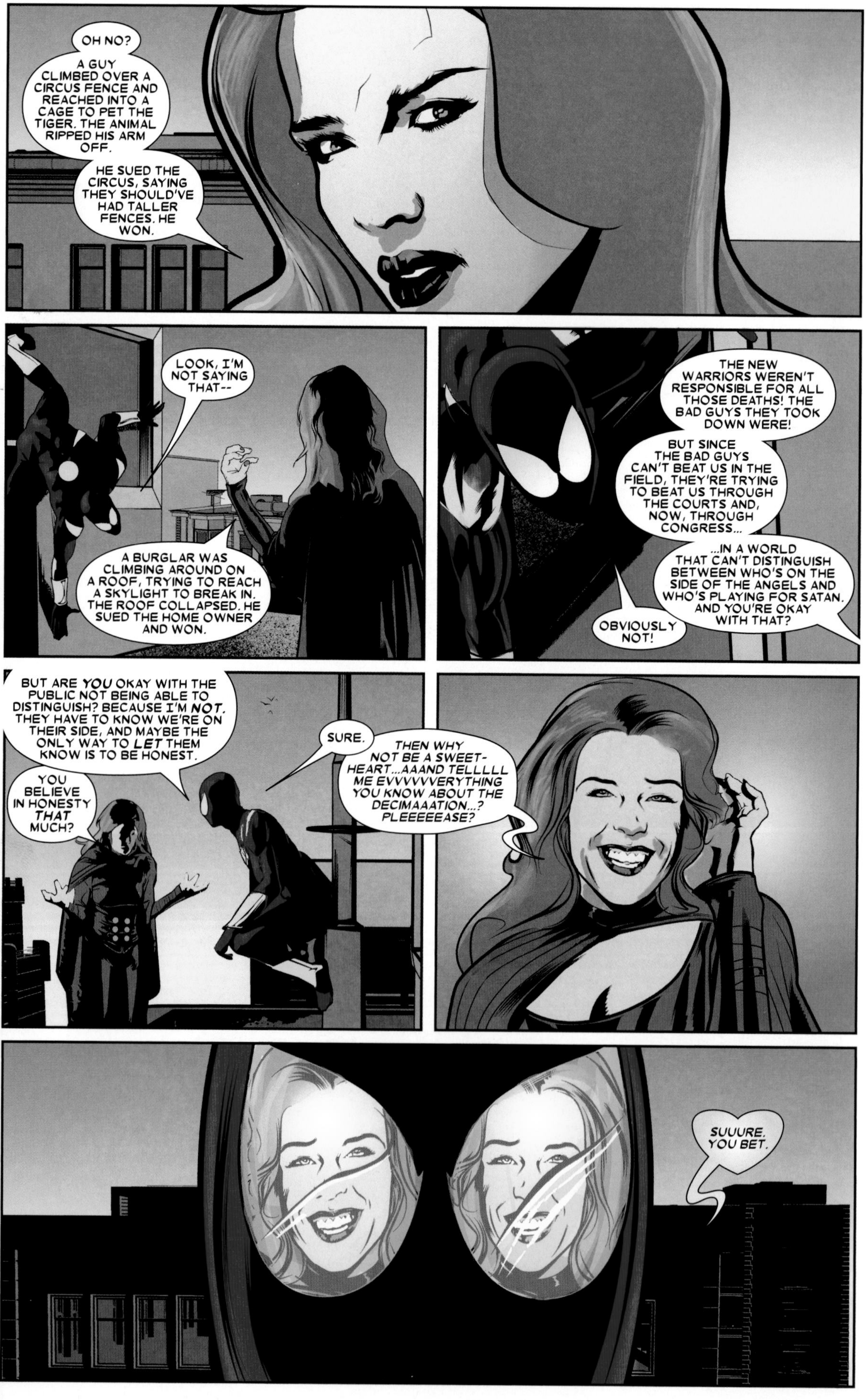
OH NO?
A GUY CLIMBED OVER A CIRCUS FENCE AND REACHED INTO A CAGE TO PET THE TIGER. THE ANIMAL RIPPED HIS ARM OFF.
HE SUED THE CIRCUS, SAYING THEY SHOULD'VE HAD TALLER FENCES. HE WON.
LOOK, I'M NOT SAYING THAT--
A BURGLAR WAS CLIMBING AROUND ON A ROOF, TRYING TO REACH A SKYLIGHT TO BREAK IN. THE ROOF COLLAPSED. HE SUED THE HOME OWNER AND WON.
THE NEW WARRIORS WEREN'T RESPONSIBLE FOR ALL THOSE DEATHS! THE BAD GUYS THEY TOOK DOWN WERE!
BUT SINCE THE BAD GUYS CAN'T BEAT US IN THE FIELD, THEY'RE TRYING TO BEAT US THROUGH THE COURTS AND, NOW, THROUGH CONGRESS...
...IN A WORLD THAT CAN'T DISTINGUISH BETWEEN WHO'S ON THE SIDE OF THE ANGELS AND WHO'S PLAYING FOR SATAN. AND YOU'RE OKAY WITH THAT?
OBVIOUSLY NOT!
BUT ARE YOU OKAY WITH THE PUBLIC NOT BEING ABLE TO DISTINGUISH? BECAUSE I'M NOT. THEY HAVE TO KNOW WE'RE ON THEIR SIDE, AND MAYBE THE ONLY WAY TO LET THEM KNOW IS TO BE HONEST.
YOU BELIEVE IN HONESTY THAT MUCH?
SURE.
THEN WHY NOT BE A SWEET-HEART...AAAND TELLLLL ME EVVVVVVERYTHING YOU KNOW ABOUT THE DECIMAAATION...? PLEEEEEASE?
SUUURE. YOU BET.

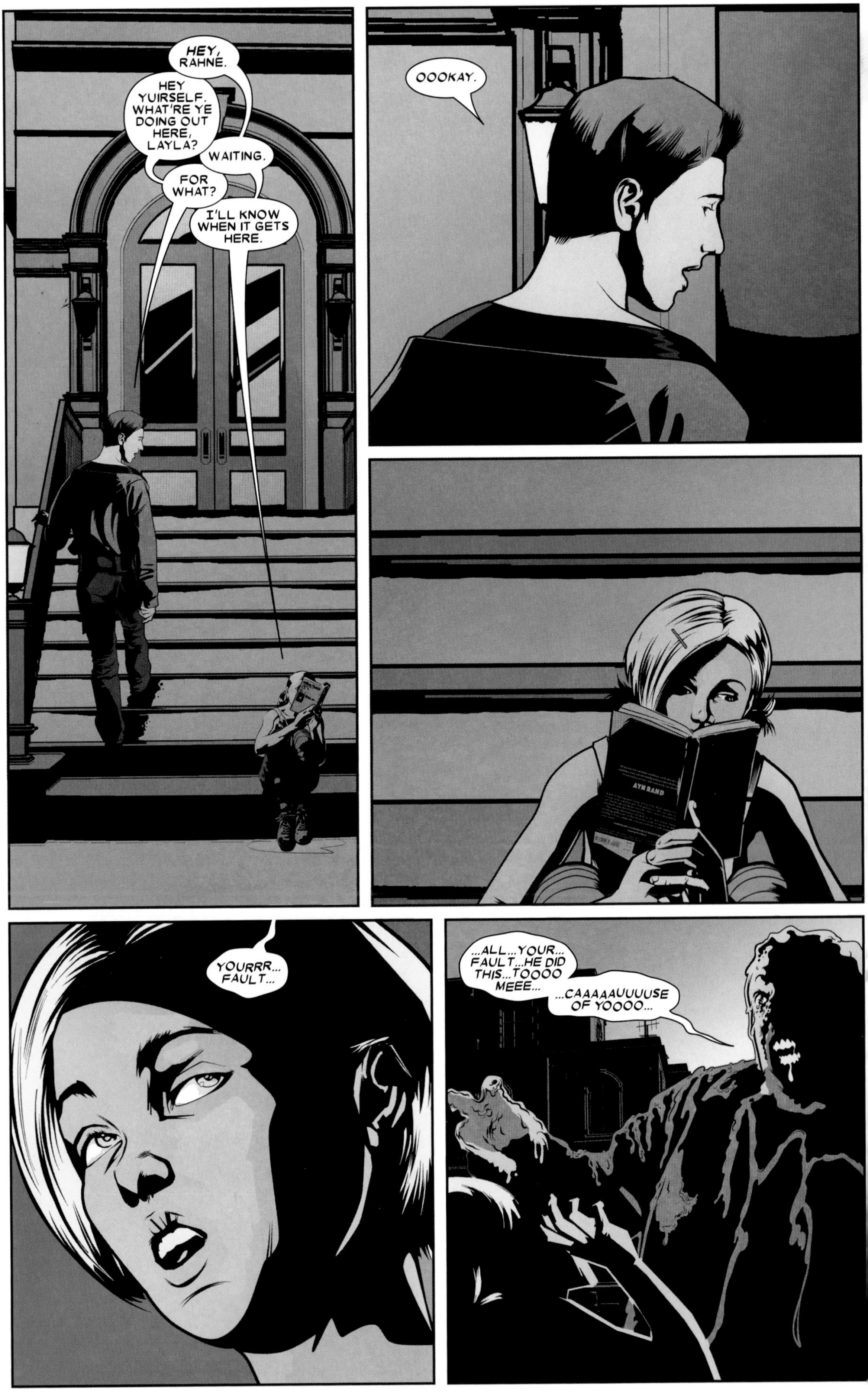
HEY, RAHNE.
HEY YUIRSELF. WHAT'RE YE DOING OUT HERE, LAYLA?
WAITING.
FOR WHAT?
I'LL KNOW WHEN IT GETS HERE.
OOOKAY.
AYN RAND
YOURRR... FAULT...
...ALL...YOUR... FAULT...HE DID THIS...TOOOO MEEE...
...CAAAAAUUUUSE OF YOOOO...

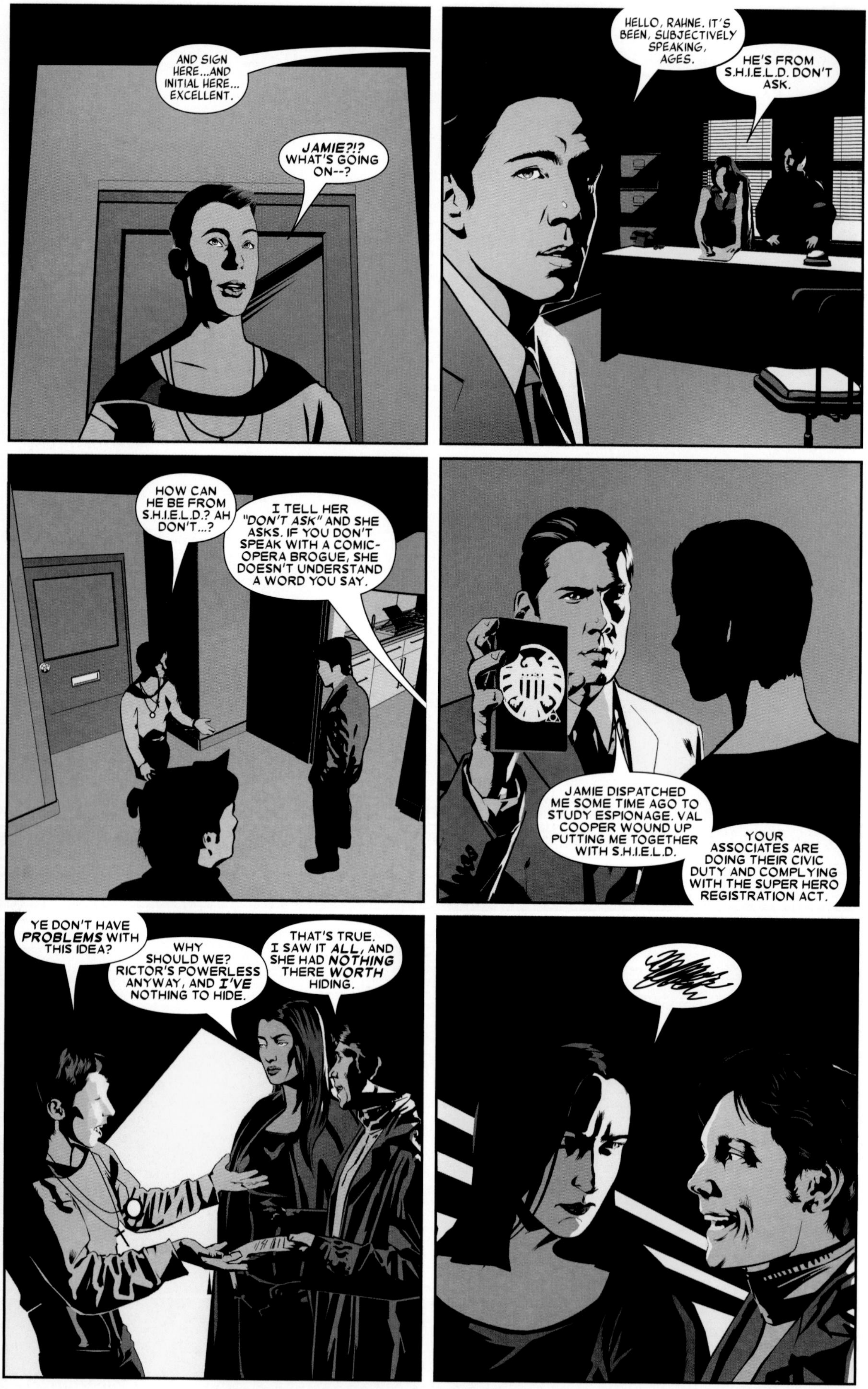
AND SIGN HERE...AND INITIAL HERE... EXCELLENT.
JAMIE?!? WHAT'S GOING ON--?
HELLO, RAHNE. IT'S BEEN, SUBJECTIVELY SPEAKING, AGES.
HE'S FROM S.H.I.E.L.D. DON'T ASK.
HOW CAN HE BE FROM S.H.I.E.L.D.? AH DON'T...?
I TELL HER "DON'T ASK" AND SHE ASKS. IF YOU DON'T SPEAK WITH A COMIC-OPERA BROGUE, SHE DOESN'T UNDERSTAND A WORD YOU SAY.
JAMIE DISPATCHED ME SOME TIME AGO TO STUDY ESPIONAGE. VAL COOPER WOUND UP PUTTING ME TOGETHER WITH S.H.I.E.L.D.
YOUR ASSOCIATES ARE DOING THEIR CIVIC DUTY AND COMPLYING WITH THE SUPER HERO REGISTRATION ACT.
YE DON'T HAVE PROBLEMS WITH THIS IDEA?
WHY SHOULD WE? RICTOR'S POWERLESS ANYWAY, AND I'VE NOTHING TO HIDE.
THAT'S TRUE. I SAW IT ALL, AND SHE HAD NOTHING THERE WORTH HIDING.

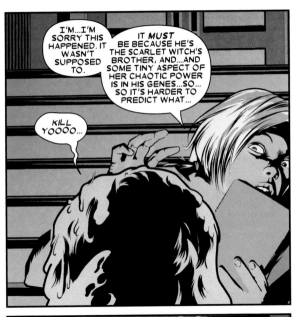

I'M...I'M SORRY THIS HAPPENED. IT WASN'T SUPPOSED TO.

IT *MUST* BE BECAUSE HE'S THE SCARLET WITCH'S BROTHER, AND...AND SOME TINY ASPECT OF HER CHAOTIC POWER IS IN HIS GENES...SO... SO IT'S HARDER TO PREDICT WHAT...

KILL YOOOO...

KILLLLL... Y--

--OOOOOOOO...

SHLUUP

EWW. GROSS.

GURGLE-GLORP

GOOD HEAVENS, YOUNG LADY. YOU LOOK SO *SERIOUS.* LIKE YOU HAVE THE WEIGHT OF THE WORLD ON YOUR SHOULDERS.

I DO.

HOW DO YOU DEAL WITH THAT?

I SHRUG.

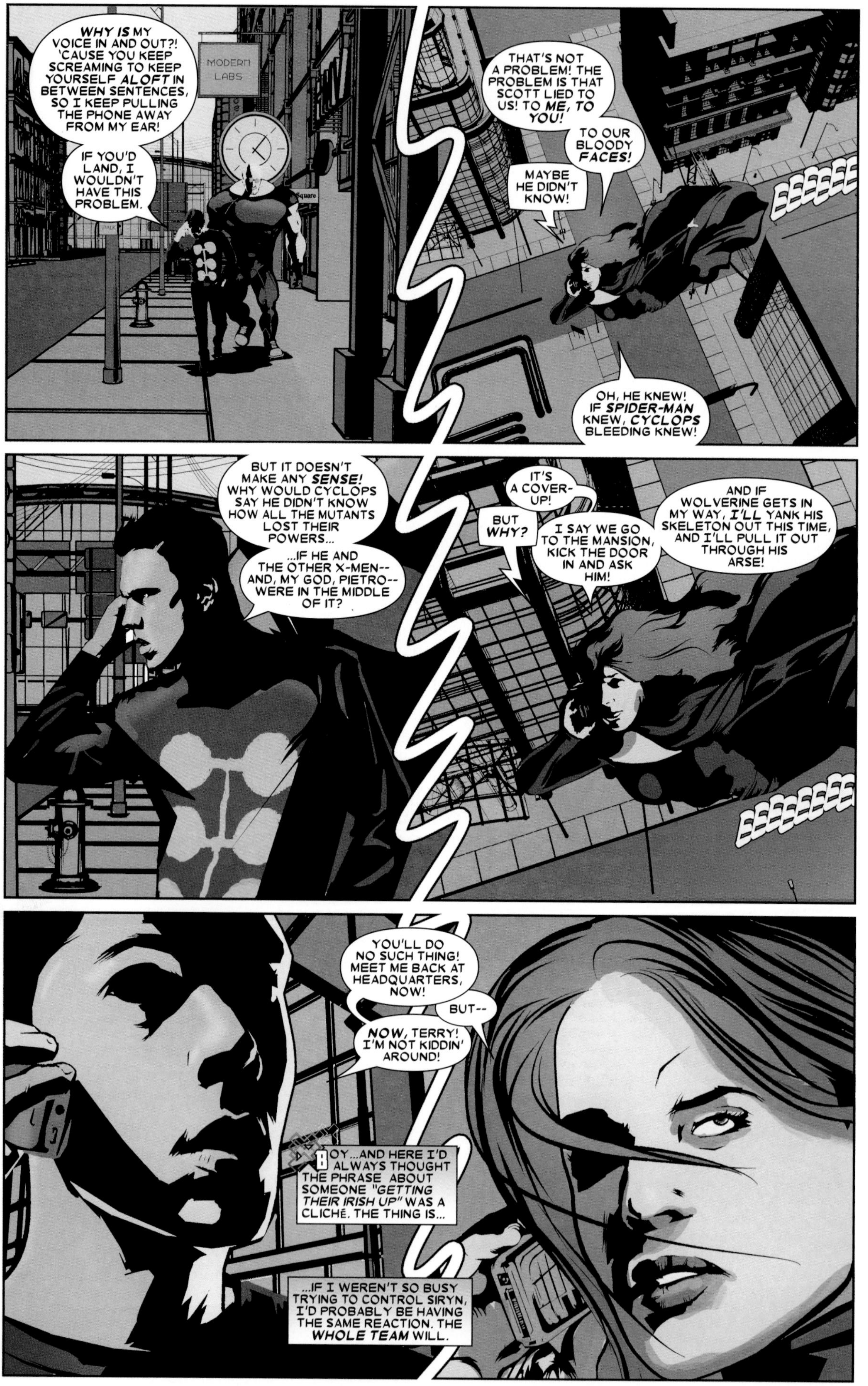
WHY IS MY VOICE IN AND OUT?! 'CAUSE YOU KEEP SCREAMING TO KEEP YOURSELF ALOFT IN BETWEEN SENTENCES, SO I KEEP PULLING THE PHONE AWAY FROM MY EAR!
IF YOU'D LAND, I WOULDN'T HAVE THIS PROBLEM.
MODERN LABS
THAT'S NOT A PROBLEM! THE PROBLEM IS THAT SCOTT LIED TO US! TO ME, TO YOU!
TO OUR BLOODY FACES!
MAYBE HE DIDN'T KNOW!
EEEEEEE
OH, HE KNEW! IF SPIDER-MAN KNEW, CYCLOPS BLEEDING KNEW!
BUT IT DOESN'T MAKE ANY SENSE! WHY WOULD CYCLOPS SAY HE DIDN'T KNOW HOW ALL THE MUTANTS LOST THEIR POWERS...
...IF HE AND THE OTHER X-MEN-- AND, MY GOD, PIETRO-- WERE IN THE MIDDLE OF IT?
IT'S A COVER-UP!
BUT WHY?
I SAY WE GO TO THE MANSION, KICK THE DOOR IN AND ASK HIM!
AND IF WOLVERINE GETS IN MY WAY, I'LL YANK HIS SKELETON OUT THIS TIME, AND I'LL PULL IT OUT THROUGH HIS ARSE!
EEEEEEEE
YOU'LL DO NO SUCH THING! MEET ME BACK AT HEADQUARTERS, NOW!
BUT--
NOW, TERRY! I'M NOT KIDDIN' AROUND!
BOY...AND HERE I'D ALWAYS THOUGHT THE PHRASE ABOUT SOMEONE "GETTING THEIR IRISH UP" WAS A CLICHÉ. THE THING IS...
...IF I WEREN'T SO BUSY TRYING TO CONTROL SIRYN, I'D PROBABLY BE HAVING THE SAME REACTION. THE WHOLE TEAM WILL.

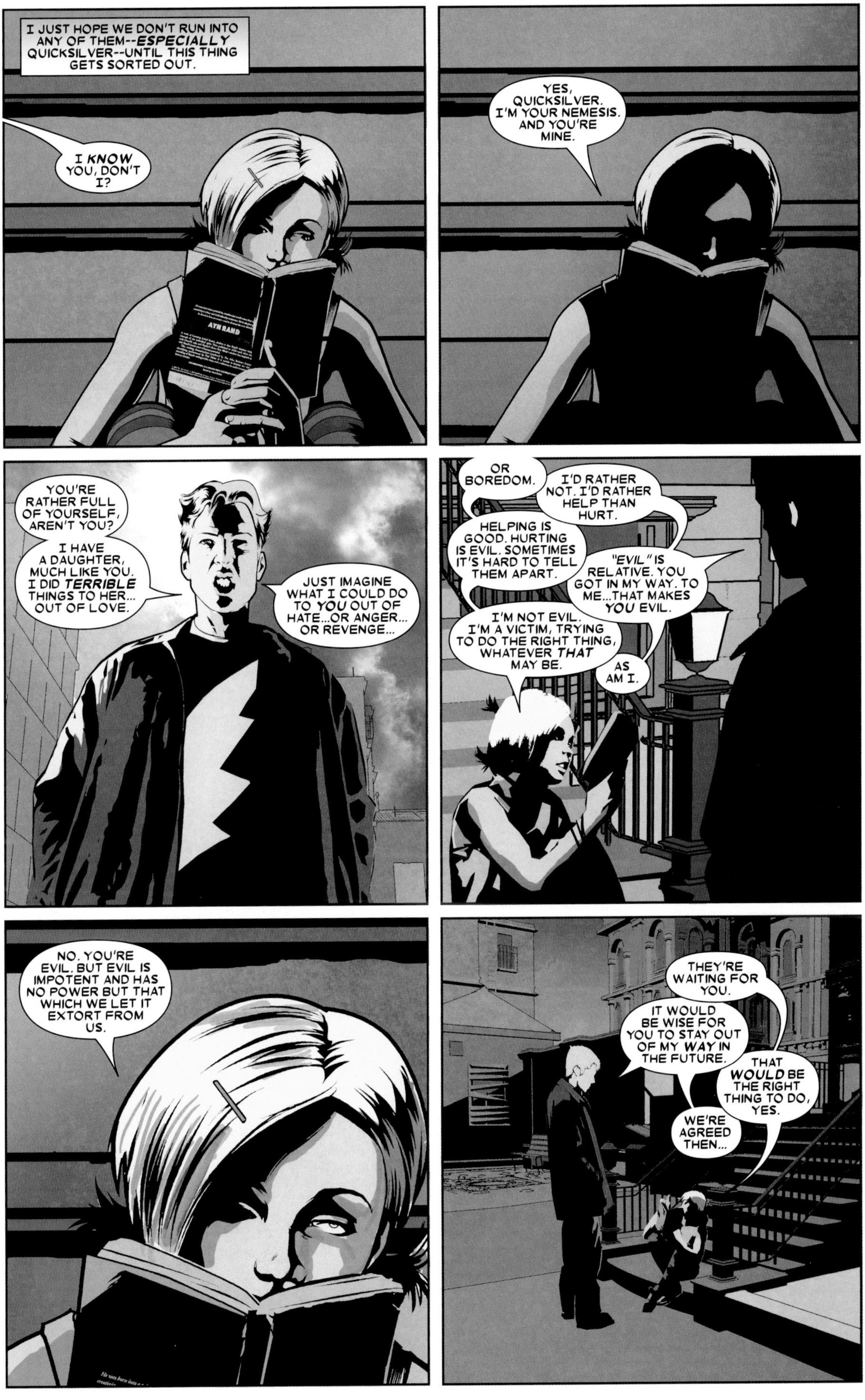
I JUST HOPE WE DON'T RUN INTO ANY OF THEM--ESPECIALLY QUICKSILVER--UNTIL THIS THING GETS SORTED OUT.
I KNOW YOU, DON'T I?
AYN RAND
YES, QUICKSILVER. I'M YOUR NEMESIS. AND YOU'RE MINE.
YOU'RE RATHER FULL OF YOURSELF, AREN'T YOU?
I HAVE A DAUGHTER, MUCH LIKE YOU. I DID TERRIBLE THINGS TO HER... OUT OF LOVE.
JUST IMAGINE WHAT I COULD DO TO YOU OUT OF HATE...OR ANGER... OR REVENGE...
OR BOREDOM.
I'D RATHER NOT. I'D RATHER HELP THAN HURT.
HELPING IS GOOD. HURTING IS EVIL. SOMETIMES IT'S HARD TO TELL THEM APART.
"EVIL" IS RELATIVE. YOU GOT IN MY WAY. TO ME...THAT MAKES YOU EVIL.
I'M NOT EVIL. I'M A VICTIM, TRYING TO DO THE RIGHT THING, WHATEVER THAT MAY BE.
AS AM I.
NO. YOU'RE EVIL. BUT EVIL IS IMPOTENT AND HAS NO POWER BUT THAT WHICH WE LET IT EXTORT FROM US.
THEY'RE WAITING FOR YOU.
IT WOULD BE WISE FOR YOU TO STAY OUT OF MY WAY IN THE FUTURE.
THAT WOULD BE THE RIGHT THING TO DO, YES.
WE'RE AGREED THEN...

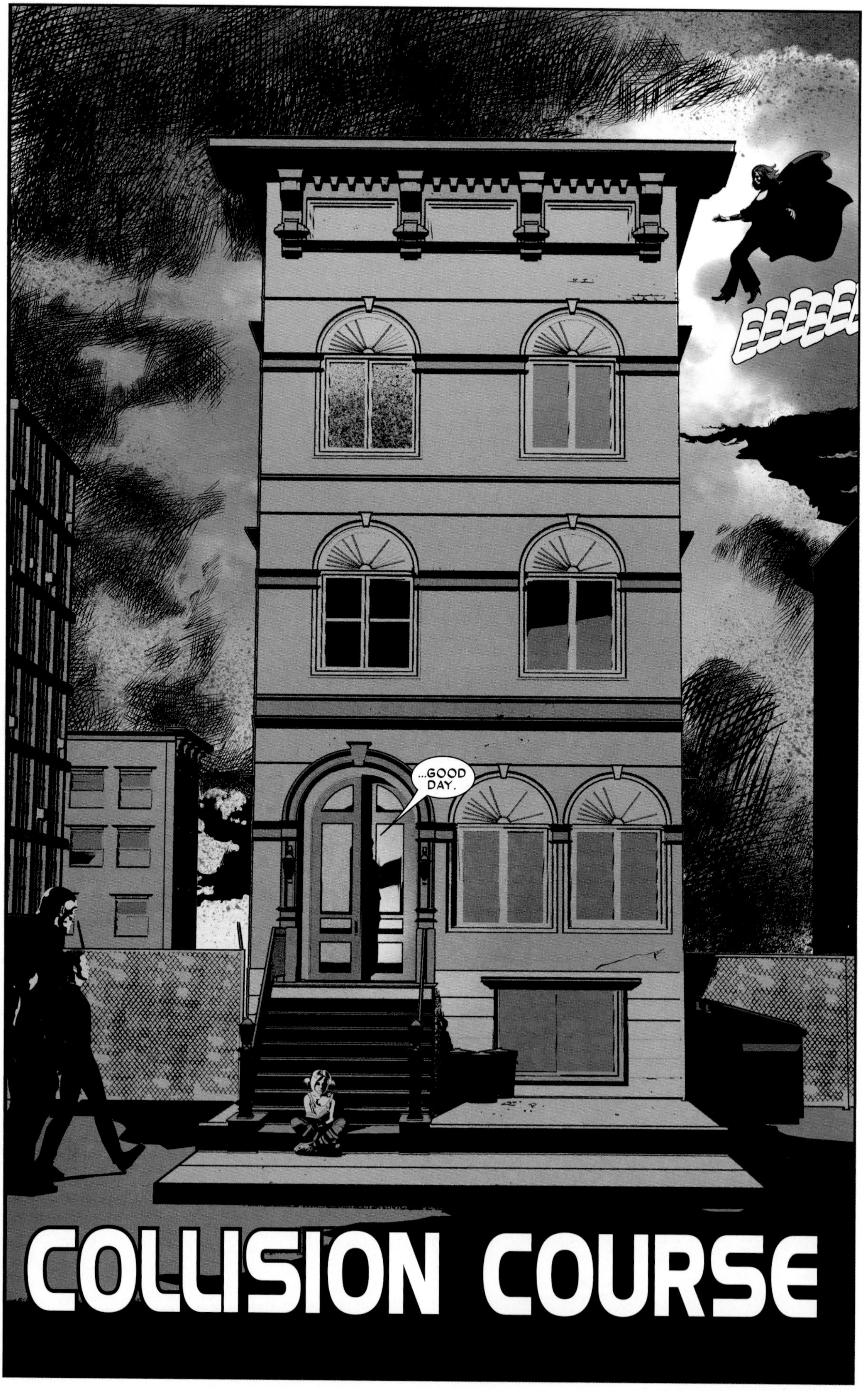
EEEEEEL
...GOOD DAY.
COLLISION COURSE

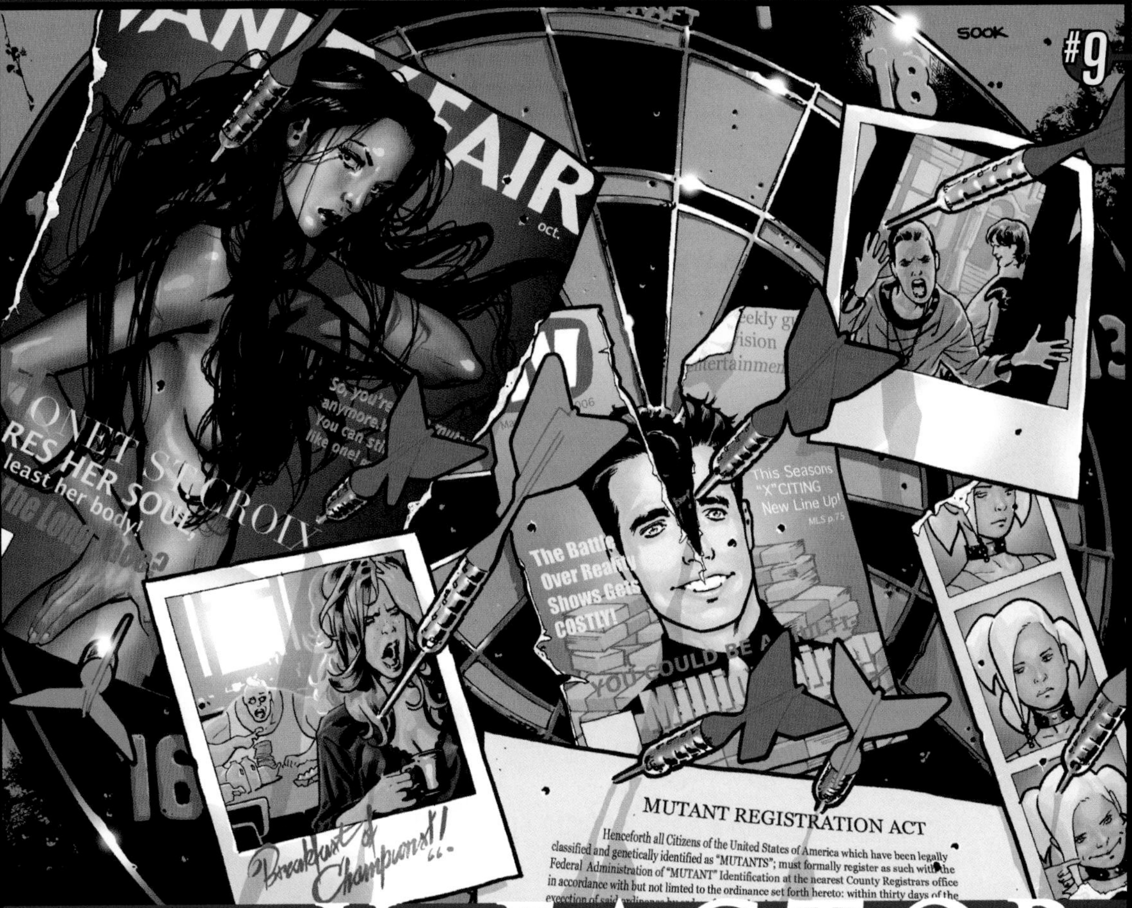

SOOK
#9
oct.
This Seasons
"X"CITING
New Line Up!
MLS p.75
COSTLY!
MUTANT REGISTRATION ACT
Henceforth all Citizens of the United States of America which have been legally
classified and genetically identified as "MUTANTS"; must formally register as such with the
Federal Administration of "MUTANT" Identification at the nearest County Registrars office
in accordance with but not limted to the ordinance set forth hereto: within thirty days of the
Breakfast of Champions!!

X-FACTOR
A MARVEL COMICS EVENT

CIVIL WAR

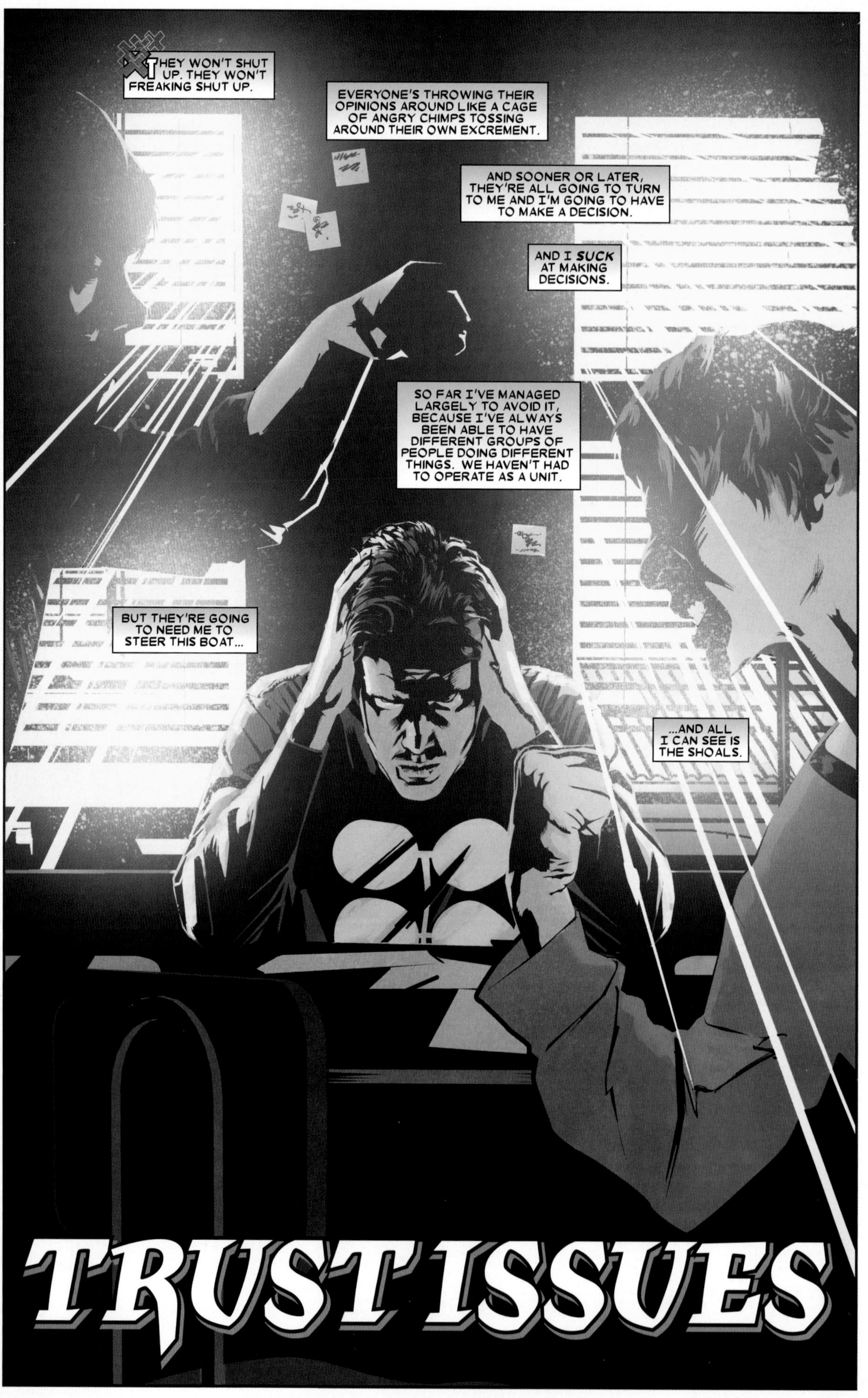

THEY WON'T SHUT UP. THEY WON'T FREAKING SHUT UP.
EVERYONE'S THROWING THEIR OPINIONS AROUND LIKE A CAGE OF ANGRY CHIMPS TOSSING AROUND THEIR OWN EXCREMENT.
AND SOONER OR LATER, THEY'RE ALL GOING TO TURN TO ME AND I'M GOING TO HAVE TO MAKE A DECISION.
AND I *SUCK* AT MAKING DECISIONS.
SO FAR I'VE MANAGED LARGELY TO AVOID IT, BECAUSE I'VE ALWAYS BEEN ABLE TO HAVE DIFFERENT GROUPS OF PEOPLE DOING DIFFERENT THINGS. WE HAVEN'T HAD TO OPERATE AS A UNIT.
BUT THEY'RE GOING TO NEED ME TO STEER THIS BOAT...
...AND ALL I CAN SEE IS THE SHOALS.
TRUST ISSUES

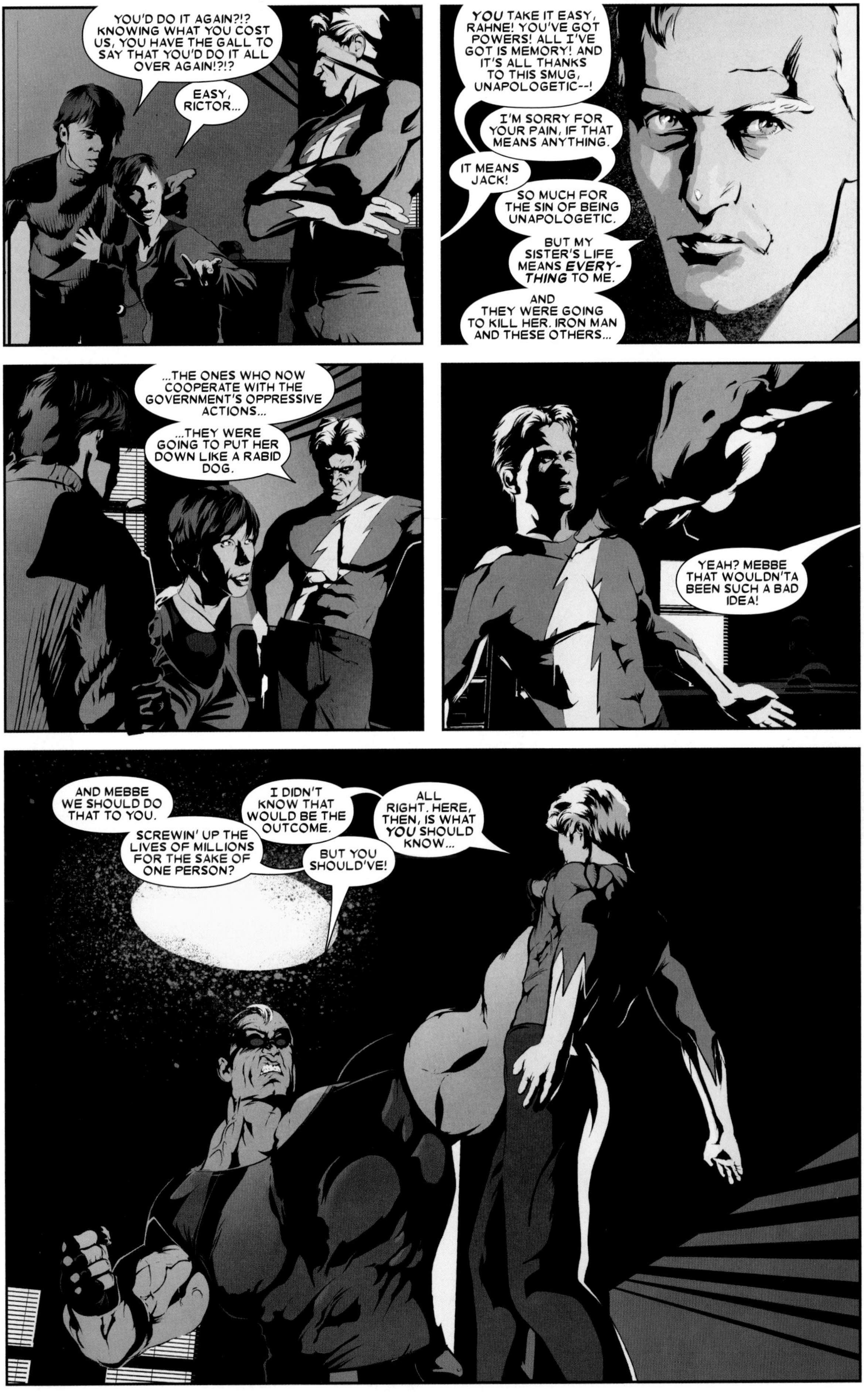
YOU'D DO IT AGAIN?!? KNOWING WHAT YOU COST US, YOU HAVE THE GALL TO SAY THAT YOU'D DO IT ALL OVER AGAIN!?!?
EASY, RICTOR...
YOU TAKE IT EASY, RAHNE! YOU'VE GOT POWERS! ALL I'VE GOT IS MEMORY! AND IT'S ALL THANKS TO THIS SMUG, UNAPOLOGETIC--!
I'M SORRY FOR YOUR PAIN, IF THAT MEANS ANYTHING.
IT MEANS JACK!
SO MUCH FOR THE SIN OF BEING UNAPOLOGETIC.
BUT MY SISTER'S LIFE MEANS EVERY-THING TO ME.
AND THEY WERE GOING TO KILL HER. IRON MAN AND THESE OTHERS...
...THE ONES WHO NOW COOPERATE WITH THE GOVERNMENT'S OPPRESSIVE ACTIONS...
...THEY WERE GOING TO PUT HER DOWN LIKE A RABID DOG.
YEAH? MEBBE THAT WOULDN'TA BEEN SUCH A BAD IDEA!
AND MEBBE WE SHOULD DO THAT TO YOU.
SCREWIN' UP THE LIVES OF MILLIONS FOR THE SAKE OF ONE PERSON?
I DIDN'T KNOW THAT WOULD BE THE OUTCOME.
BUT YOU SHOULD'VE!
ALL RIGHT. HERE, THEN, IS WHAT YOU SHOULD KNOW...

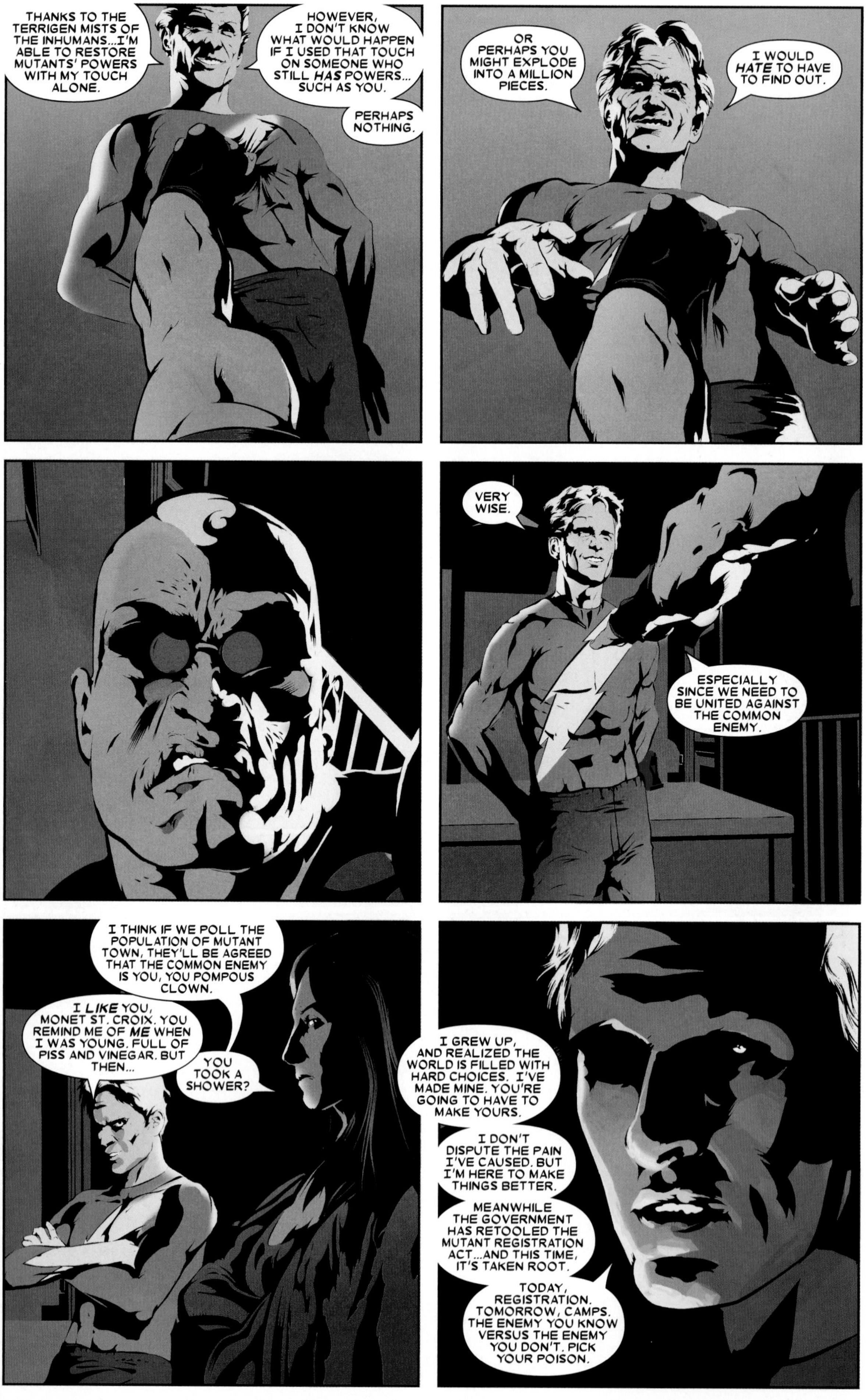
THANKS TO THE TERRIGEN MISTS OF THE INHUMANS...I'M ABLE TO RESTORE MUTANTS' POWERS WITH MY TOUCH ALONE.
HOWEVER, I DON'T KNOW WHAT WOULD HAPPEN IF I USED THAT TOUCH ON SOMEONE WHO STILL *HAS* POWERS... SUCH AS YOU.
PERHAPS NOTHING.
OR PERHAPS YOU MIGHT EXPLODE INTO A MILLION PIECES.
I WOULD *HATE* TO HAVE TO FIND OUT.
VERY WISE.
ESPECIALLY SINCE WE NEED TO BE UNITED AGAINST THE COMMON ENEMY.
I THINK IF WE POLL THE POPULATION OF MUTANT TOWN, THEY'LL BE AGREED THAT THE COMMON ENEMY IS YOU, YOU POMPOUS CLOWN.
I *LIKE* YOU, MONET ST. CROIX. YOU REMIND ME OF *ME* WHEN I WAS YOUNG. FULL OF PISS AND VINEGAR. BUT THEN...
YOU TOOK A SHOWER?
I GREW UP, AND REALIZED THE WORLD IS FILLED WITH HARD CHOICES. I'VE MADE MINE. YOU'RE GOING TO HAVE TO MAKE YOURS.
I DON'T DISPUTE THE PAIN I'VE CAUSED. BUT I'M HERE TO MAKE THINGS BETTER.
MEANWHILE THE GOVERNMENT HAS RETOOLED THE MUTANT REGISTRATION ACT...AND THIS TIME, IT'S TAKEN ROOT.
TODAY, REGISTRATION. TOMORROW, CAMPS. THE ENEMY YOU KNOW VERSUS THE ENEMY YOU DON'T. PICK YOUR POISON.

OH GOD...

JAMIE...

HERE IT COMES.

...WHAT DO *YOU* THINK?

YEAH. WHAT'S YOUR TAKE ON THIS?

WHOSE SIDE IS X-FACTOR ON, ANYWAY?

DO WE TELL EVERYONE WHAT HAPPENED?

SHOULD WE LET FAST-FEET SET UP SHOP HERE?

AS IF YOU COULD STOP ME.

SHOULD WE *TRY* TO STOP HIM?

WHAT ABOUT THE REG ACT? WHAT ABOUT THAT?

SO, MADROX. WHAT'S--?

X-FACTOR DETECTIVE AGENCY

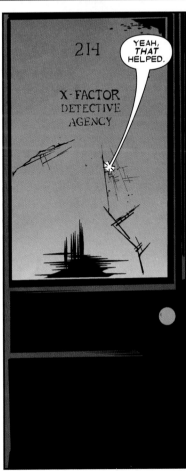

YEAH, *THAT* HELPED.

X-FACTOR DETECTIVE AGENCY

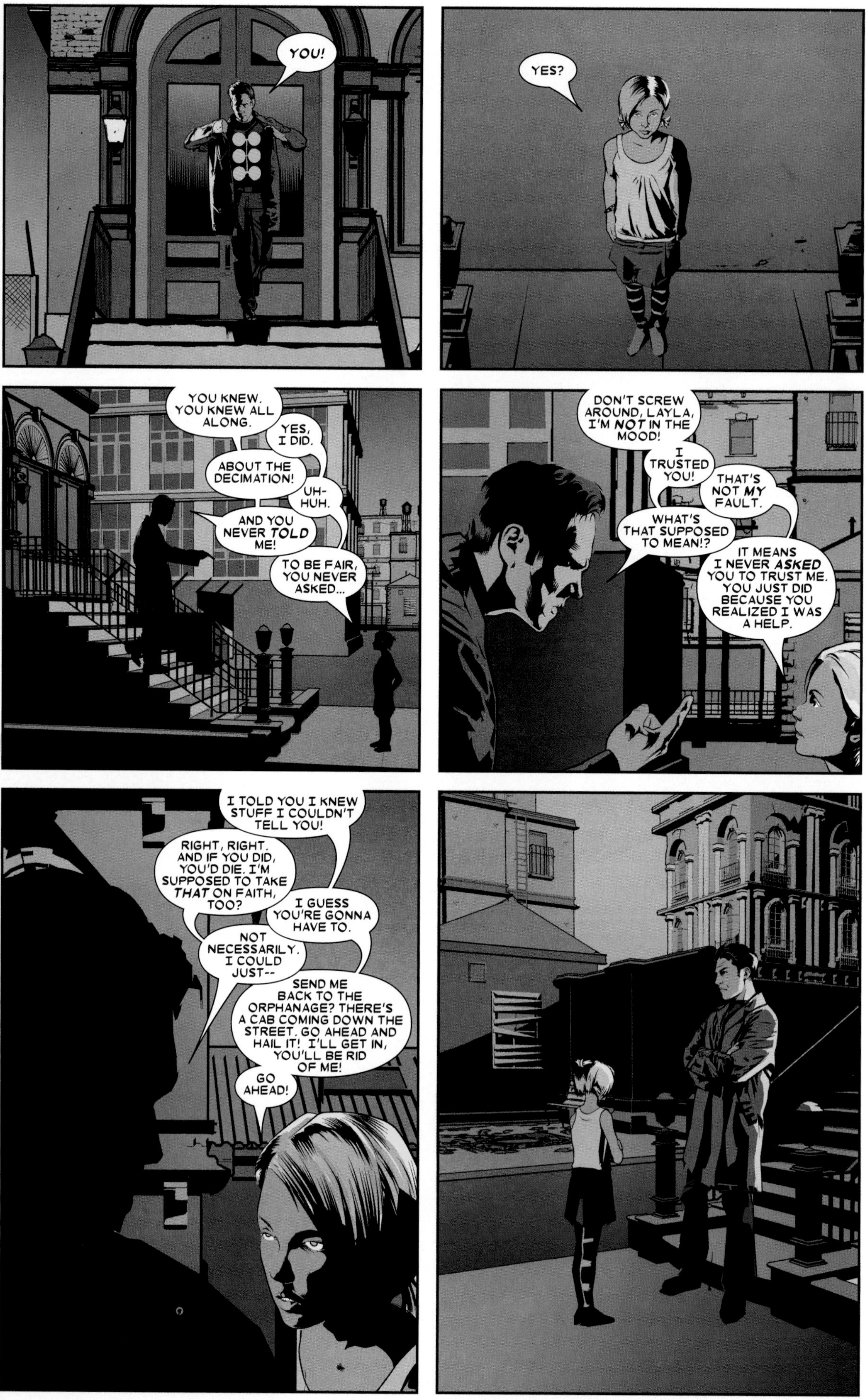
YOU!
YES?
YOU KNEW. YOU KNEW ALL ALONG.
YES, I DID.
ABOUT THE DECIMATION!
UH-HUH.
AND YOU NEVER *TOLD* ME!
TO BE FAIR, YOU NEVER ASKED...
DON'T SCREW AROUND, LAYLA, I'M *NOT* IN THE MOOD!
I TRUSTED YOU!
THAT'S NOT *MY* FAULT.
WHAT'S THAT SUPPOSED TO MEAN!?
IT MEANS I NEVER *ASKED* YOU TO TRUST ME. YOU JUST DID BECAUSE YOU REALIZED I WAS A HELP.
I TOLD YOU I KNEW STUFF I COULDN'T TELL YOU!
RIGHT, RIGHT. AND IF YOU DID, YOU'D DIE. I'M SUPPOSED TO TAKE *THAT* ON FAITH, TOO?
I GUESS YOU'RE GONNA HAVE TO.
NOT NECESSARILY. I COULD JUST--
SEND ME BACK TO THE ORPHANAGE? THERE'S A CAB COMING DOWN THE STREET. GO AHEAD AND HAIL IT! I'LL GET IN, YOU'LL BE RID OF ME!
GO AHEAD!

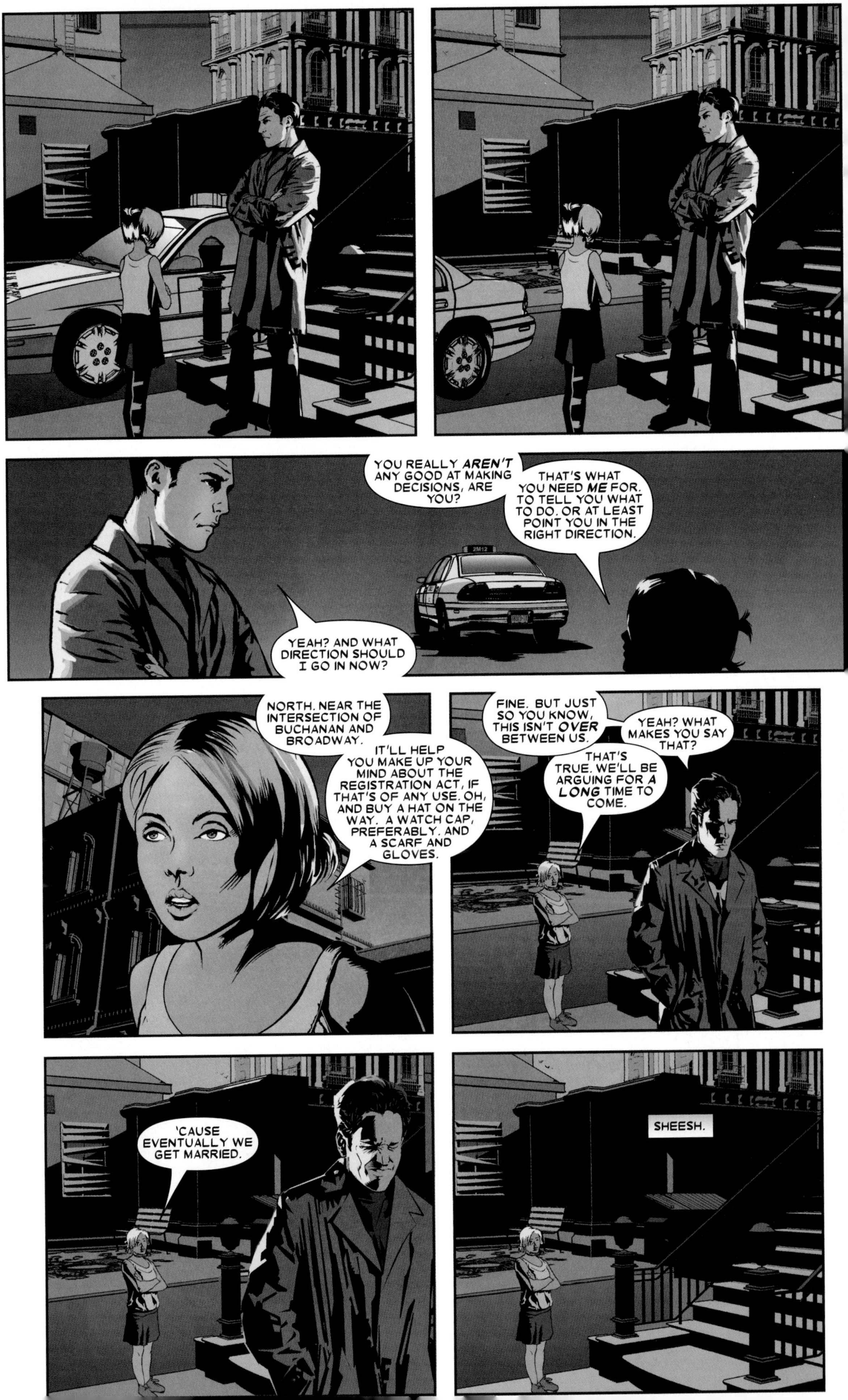
YOU REALLY AREN'T ANY GOOD AT MAKING DECISIONS, ARE YOU?
THAT'S WHAT YOU NEED ME FOR. TO TELL YOU WHAT TO DO. OR AT LEAST POINT YOU IN THE RIGHT DIRECTION.
YEAH? AND WHAT DIRECTION SHOULD I GO IN NOW?
NORTH. NEAR THE INTERSECTION OF BUCHANAN AND BROADWAY.
IT'LL HELP YOU MAKE UP YOUR MIND ABOUT THE REGISTRATION ACT, IF THAT'S OF ANY USE. OH, AND BUY A HAT ON THE WAY. A WATCH CAP, PREFERABLY. AND A SCARF AND GLOVES.
FINE. BUT JUST SO YOU KNOW, THIS ISN'T OVER BETWEEN US.
YEAH? WHAT MAKES YOU SAY THAT?
THAT'S TRUE. WE'LL BE ARGUING FOR A LONG TIME TO COME.
'CAUSE EVENTUALLY WE GET MARRIED.
SHEESH.

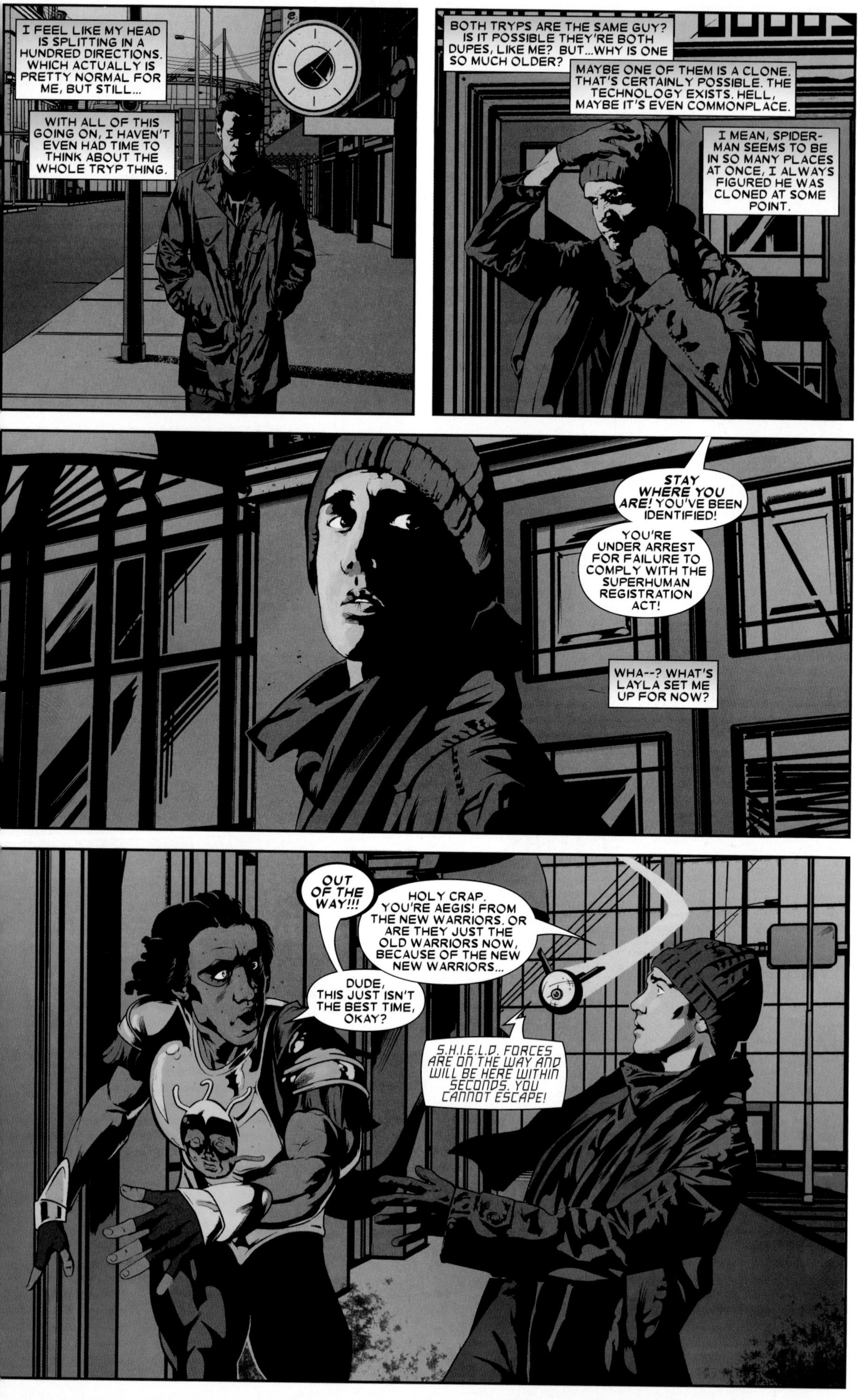
I FEEL LIKE MY HEAD IS SPLITTING IN A HUNDRED DIRECTIONS. WHICH ACTUALLY IS PRETTY NORMAL FOR ME, BUT STILL...
WITH ALL OF THIS GOING ON, I HAVEN'T EVEN HAD TIME TO THINK ABOUT THE WHOLE TRYP THING.
BOTH TRYPS ARE THE SAME GUY? IS IT POSSIBLE THEY'RE BOTH DUPES, LIKE ME? BUT...WHY IS ONE SO MUCH OLDER?
MAYBE ONE OF THEM IS A CLONE. THAT'S CERTAINLY POSSIBLE. THE TECHNOLOGY EXISTS. HELL, MAYBE IT'S EVEN COMMONPLACE.
I MEAN, SPIDER-MAN SEEMS TO BE IN SO MANY PLACES AT ONCE, I ALWAYS FIGURED HE WAS CLONED AT SOME POINT.
STAY WHERE YOU ARE! YOU'VE BEEN IDENTIFIED!
YOU'RE UNDER ARREST FOR FAILURE TO COMPLY WITH THE SUPERHUMAN REGISTRATION ACT!
WHA--? WHAT'S LAYLA SET ME UP FOR NOW?
OUT OF THE WAY!!!
HOLY CRAP. YOU'RE AEGIS! FROM THE NEW WARRIORS. OR ARE THEY JUST THE OLD WARRIORS NOW, BECAUSE OF THE NEW NEW WARRIORS...
DUDE, THIS JUST ISN'T THE BEST TIME, OKAY?
S.H.I.E.L.D. FORCES ARE ON THE WAY AND WILL BE HERE WITHIN SECONDS. YOU CANNOT ESCAPE!

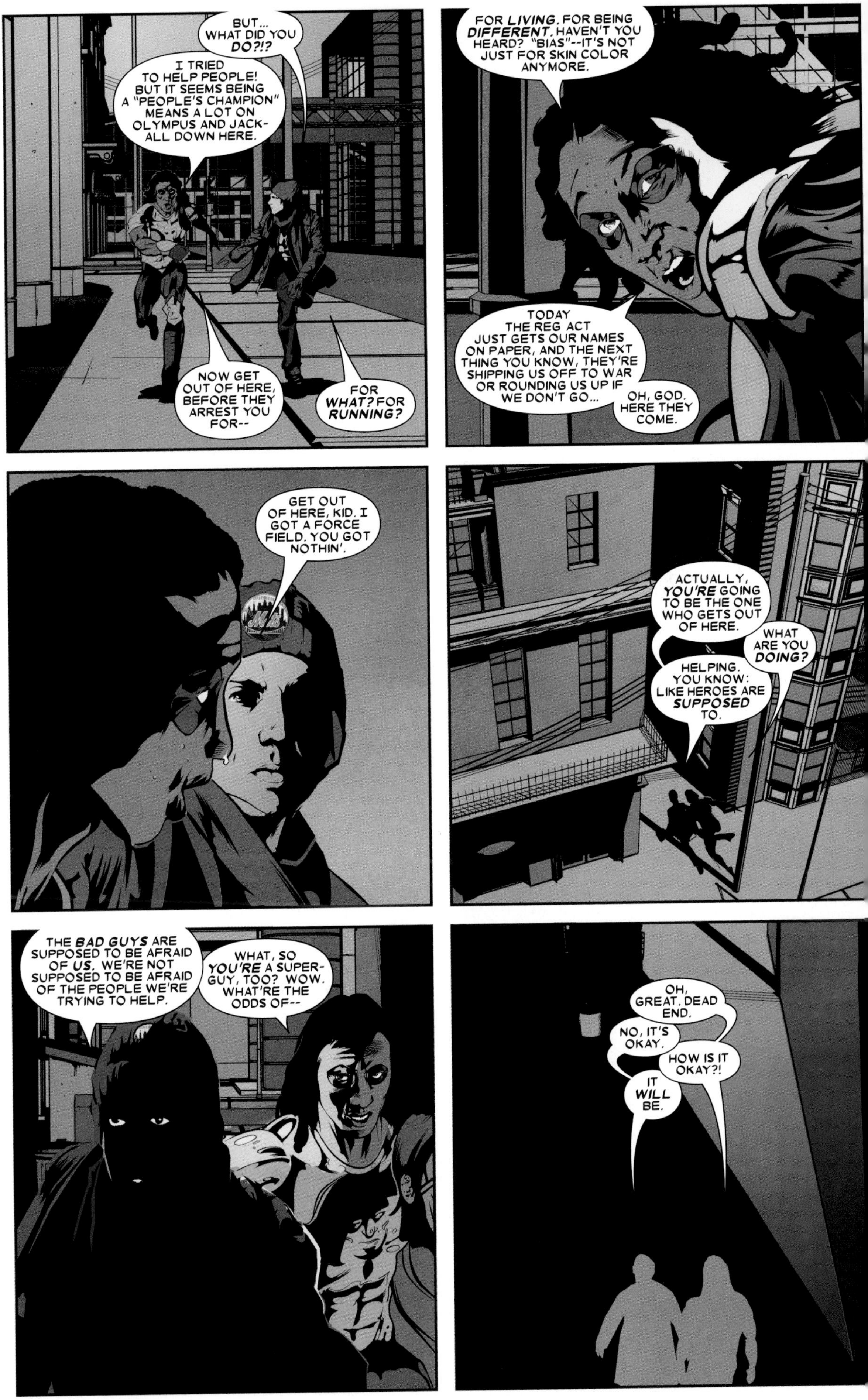
BUT... WHAT DID YOU DO?!?
I TRIED TO HELP PEOPLE! BUT IT SEEMS BEING A "PEOPLE'S CHAMPION" MEANS A LOT ON OLYMPUS AND JACK-ALL DOWN HERE.
NOW GET OUT OF HERE, BEFORE THEY ARREST YOU FOR--
FOR WHAT? FOR RUNNING?
FOR LIVING. FOR BEING DIFFERENT. HAVEN'T YOU HEARD? "BIAS"--IT'S NOT JUST FOR SKIN COLOR ANYMORE.
TODAY THE REG ACT JUST GETS OUR NAMES ON PAPER, AND THE NEXT THING YOU KNOW, THEY'RE SHIPPING US OFF TO WAR OR ROUNDING US UP IF WE DON'T GO...
OH, GOD. HERE THEY COME.
GET OUT OF HERE, KID. I GOT A FORCE FIELD. YOU GOT NOTHIN'.
ACTUALLY, YOU'RE GOING TO BE THE ONE WHO GETS OUT OF HERE.
WHAT ARE YOU DOING?
HELPING. YOU KNOW: LIKE HEROES ARE SUPPOSED TO.
THE BAD GUYS ARE SUPPOSED TO BE AFRAID OF US. WE'RE NOT SUPPOSED TO BE AFRAID OF THE PEOPLE WE'RE TRYING TO HELP.
WHAT, SO YOU'RE A SUPER-GUY, TOO? WOW. WHAT'RE THE ODDS OF--
OH, GREAT. DEAD END.
NO, IT'S OKAY.
HOW IS IT OKAY?!
IT WILL BE.

AEGIS! COME OUT SLOWLY AND MAKE NO SUDDEN MOVES.

WE HAVE WEAPONS THAT CAN PUNCH THROUGH EVEN YOUR FORCE FIELD, SON. BUT YOU WON'T BE INJURED IF YOU SURRENDER IMMEDIATELY!

COMPLY WITH THE LAW, OR WE WILL BE FORCED TO--

DO YOU HEAR SOMETHING? LIKE... THE GROUND RUMBLING?

SOUNDS LIKE... A STAMPEDE.

GIVE ME A VIDEO REPORT FROM THE 'BOT!

SCANNING NOW, SIR.

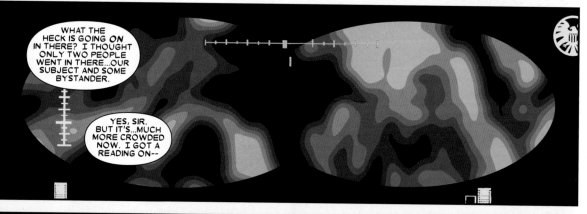

WHAT THE HECK IS GOING ON IN THERE? I THOUGHT ONLY TWO PEOPLE WENT IN THERE... OUR SUBJECT AND SOME BYSTANDER.

YES, SIR. BUT IT'S... MUCH MORE CROWDED NOW. I GOT A READING ON--

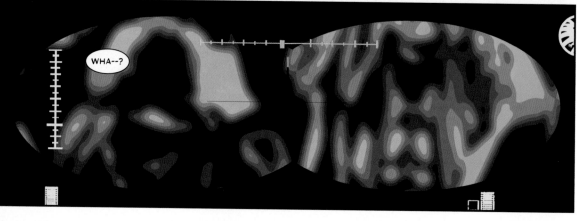

WHA--?

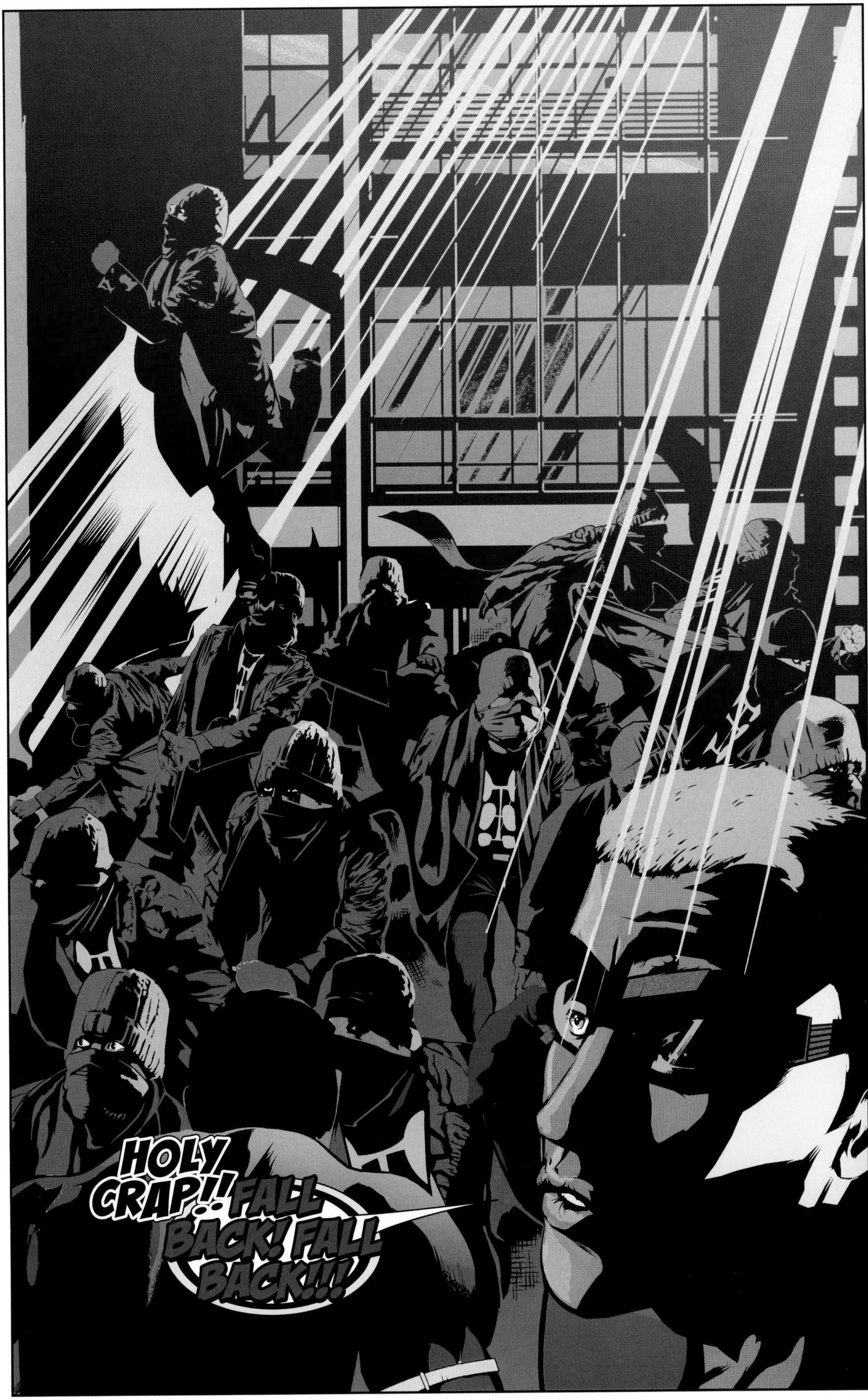
HOLY CRAP!! FALL BACK! FALL BACK!!!

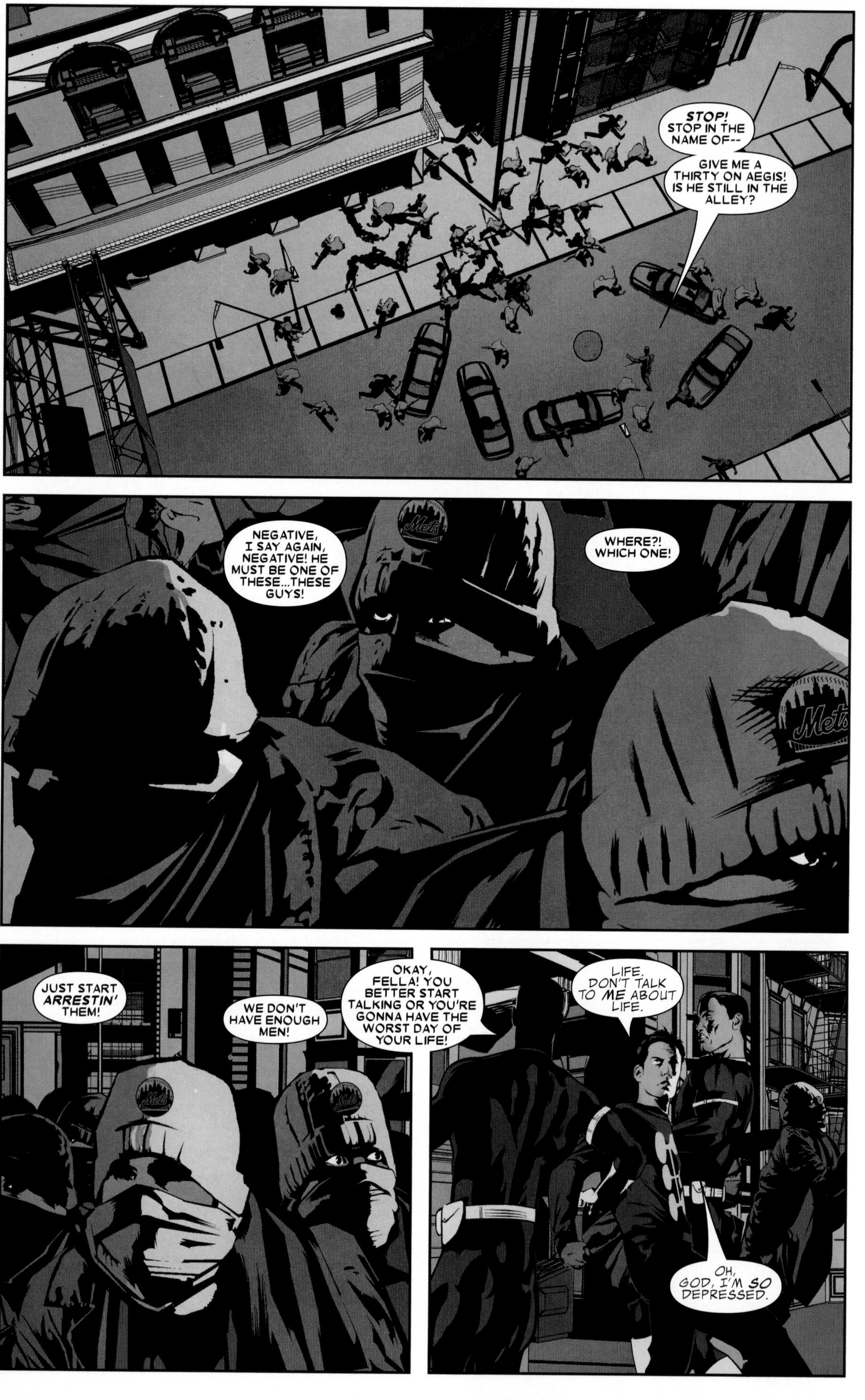
STOP! STOP IN THE NAME OF--
GIVE ME A THIRTY ON AEGIS! IS HE STILL IN THE ALLEY?
NEGATIVE, I SAY AGAIN, NEGATIVE! HE MUST BE ONE OF THESE...THESE GUYS!
WHERE?! WHICH ONE!
JUST START *ARRESTIN'* THEM!
WE DON'T HAVE ENOUGH MEN!
OKAY, FELLA! YOU BETTER START TALKING OR YOU'RE GONNA HAVE THE WORST DAY OF YOUR LIFE!
LIFE. DON'T TALK TO *ME* ABOUT LIFE.
OH, GOD, I'M *SO* DEPRESSED.

YOU'RE OUT OF YOUR MIND! YOU GOTTA BE!

I HEAR THAT A LOT. I THINK WE'RE IN THE CLEAR.

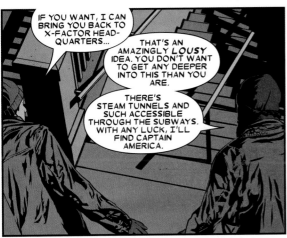

IF YOU WANT, I CAN BRING YOU BACK TO X-FACTOR HEAD-QUARTERS...

THAT'S AN AMAZINGLY *LOUSY* IDEA. YOU DON'T WANT TO GET ANY DEEPER INTO THIS THAN YOU ARE.

THERE'S STEAM TUNNELS AND SUCH ACCESSIBLE THROUGH THE SUBWAYS. WITH ANY LUCK, I'LL FIND CAPTAIN AMERICA.

THANKS. I OWE YOU.

YOU DON'T OWE ME A THING.

OKAY, GOOD, 'CAUSE I'M NOT REALLY SURE HOW I'D REPAY YOU, SO...

LATER.

HE WAS JUST TRYING TO HELP PEOPLE, AND THEY'RE TREATING HIM LIKE HE'S A TERRORIST OR WORSE.

IT'S LIKE BEING TRAPPED AT THE MAD TEA PARTY.

OKAY, FIRST THINGS FIRST. TIME TO CALL ALLY-ALLY-OUT-ARE-IN-FREE.

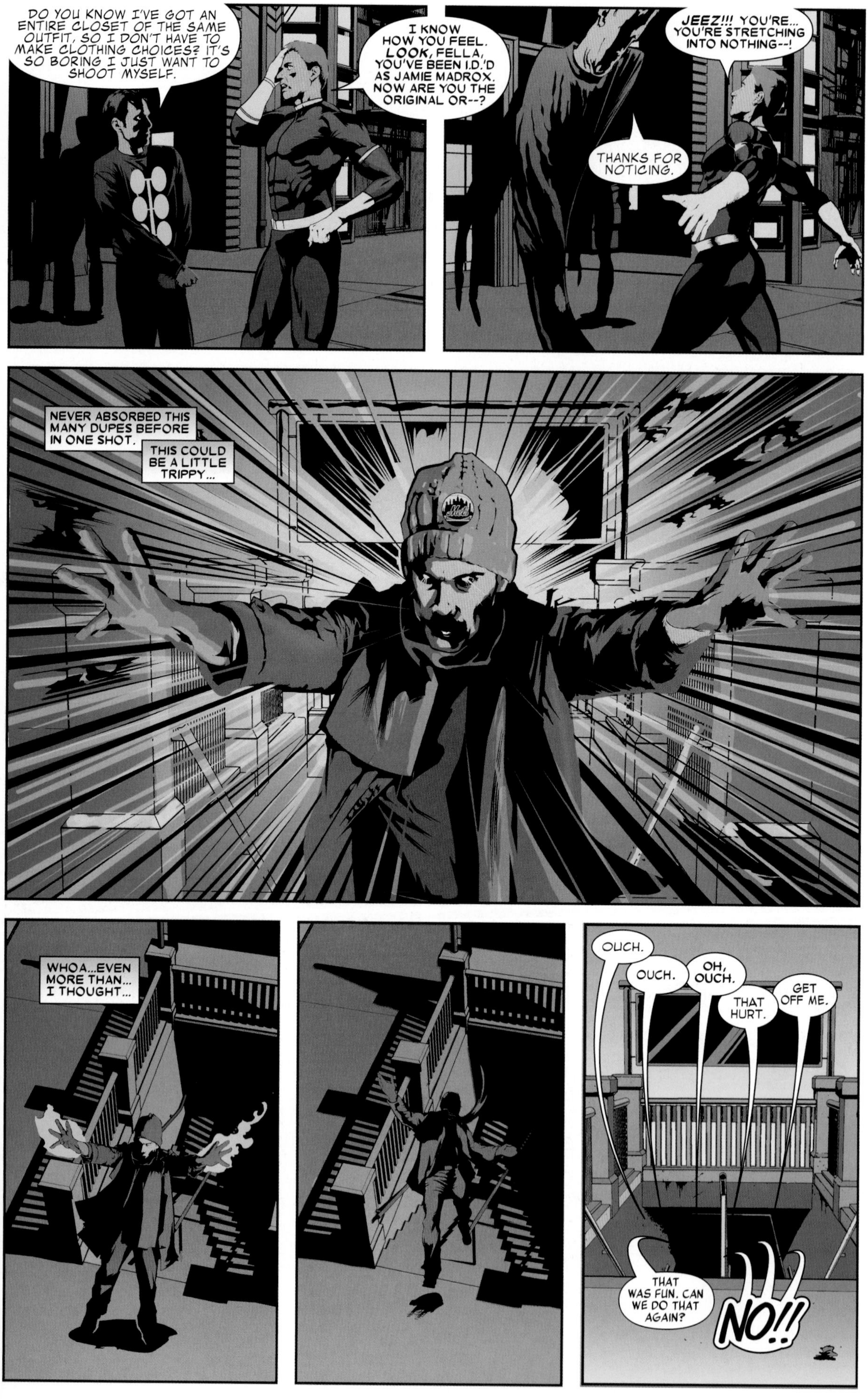

DO YOU KNOW I'VE GOT AN ENTIRE CLOSET OF THE SAME OUTFIT, SO I DON'T HAVE TO MAKE CLOTHING CHOICES? IT'S SO BORING I JUST WANT TO SHOOT MYSELF.
I KNOW HOW YOU FEEL. LOOK, FELLA, YOU'VE BEEN I.D.'D AS JAMIE MADROX. NOW ARE YOU THE ORIGINAL OR--?
JEEZ!!! YOU'RE... YOU'RE STRETCHING INTO NOTHING--!
THANKS FOR NOTICING.
NEVER ABSORBED THIS MANY DUPES BEFORE IN ONE SHOT.
THIS COULD BE A LITTLE TRIPPY...
WHOA...EVEN MORE THAN... I THOUGHT...
OUCH.
OUCH.
OH, OUCH.
THAT HURT.
GET OFF ME.
THAT WAS FUN. CAN WE DO THAT AGAIN?
NO!!

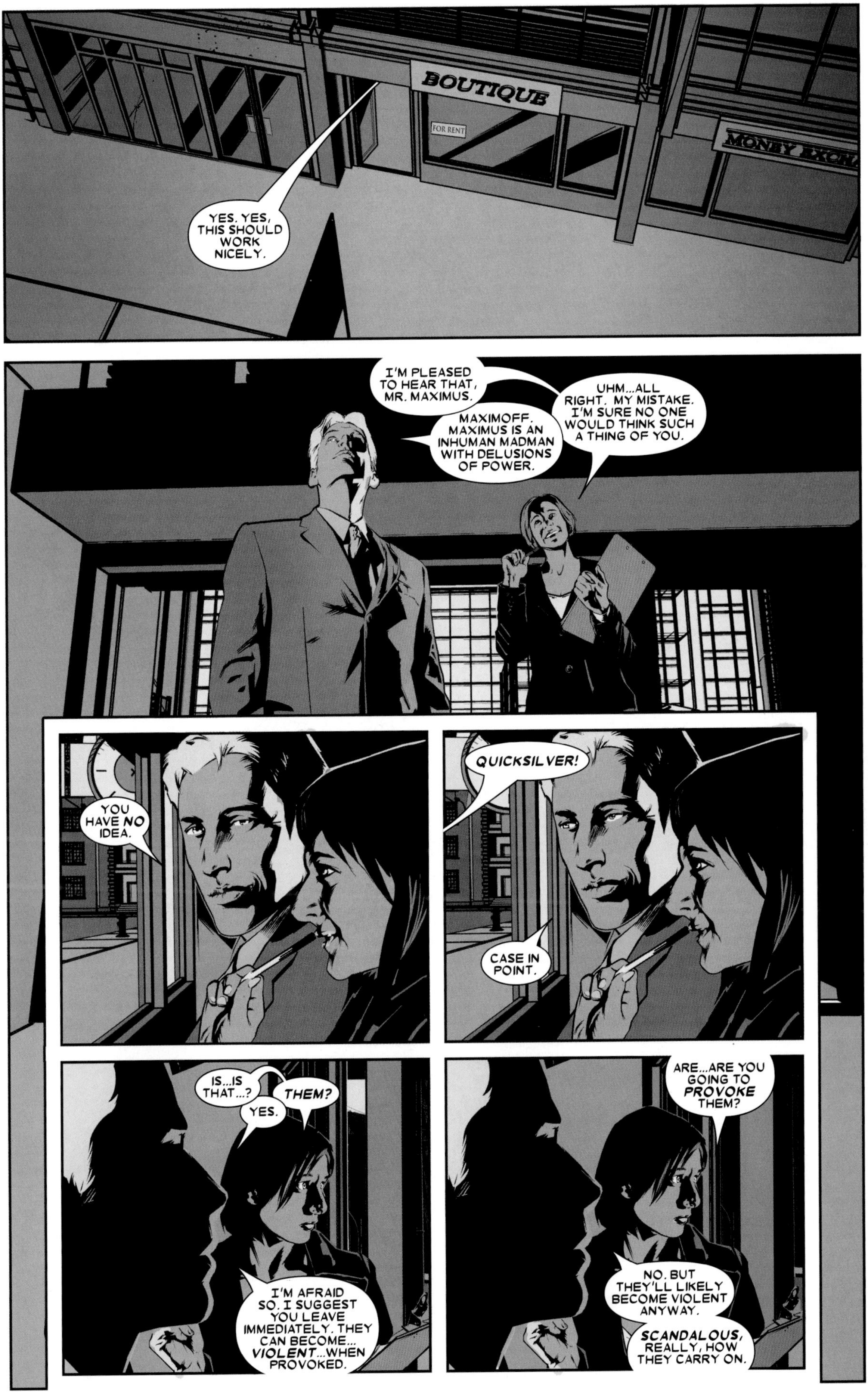
BOUTIQUE
FOR RENT
MONEY EXCHA
YES. YES, THIS SHOULD WORK NICELY.
I'M PLEASED TO HEAR THAT, MR. MAXIMUS.
MAXIMOFF. MAXIMUS IS AN INHUMAN MADMAN WITH DELUSIONS OF POWER.
UHM...ALL RIGHT. MY MISTAKE. I'M SURE NO ONE WOULD THINK SUCH A THING OF YOU.
YOU HAVE NO IDEA.
QUICKSILVER!
CASE IN POINT.
IS...IS THAT...?
THEM?
YES.
I'M AFRAID SO. I SUGGEST YOU LEAVE IMMEDIATELY. THEY CAN BECOME... VIOLENT...WHEN PROVOKED.
ARE...ARE YOU GOING TO PROVOKE THEM?
NO. BUT THEY'LL LIKELY BECOME VIOLENT ANYWAY.
SCANDALOUS, REALLY, HOW THEY CARRY ON.

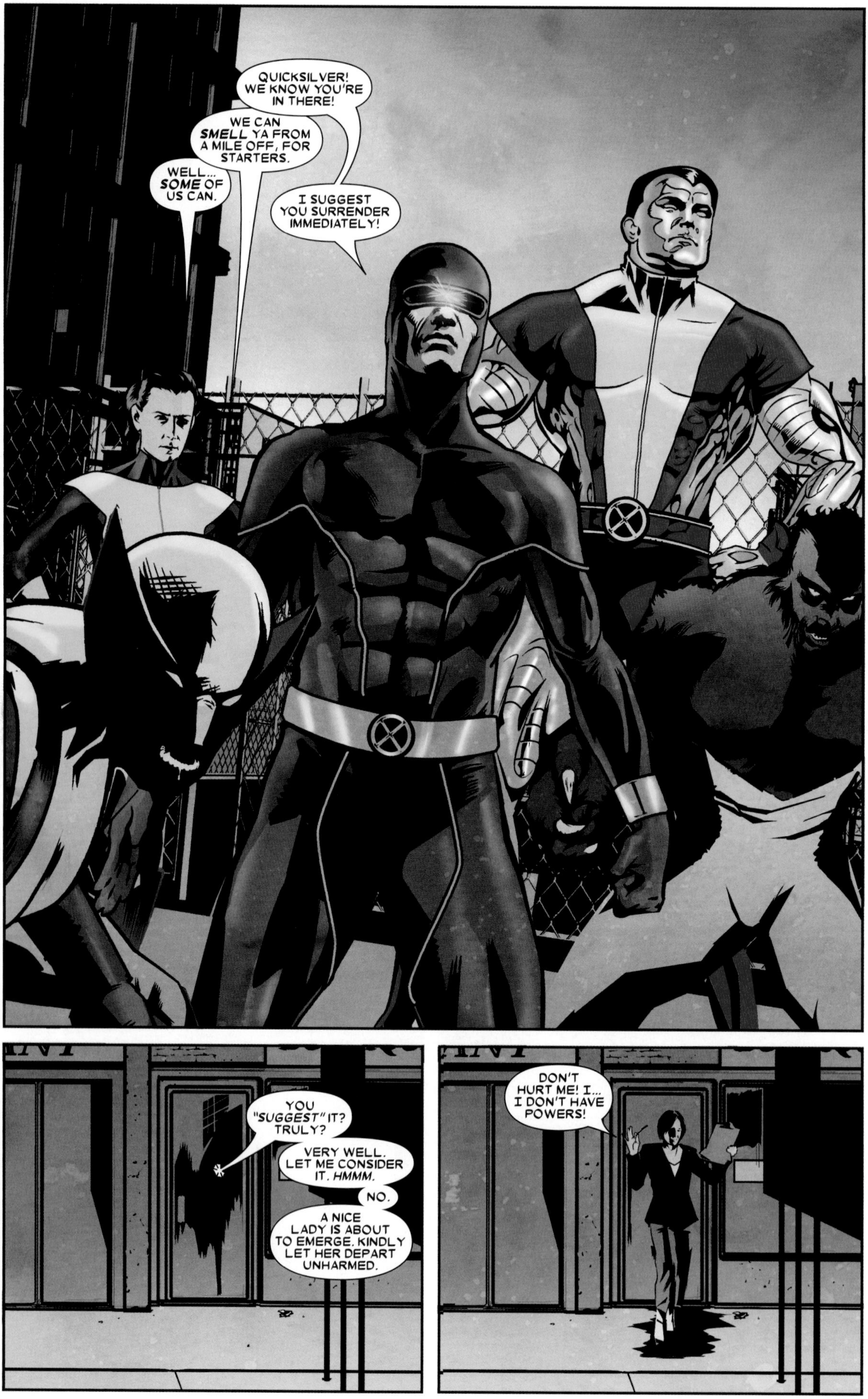
QUICKSILVER! WE KNOW YOU'RE IN THERE!
WE CAN SMELL YA FROM A MILE OFF, FOR STARTERS.
WELL... SOME OF US CAN.
I SUGGEST YOU SURRENDER IMMEDIATELY!
YOU "SUGGEST" IT? TRULY?
VERY WELL. LET ME CONSIDER IT. HMMM.
NO.
A NICE LADY IS ABOUT TO EMERGE. KINDLY LET HER DEPART UNHARMED.
DON'T HURT ME! I... I DON'T HAVE POWERS!

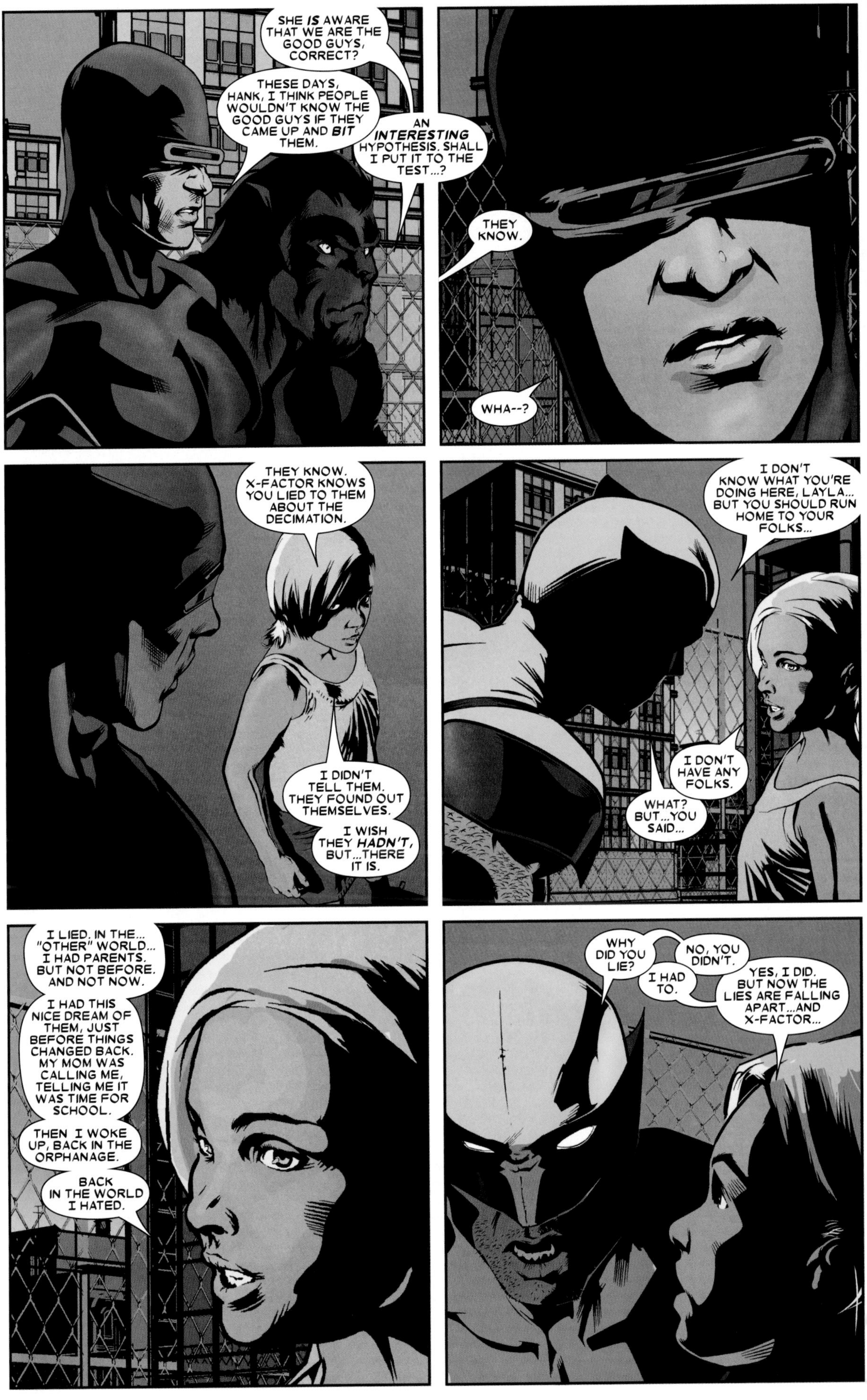
SHE IS AWARE THAT WE ARE THE GOOD GUYS, CORRECT?
THESE DAYS, HANK, I THINK PEOPLE WOULDN'T KNOW THE GOOD GUYS IF THEY CAME UP AND BIT THEM.
AN INTERESTING HYPOTHESIS. SHALL I PUT IT TO THE TEST...?
THEY KNOW.
WHA--?
THEY KNOW. X-FACTOR KNOWS YOU LIED TO THEM ABOUT THE DECIMATION.
I DIDN'T TELL THEM. THEY FOUND OUT THEMSELVES.
I WISH THEY HADN'T, BUT...THERE IT IS.
I DON'T KNOW WHAT YOU'RE DOING HERE, LAYLA... BUT YOU SHOULD RUN HOME TO YOUR FOLKS...
I DON'T HAVE ANY FOLKS.
WHAT? BUT...YOU SAID...
I LIED. IN THE... "OTHER" WORLD... I HAD PARENTS. BUT NOT BEFORE. AND NOT NOW.
I HAD THIS NICE DREAM OF THEM, JUST BEFORE THINGS CHANGED BACK. MY MOM WAS CALLING ME, TELLING ME IT WAS TIME FOR SCHOOL.
THEN I WOKE UP, BACK IN THE ORPHANAGE.
BACK IN THE WORLD I HATED.
WHY DID YOU LIE?
NO, YOU DIDN'T.
I HAD TO.
YES, I DID. BUT NOW THE LIES ARE FALLING APART...AND X-FACTOR...

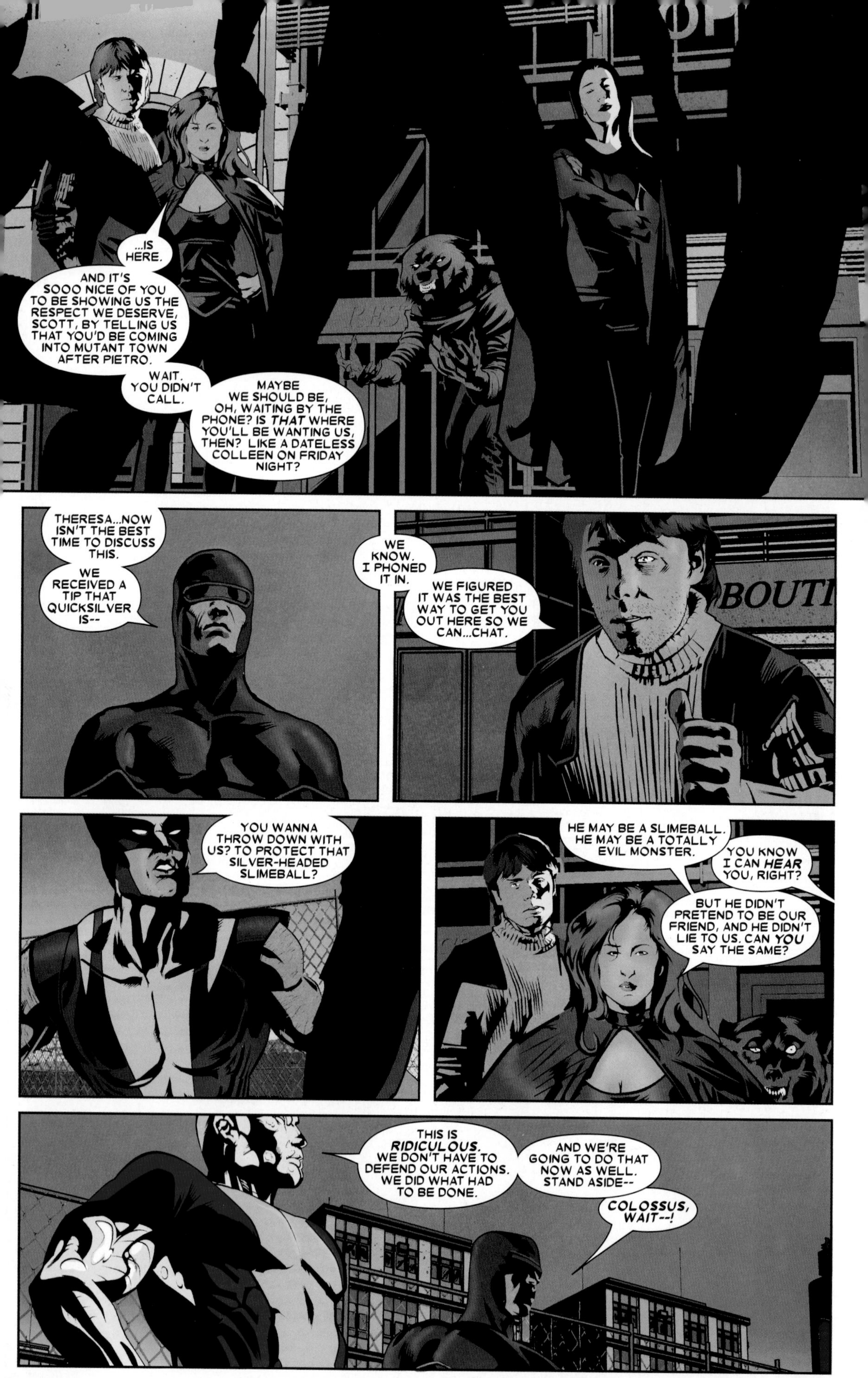
...IS HERE.
AND IT'S SOOO NICE OF YOU TO BE SHOWING US THE RESPECT WE DESERVE, SCOTT, BY TELLING US THAT YOU'D BE COMING INTO MUTANT TOWN AFTER PIETRO.
WAIT. YOU DIDN'T CALL.
MAYBE WE SHOULD BE, OH, WAITING BY THE PHONE? IS *THAT* WHERE YOU'LL BE WANTING US, THEN? LIKE A DATELESS COLLEEN ON FRIDAY NIGHT?
THERESA...NOW ISN'T THE BEST TIME TO DISCUSS THIS.
WE RECEIVED A TIP THAT QUICKSILVER IS--
WE KNOW. I PHONED IT IN.
WE FIGURED IT WAS THE BEST WAY TO GET YOU OUT HERE SO WE CAN...CHAT.
BOUTI
YOU WANNA THROW DOWN WITH US? TO PROTECT THAT SILVER-HEADED SLIMEBALL?
HE MAY BE A SLIMEBALL. HE MAY BE A TOTALLY EVIL MONSTER.
YOU KNOW I CAN *HEAR* YOU, RIGHT?
BUT HE DIDN'T PRETEND TO BE OUR FRIEND, AND HE DIDN'T LIE TO US. CAN *YOU* SAY THE SAME?
THIS IS *RIDICULOUS.* WE DON'T HAVE TO DEFEND OUR ACTIONS. WE DID WHAT HAD TO BE DONE.
AND WE'RE GOING TO DO THAT NOW AS WELL. STAND ASIDE--
COLOSSUS, WAIT--!

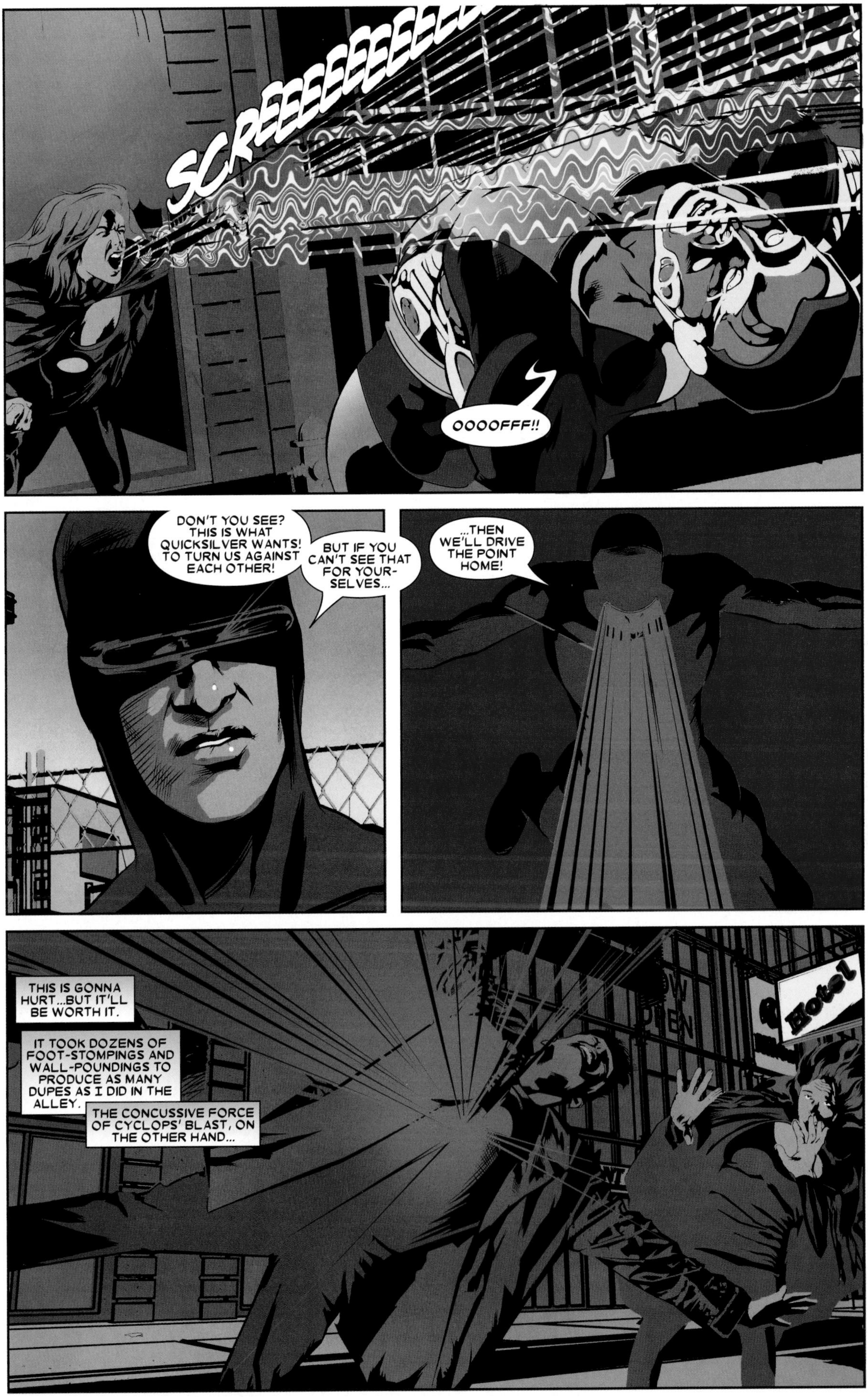
SCREEEEEEEEEE
OOOOFFF!!
DON'T YOU SEE? THIS IS WHAT QUICKSILVER WANTS! TO TURN US AGAINST EACH OTHER!
BUT IF YOU CAN'T SEE THAT FOR YOURSELVES...
...THEN WE'LL DRIVE THE POINT HOME!
THIS IS GONNA HURT...BUT IT'LL BE WORTH IT.
IT TOOK DOZENS OF FOOT-STOMPINGS AND WALL-POUNDINGS TO PRODUCE AS MANY DUPES AS I DID IN THE ALLEY.
THE CONCUSSIVE FORCE OF CYCLOPS' BLAST, ON THE OTHER HAND...
Hotel

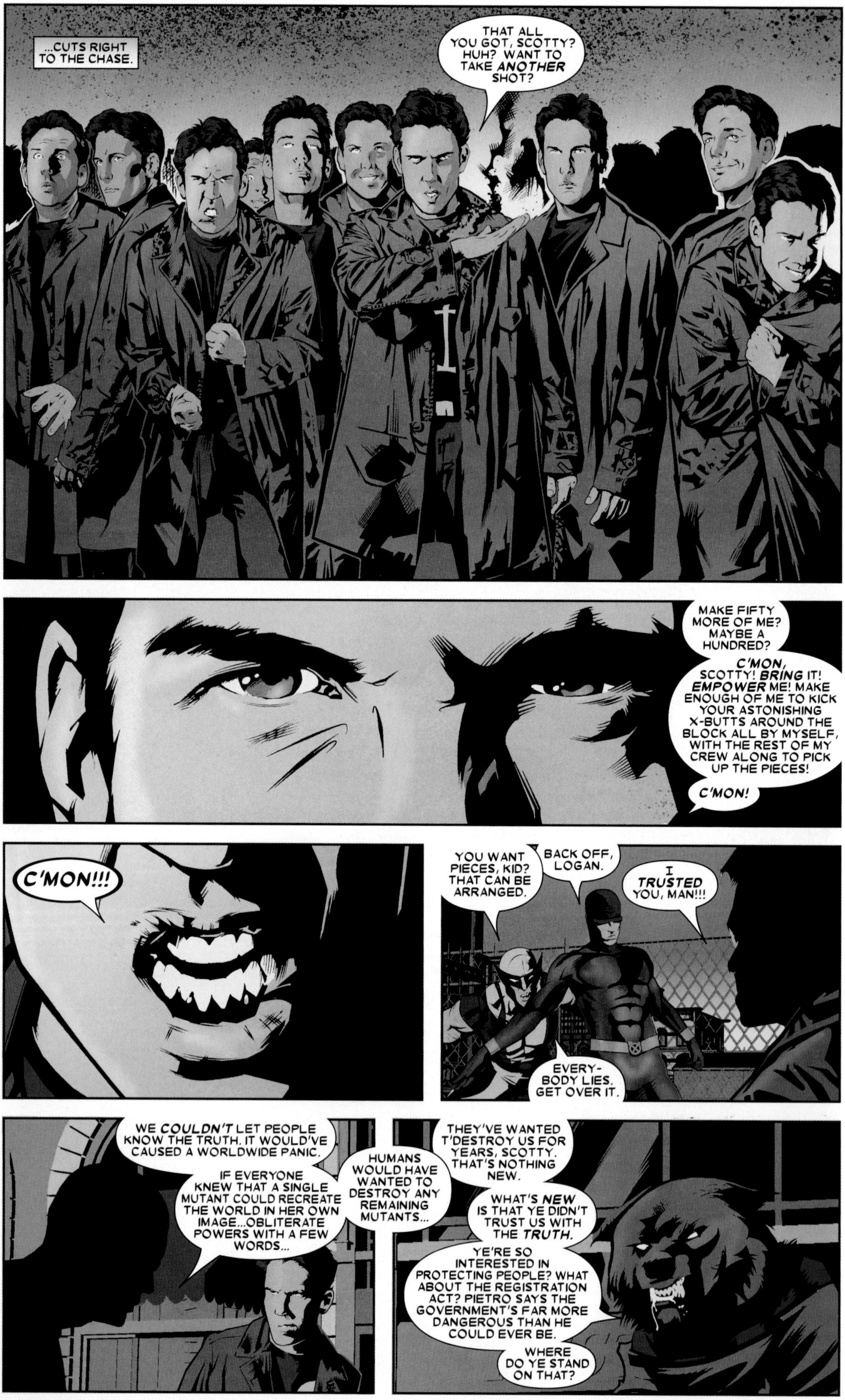
...CUTS RIGHT TO THE CHASE.
THAT ALL YOU GOT, SCOTTY? HUH? WANT TO TAKE ANOTHER SHOT?
MAKE FIFTY MORE OF ME? MAYBE A HUNDRED?
C'MON, SCOTTY! BRING IT! EMPOWER ME! MAKE ENOUGH OF ME TO KICK YOUR ASTONISHING X-BUTTS AROUND THE BLOCK ALL BY MYSELF, WITH THE REST OF MY CREW ALONG TO PICK UP THE PIECES!
C'MON!
C'MON!!!
YOU WANT PIECES, KID? THAT CAN BE ARRANGED.
BACK OFF, LOGAN.
I TRUSTED YOU, MAN!!!
EVERY-BODY LIES. GET OVER IT.
WE COULDN'T LET PEOPLE KNOW THE TRUTH. IT WOULD'VE CAUSED A WORLDWIDE PANIC.
IF EVERYONE KNEW THAT A SINGLE MUTANT COULD RECREATE THE WORLD IN HER OWN IMAGE...OBLITERATE POWERS WITH A FEW WORDS...
HUMANS WOULD HAVE WANTED TO DESTROY ANY REMAINING MUTANTS...
THEY'VE WANTED T'DESTROY US FOR YEARS, SCOTTY. THAT'S NOTHING NEW.
WHAT'S NEW IS THAT YE DIDN'T TRUST US WITH THE TRUTH.
YE'RE SO INTERESTED IN PROTECTING PEOPLE? WHAT ABOUT THE REGISTRATION ACT? PIETRO SAYS THE GOVERNMENT'S FAR MORE DANGEROUS THAN HE COULD EVER BE.
WHERE DO YE STAND ON THAT?

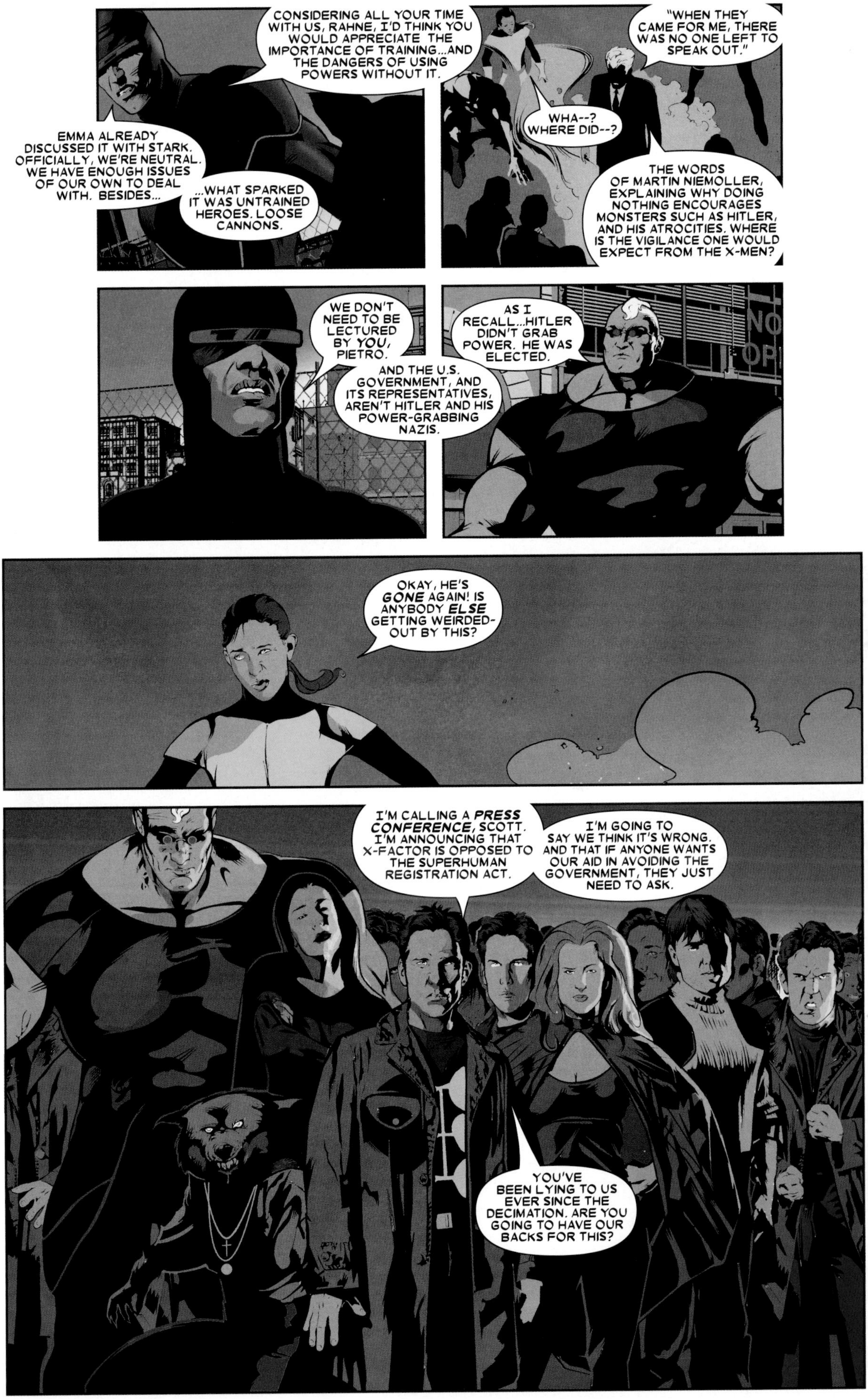
CONSIDERING ALL YOUR TIME WITH US, RAHNE, I'D THINK YOU WOULD APPRECIATE THE IMPORTANCE OF TRAINING...AND THE DANGERS OF USING POWERS WITHOUT IT.
EMMA ALREADY DISCUSSED IT WITH STARK. OFFICIALLY, WE'RE NEUTRAL. WE HAVE ENOUGH ISSUES OF OUR OWN TO DEAL WITH. BESIDES...
...WHAT SPARKED IT WAS UNTRAINED HEROES. LOOSE CANNONS.
"WHEN THEY CAME FOR ME, THERE WAS NO ONE LEFT TO SPEAK OUT."
WHA--? WHERE DID--?
THE WORDS OF MARTIN NIEMOLLER, EXPLAINING WHY DOING NOTHING ENCOURAGES MONSTERS SUCH AS HITLER, AND HIS ATROCITIES. WHERE IS THE VIGILANCE ONE WOULD EXPECT FROM THE X-MEN?
WE DON'T NEED TO BE LECTURED BY *YOU*, PIETRO.
AND THE U.S. GOVERNMENT, AND ITS REPRESENTATIVES, AREN'T HITLER AND HIS POWER-GRABBING NAZIS.
AS I RECALL...HITLER DIDN'T GRAB POWER. HE WAS ELECTED.
OKAY, HE'S *GONE* AGAIN! IS ANYBODY *ELSE* GETTING WEIRDED-OUT BY THIS?
I'M CALLING A ***PRESS CONFERENCE,*** SCOTT. I'M ANNOUNCING THAT X-FACTOR IS OPPOSED TO THE SUPERHUMAN REGISTRATION ACT.
I'M GOING TO SAY WE THINK IT'S WRONG. AND THAT IF ANYONE WANTS OUR AID IN AVOIDING THE GOVERNMENT, THEY JUST NEED TO ASK.
YOU'VE BEEN LYING TO US EVER SINCE THE DECIMATION. ARE YOU GOING TO HAVE OUR BACKS FOR THIS?

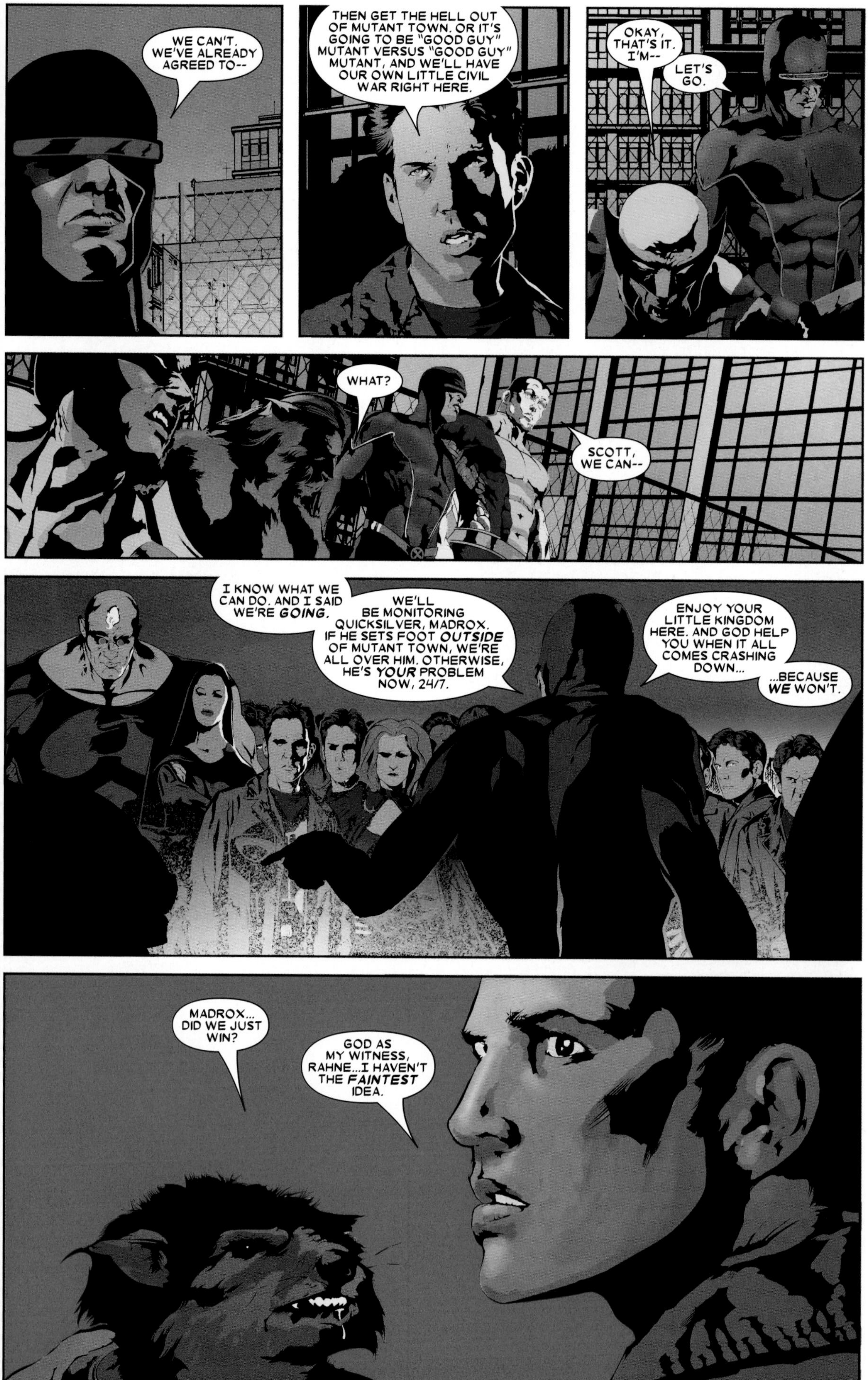
WE CAN'T. WE'VE ALREADY AGREED TO--
THEN GET THE HELL OUT OF MUTANT TOWN. OR IT'S GOING TO BE "GOOD GUY" MUTANT VERSUS "GOOD GUY" MUTANT, AND WE'LL HAVE OUR OWN LITTLE CIVIL WAR RIGHT HERE.
OKAY, THAT'S IT. I'M--
LET'S GO.
WHAT?
SCOTT, WE CAN--
I KNOW WHAT WE CAN DO. AND I SAID WE'RE GOING.
WE'LL BE MONITORING QUICKSILVER, MADROX. IF HE SETS FOOT OUTSIDE OF MUTANT TOWN, WE'RE ALL OVER HIM. OTHERWISE, HE'S YOUR PROBLEM NOW, 24/7.
ENJOY YOUR LITTLE KINGDOM HERE. AND GOD HELP YOU WHEN IT ALL COMES CRASHING DOWN...
...BECAUSE WE WON'T.
MADROX... DID WE JUST WIN?
GOD AS MY WITNESS, RAHNE...I HAVEN'T THE FAINTEST IDEA.

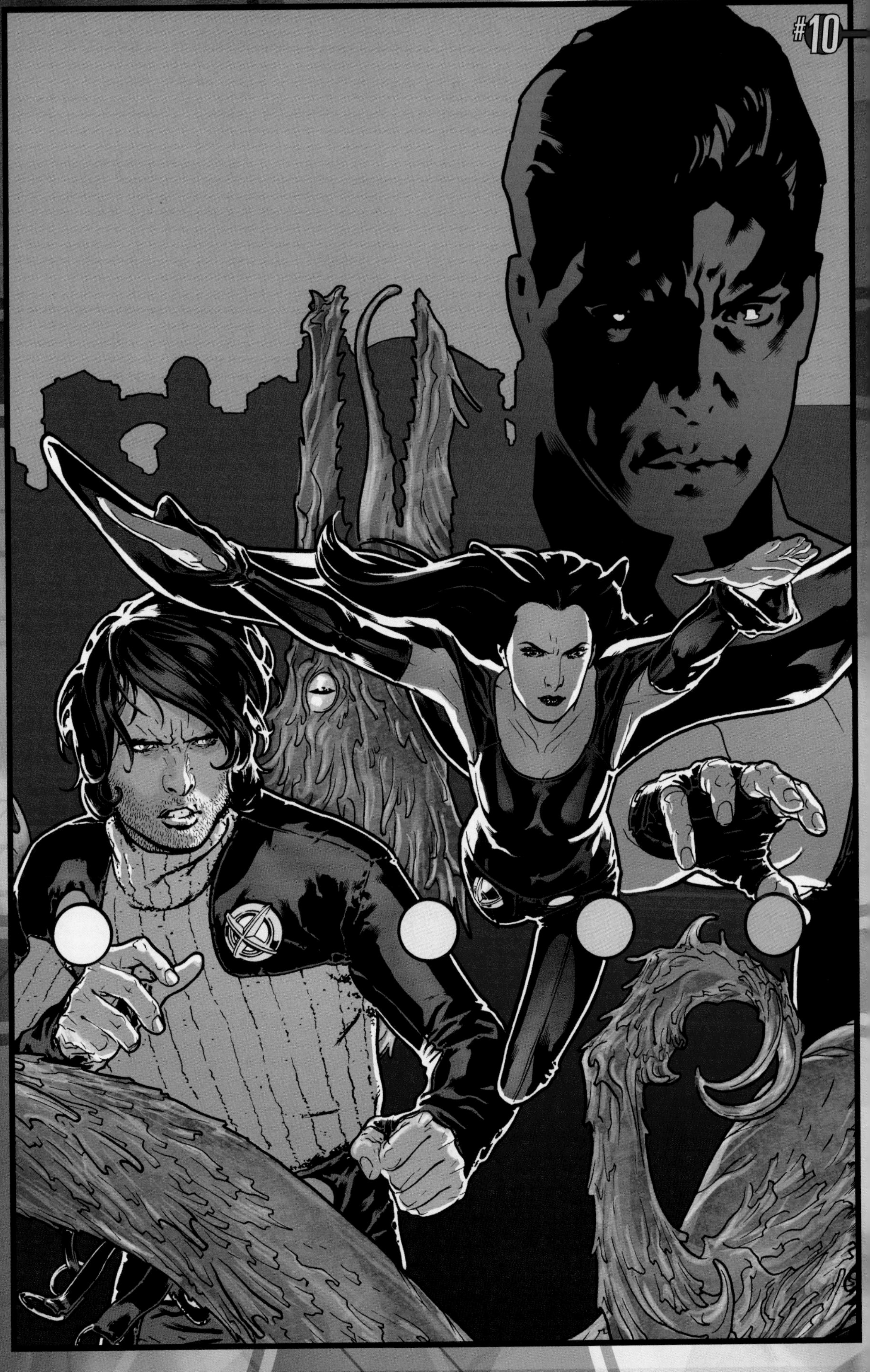
#10

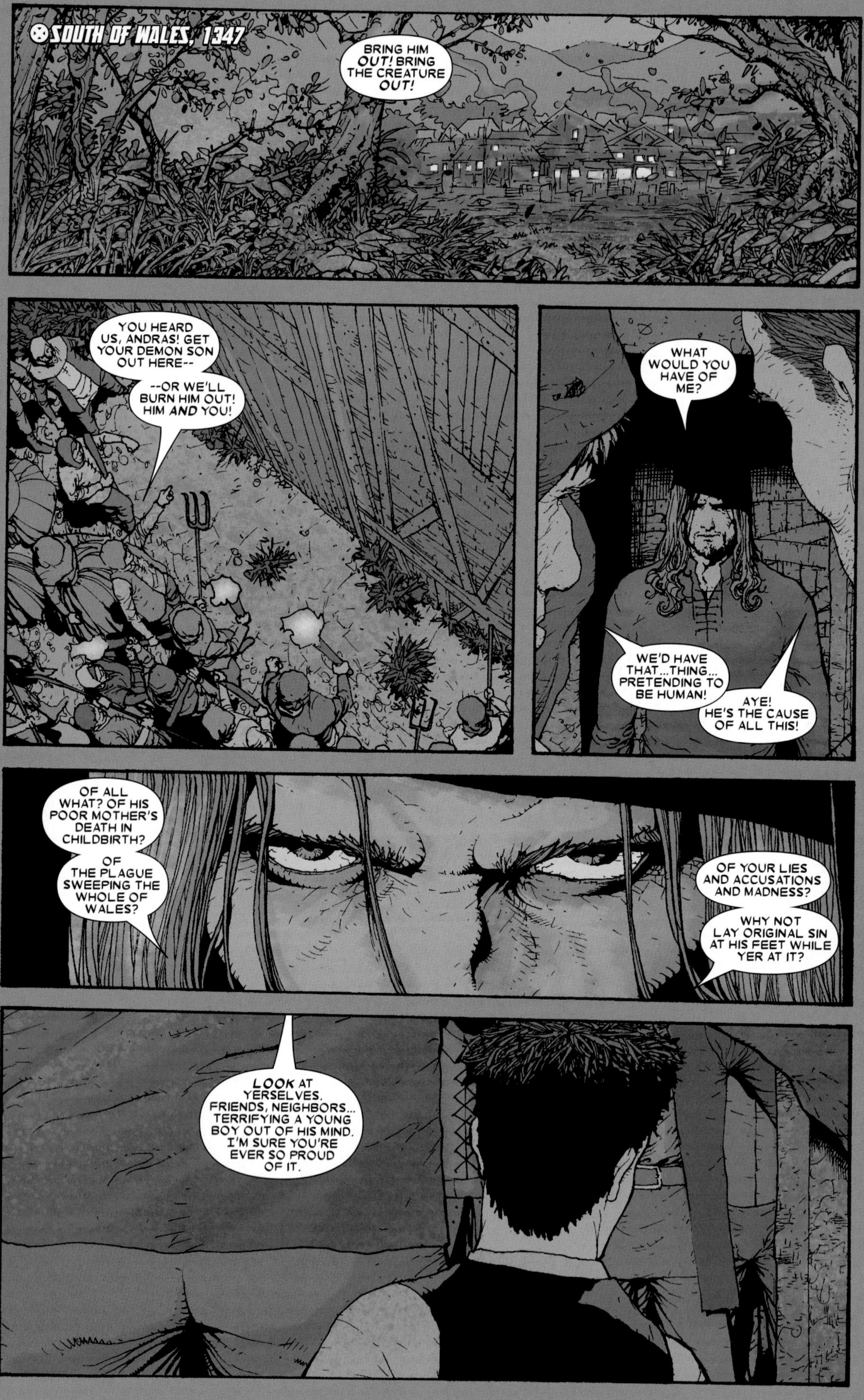
SOUTH OF WALES, 1347
BRING HIM OUT! BRING THE CREATURE OUT!
YOU HEARD US, ANDRAS! GET YOUR DEMON SON OUT HERE--
--OR WE'LL BURN HIM OUT! HIM AND YOU!
WHAT WOULD YOU HAVE OF ME?
WE'D HAVE THAT...THING... PRETENDING TO BE HUMAN!
AYE! HE'S THE CAUSE OF ALL THIS!
OF ALL WHAT? OF HIS POOR MOTHER'S DEATH IN CHILDBIRTH?
OF THE PLAGUE SWEEPING THE WHOLE OF WALES?
OF YOUR LIES AND ACCUSATIONS AND MADNESS?
WHY NOT LAY ORIGINAL SIN AT HIS FEET WHILE YER AT IT?
LOOK AT YERSELVES. FRIENDS, NEIGHBORS... TERRIFYING A YOUNG BOY OUT OF HIS MIND. I'M SURE YOU'RE EVER SO PROUD OF IT.

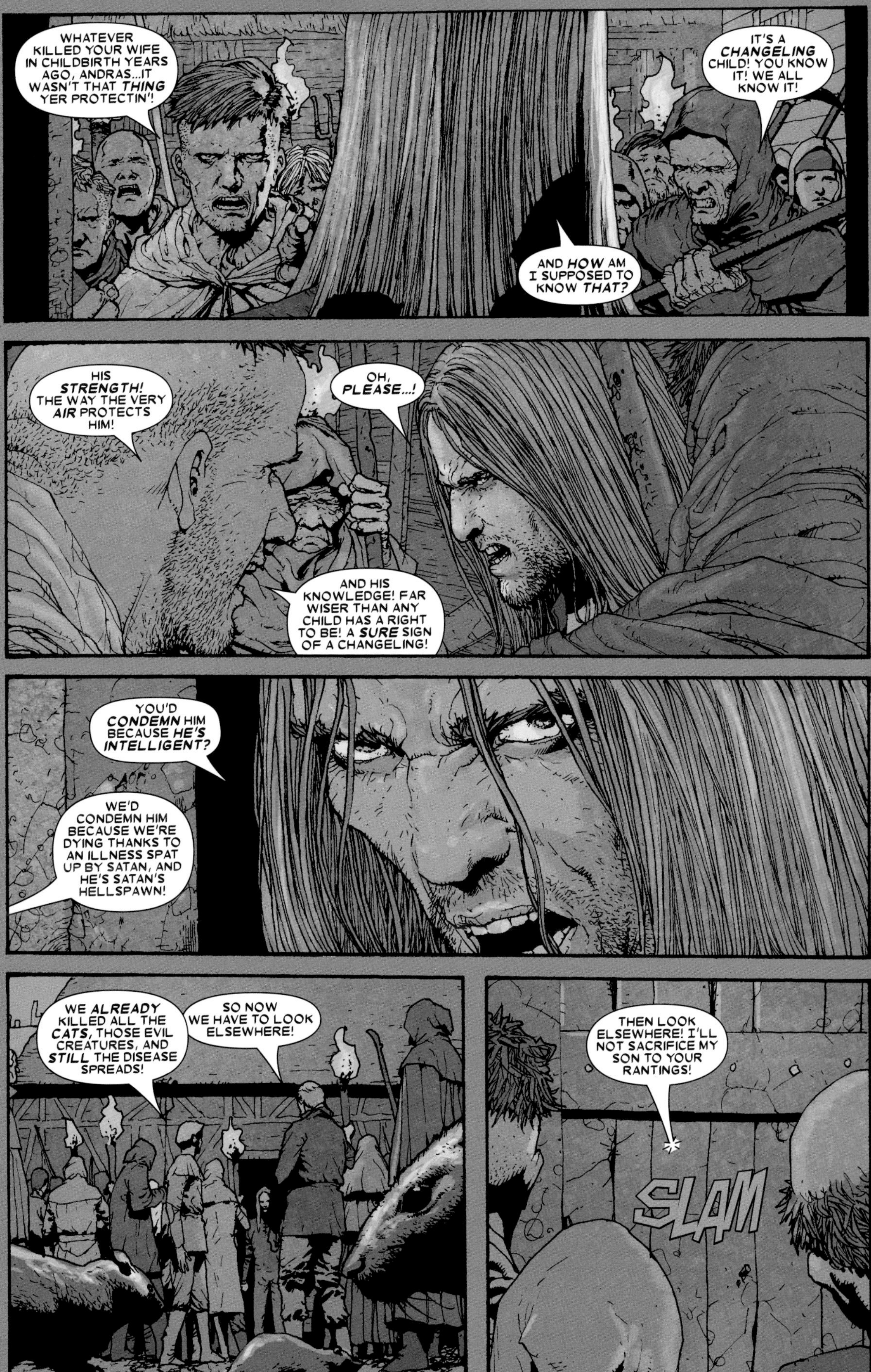

WHATEVER KILLED YOUR WIFE IN CHILDBIRTH YEARS AGO, ANDRAS...IT WASN'T THAT THING YER PROTECTIN'!
IT'S A CHANGELING CHILD! YOU KNOW IT! WE ALL KNOW IT!
AND HOW AM I SUPPOSED TO KNOW THAT?
HIS STRENGTH! THE WAY THE VERY AIR PROTECTS HIM!
OH, PLEASE...!
AND HIS KNOWLEDGE! FAR WISER THAN ANY CHILD HAS A RIGHT TO BE! A SURE SIGN OF A CHANGELING!
YOU'D CONDEMN HIM BECAUSE HE'S INTELLIGENT?
WE'D CONDEMN HIM BECAUSE WE'RE DYING THANKS TO AN ILLNESS SPAT UP BY SATAN, AND HE'S SATAN'S HELLSPAWN!
WE ALREADY KILLED ALL THE CATS, THOSE EVIL CREATURES, AND STILL THE DISEASE SPREADS!
SO NOW WE HAVE TO LOOK ELSEWHERE!
THEN LOOK ELSEWHERE! I'LL NOT SACRIFICE MY SON TO YOUR RANTINGS!
SLAM

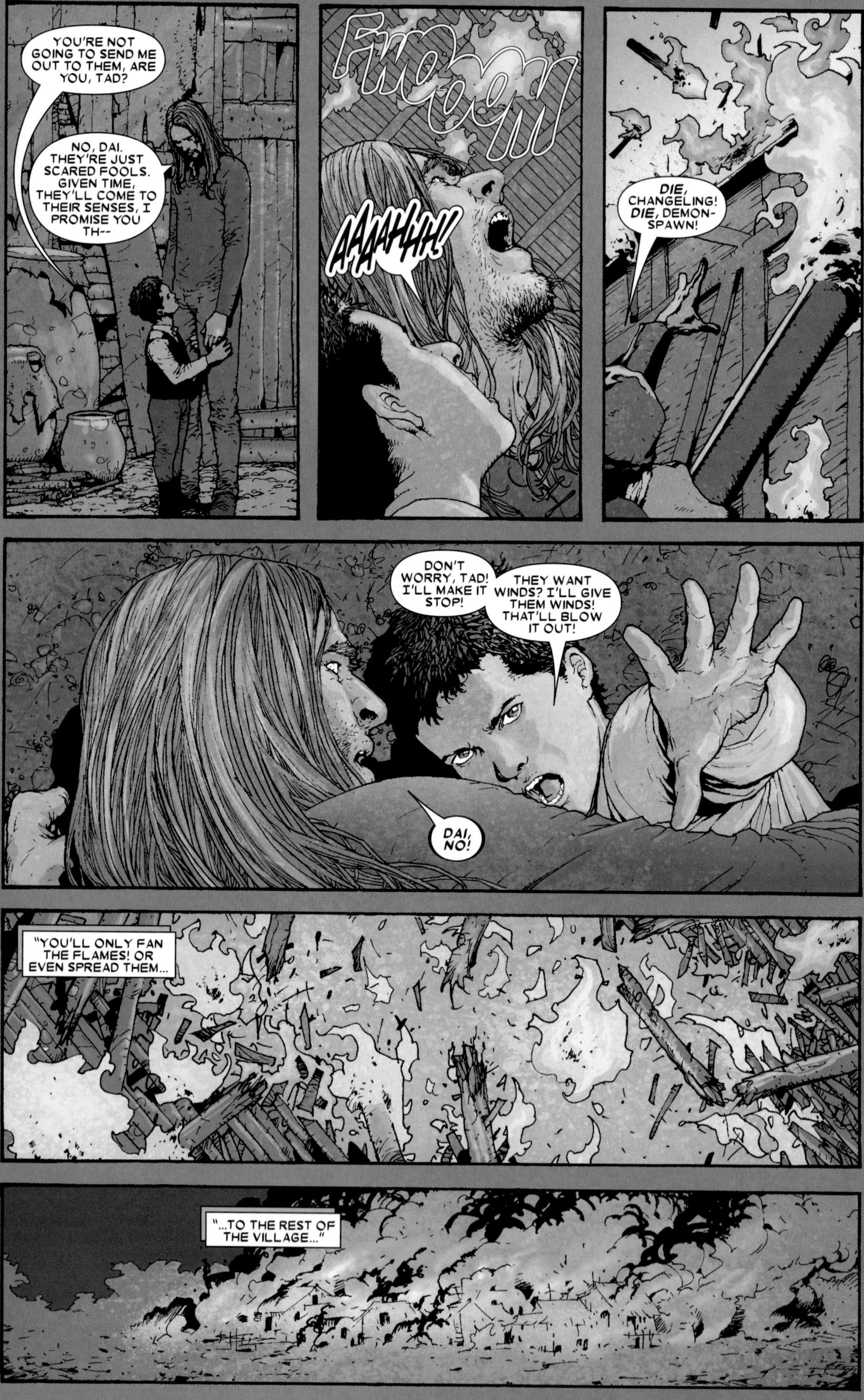
YOU'RE NOT GOING TO SEND ME OUT TO THEM, ARE YOU, TAD?
NO, DAI. THEY'RE JUST SCARED FOOLS. GIVEN TIME, THEY'LL COME TO THEIR SENSES, I PROMISE YOU TH--
FWOOOM
AAAAHHH!
DIE, CHANGELING! DIE, DEMON-SPAWN!
DON'T WORRY, TAD! I'LL MAKE IT STOP!
THEY WANT WINDS? I'LL GIVE THEM WINDS! THAT'LL BLOW IT OUT!
DAI, NO!
"YOU'LL ONLY FAN THE FLAMES! OR EVEN SPREAD THEM...
"...TO THE REST OF THE VILLAGE..."

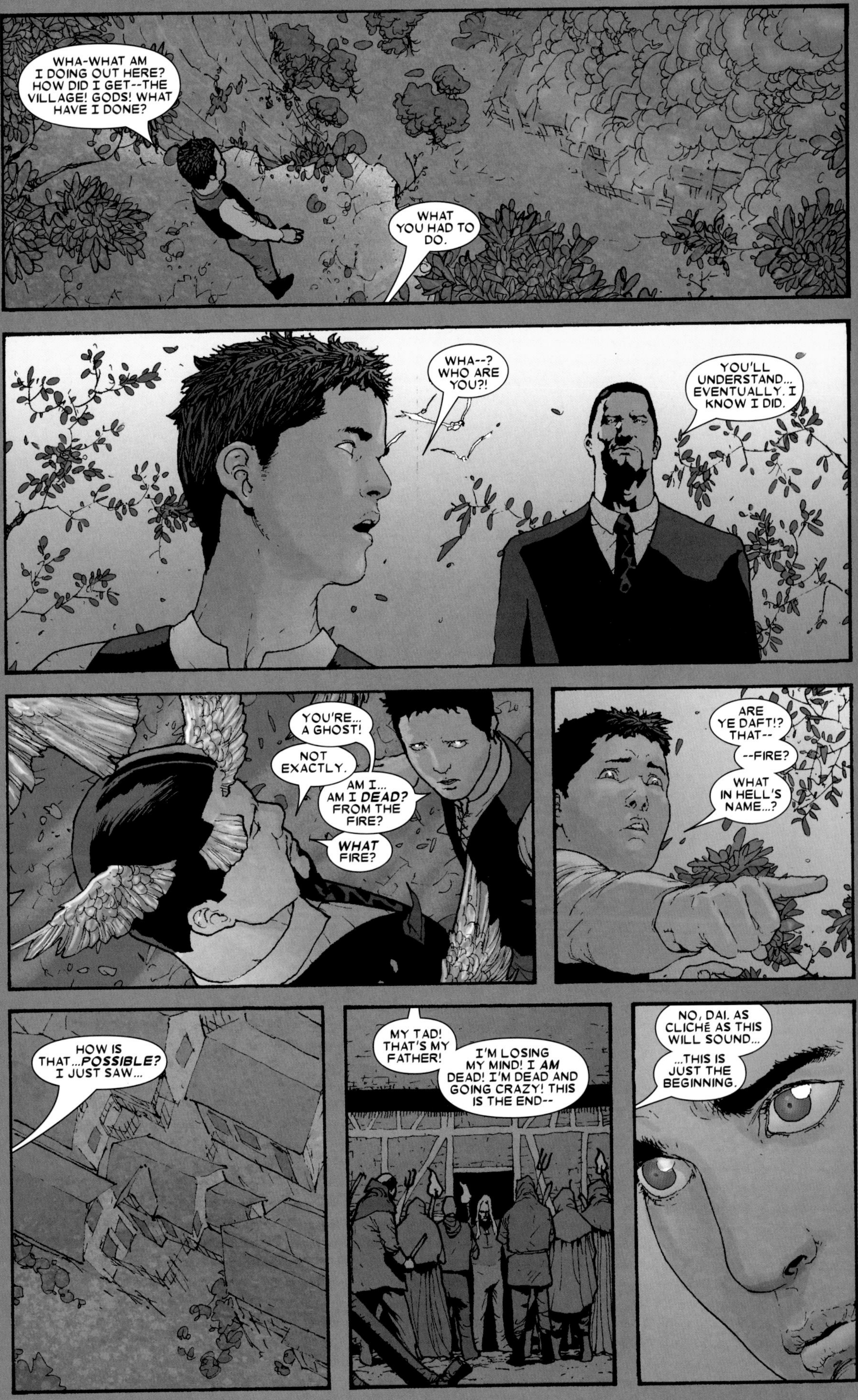
WHA-WHAT AM I DOING OUT HERE? HOW DID I GET--THE VILLAGE! GODS! WHAT HAVE I DONE?
WHAT YOU HAD TO DO.
WHA--? WHO ARE YOU?!
YOU'LL UNDERSTAND... EVENTUALLY. I KNOW I DID.
YOU'RE... A GHOST!
NOT EXACTLY.
AM I... AM I *DEAD?* FROM THE FIRE?
WHAT FIRE?
ARE YE DAFT!? THAT--
--FIRE?
WHAT IN HELL'S NAME...?
HOW IS THAT...***POSSIBLE?*** I JUST SAW...
MY TAD! THAT'S MY FATHER!
I'M LOSING MY MIND! I *AM* DEAD! I'M DEAD AND GOING CRAZY! THIS IS THE END--
NO, DAI. AS CLICHÉ AS THIS WILL SOUND...
...THIS IS JUST THE BEGINNING.

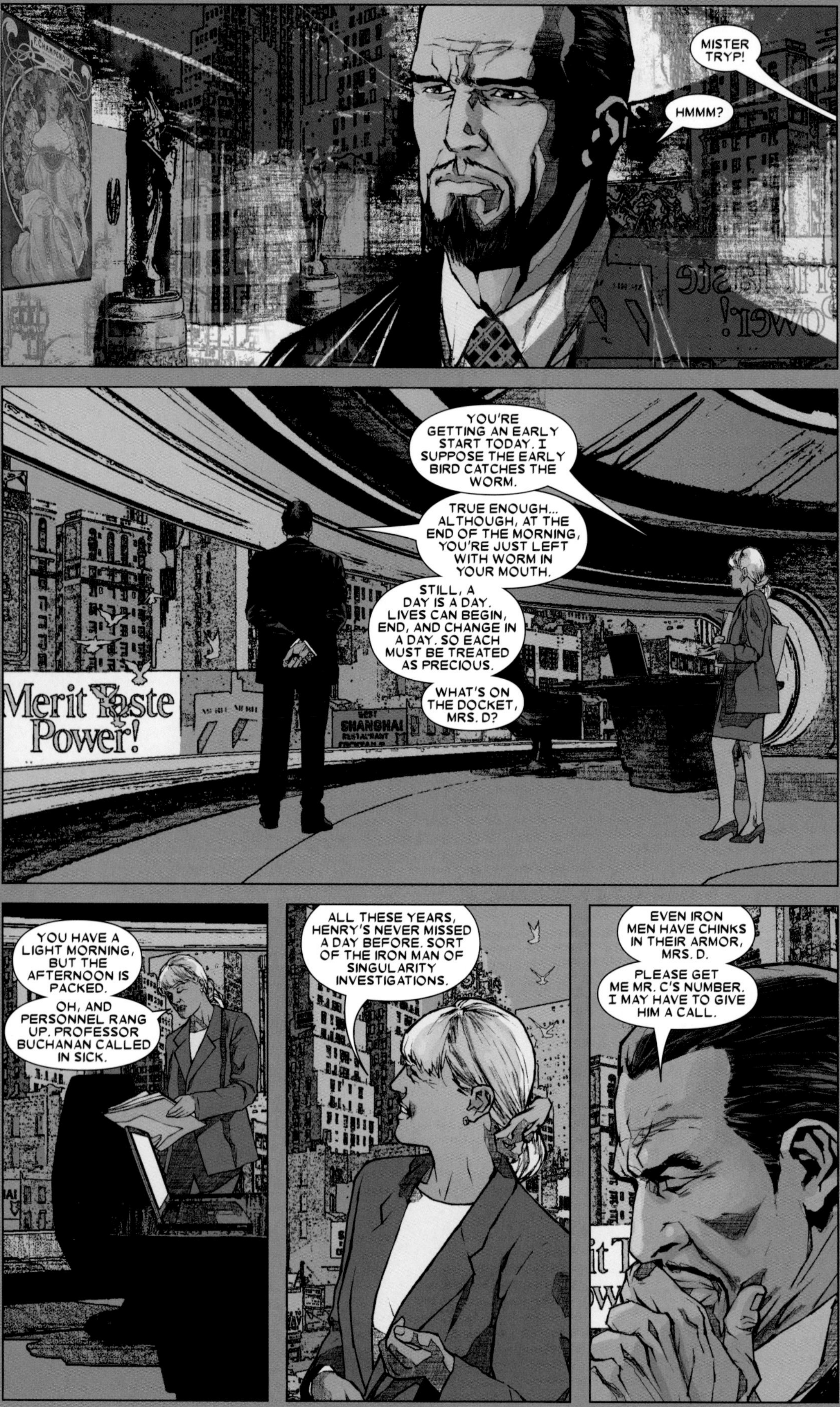
MISTER TRYP!
HMMM?
YOU'RE GETTING AN EARLY START TODAY. I SUPPOSE THE EARLY BIRD CATCHES THE WORM.
TRUE ENOUGH... ALTHOUGH, AT THE END OF THE MORNING, YOU'RE JUST LEFT WITH WORM IN YOUR MOUTH.
STILL, A DAY IS A DAY. LIVES CAN BEGIN, END, AND CHANGE IN A DAY. SO EACH MUST BE TREATED AS PRECIOUS.
WHAT'S ON THE DOCKET, MRS. D?
SHANGHAI
YOU HAVE A LIGHT MORNING, BUT THE AFTERNOON IS PACKED.
OH, AND PERSONNEL RANG UP. PROFESSOR BUCHANAN CALLED IN SICK.
ALL THESE YEARS, HENRY'S NEVER MISSED A DAY BEFORE. SORT OF THE IRON MAN OF SINGULARITY INVESTIGATIONS.
EVEN IRON MEN HAVE CHINKS IN THEIR ARMOR, MRS. D.
PLEASE GET ME MR. C'S NUMBER. I MAY HAVE TO GIVE HIM A CALL.

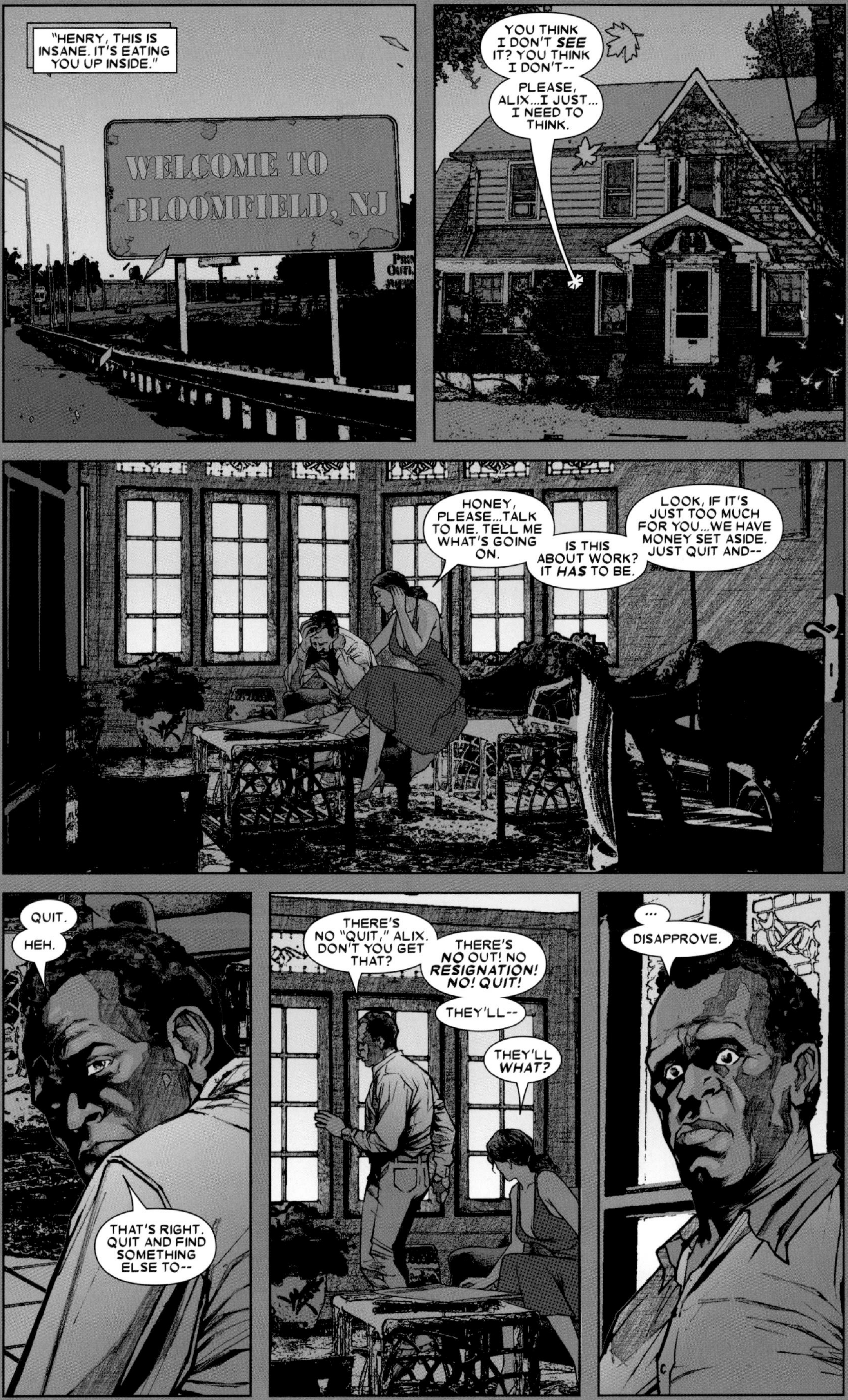
"HENRY, THIS IS INSANE. IT'S EATING YOU UP INSIDE."
WELCOME TO BLOOMFIELD, NJ
YOU THINK I DON'T SEE IT? YOU THINK I DON'T--
PLEASE, ALIX...I JUST... I NEED TO THINK.
HONEY, PLEASE...TALK TO ME. TELL ME WHAT'S GOING ON.
IS THIS ABOUT WORK? IT HAS TO BE.
LOOK, IF IT'S JUST TOO MUCH FOR YOU...WE HAVE MONEY SET ASIDE. JUST QUIT AND--
QUIT.
HEH.
THAT'S RIGHT. QUIT AND FIND SOMETHING ELSE TO--
THERE'S NO "QUIT," ALIX. DON'T YOU GET THAT?
THERE'S NO OUT! NO RESIGNATION! NO! QUIT!
THEY'LL--
THEY'LL WHAT?
...
DISAPPROVE.

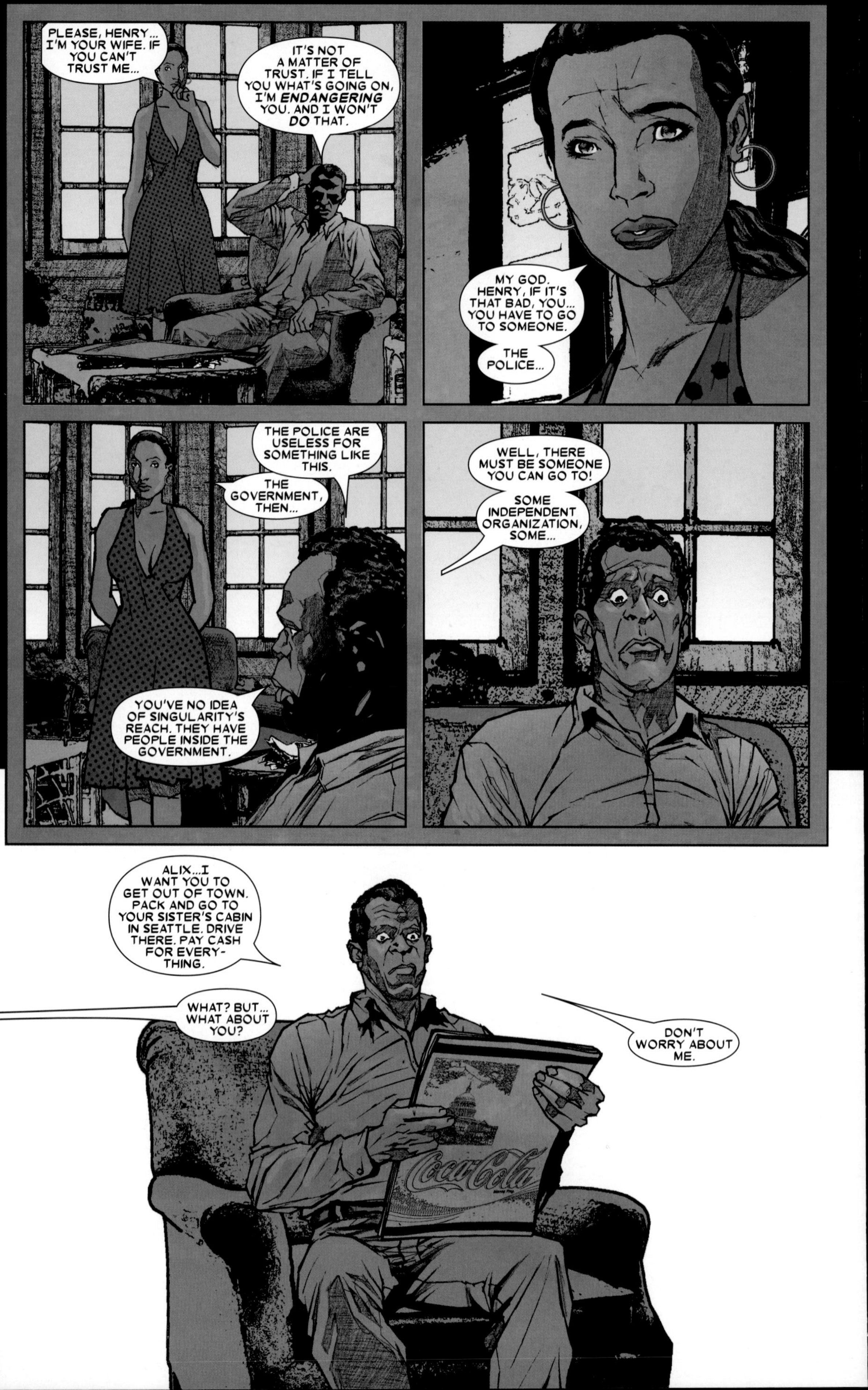
PLEASE, HENRY... I'M YOUR WIFE. IF YOU CAN'T TRUST ME...
IT'S NOT A MATTER OF TRUST. IF I TELL YOU WHAT'S GOING ON, I'M *ENDANGERING* YOU. AND I WON'T *DO* THAT.
MY GOD. HENRY, IF IT'S THAT BAD, YOU... YOU HAVE TO GO TO SOMEONE.
THE POLICE...
THE POLICE ARE USELESS FOR SOMETHING LIKE THIS.
THE GOVERNMENT, THEN...
YOU'VE NO IDEA OF SINGULARITY'S REACH. THEY HAVE PEOPLE INSIDE THE GOVERNMENT.
WELL, THERE MUST BE SOMEONE YOU CAN GO TO!
SOME INDEPENDENT ORGANIZATION, SOME...
ALIX...I WANT YOU TO GET OUT OF TOWN. PACK AND GO TO YOUR SISTER'S CABIN IN SEATTLE. DRIVE THERE. PAY CASH FOR EVERY-THING.
WHAT? BUT... WHAT ABOUT YOU?
DON'T WORRY ABOUT ME.
Coca-Cola

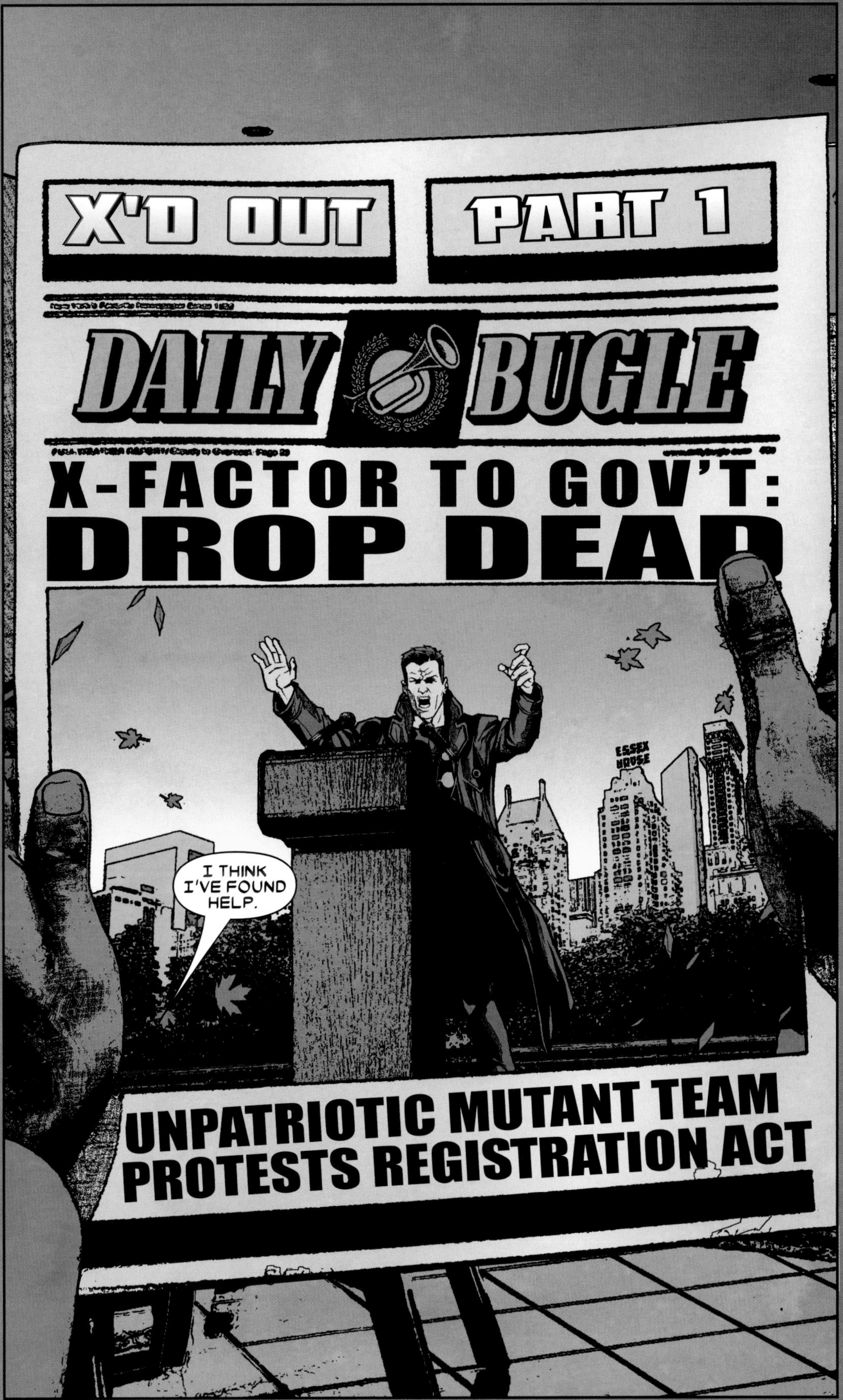
X'D OUT
PART 1
DAILY BUGLE
X-FACTOR TO GOV'T:
DROP DEAD
ESSEX HOUSE
I THINK I'VE FOUND HELP.
UNPATRIOTIC MUTANT TEAM PROTESTS REGISTRATION ACT

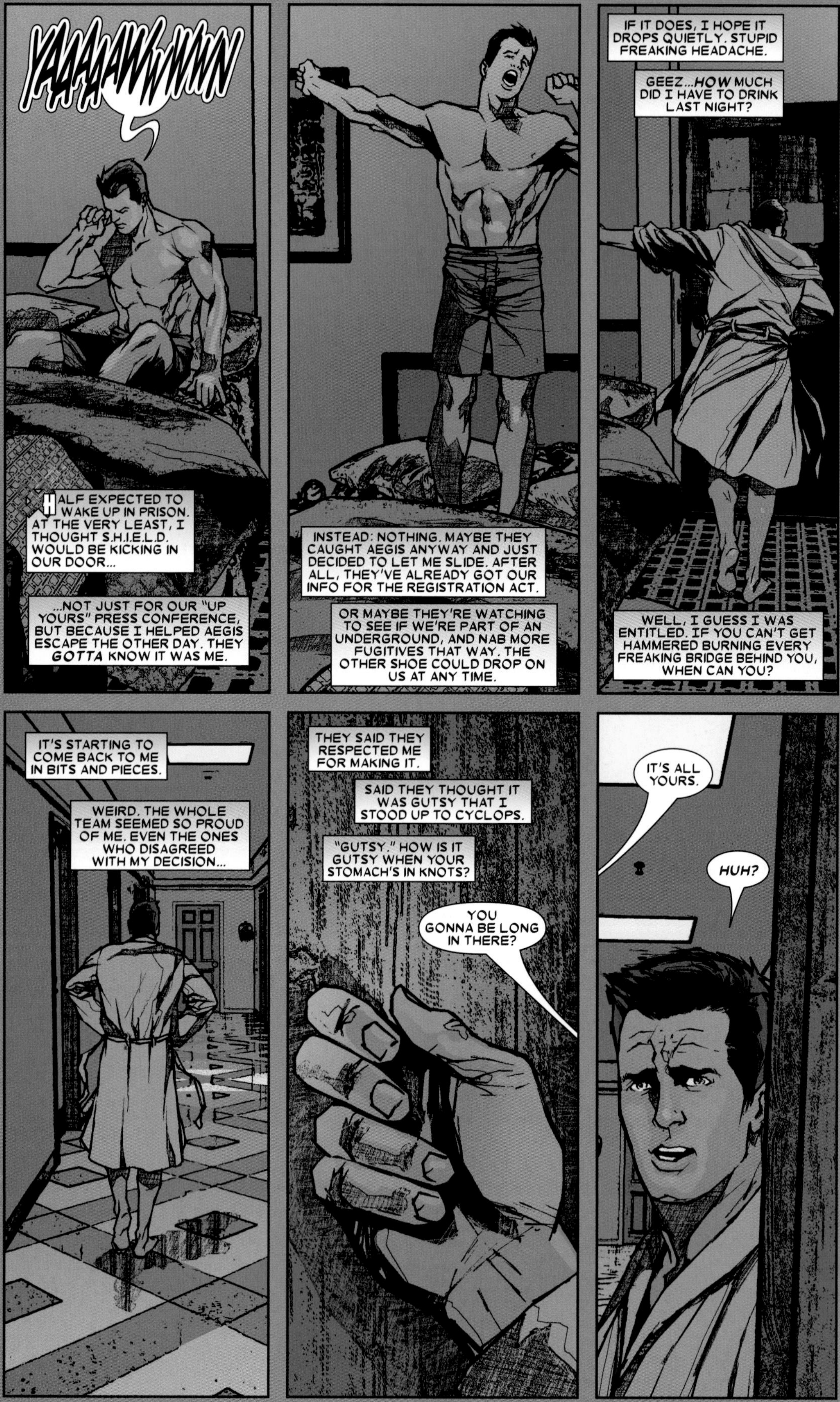

YAAAAAWWWWN
HALF EXPECTED TO WAKE UP IN PRISON. AT THE VERY LEAST, I THOUGHT S.H.I.E.L.D. WOULD BE KICKING IN OUR DOOR...
...NOT JUST FOR OUR "UP YOURS" PRESS CONFERENCE, BUT BECAUSE I HELPED AEGIS ESCAPE THE OTHER DAY. THEY GOTTA KNOW IT WAS ME.
INSTEAD: NOTHING. MAYBE THEY CAUGHT AEGIS ANYWAY AND JUST DECIDED TO LET ME SLIDE. AFTER ALL, THEY'VE ALREADY GOT OUR INFO FOR THE REGISTRATION ACT.
OR MAYBE THEY'RE WATCHING TO SEE IF WE'RE PART OF AN UNDERGROUND, AND NAB MORE FUGITIVES THAT WAY. THE OTHER SHOE COULD DROP ON US AT ANY TIME.
IF IT DOES, I HOPE IT DROPS QUIETLY. STUPID FREAKING HEADACHE.
GEEZ...HOW MUCH DID I HAVE TO DRINK LAST NIGHT?
WELL, I GUESS I WAS ENTITLED. IF YOU CAN'T GET HAMMERED BURNING EVERY FREAKING BRIDGE BEHIND YOU, WHEN CAN YOU?
IT'S STARTING TO COME BACK TO ME IN BITS AND PIECES.
WEIRD. THE WHOLE TEAM SEEMED SO PROUD OF ME. EVEN THE ONES WHO DISAGREED WITH MY DECISION...
THEY SAID THEY RESPECTED ME FOR MAKING IT.
SAID THEY THOUGHT IT WAS GUTSY THAT I STOOD UP TO CYCLOPS.
"GUTSY." HOW IS IT GUTSY WHEN YOUR STOMACH'S IN KNOTS?
YOU GONNA BE LONG IN THERE?
IT'S ALL YOURS.
HUH?

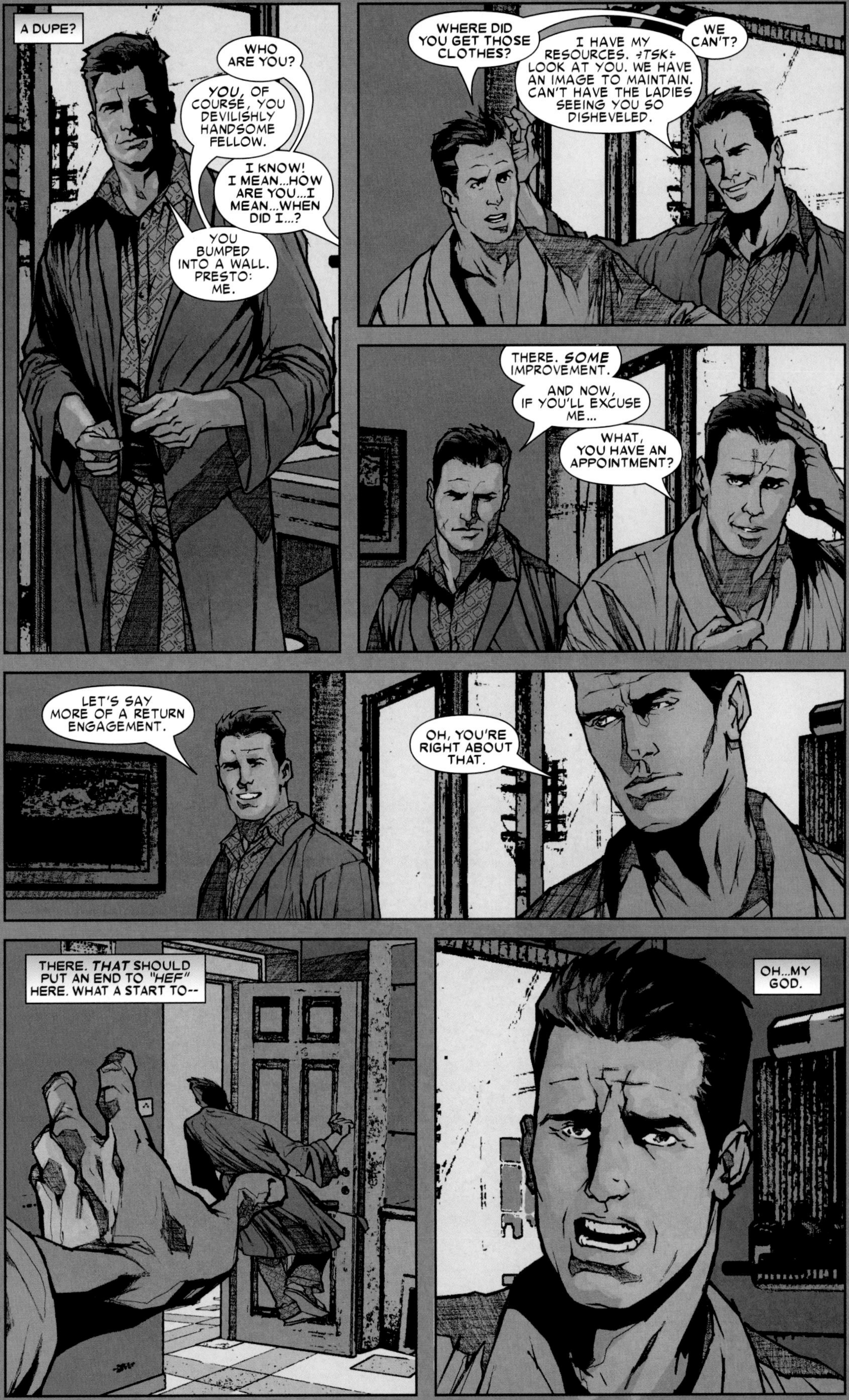
A DUPE?
WHO ARE YOU?
YOU, OF COURSE, YOU DEVILISHLY HANDSOME FELLOW.
I KNOW! I MEAN...HOW ARE YOU...I MEAN...WHEN DID I...?
YOU BUMPED INTO A WALL. PRESTO: ME.
WHERE DID YOU GET THOSE CLOTHES?
I HAVE MY RESOURCES. *TSK* LOOK AT YOU. WE HAVE AN IMAGE TO MAINTAIN. CAN'T HAVE THE LADIES SEEING YOU SO DISHEVELED.
WE CAN'T?
THERE. *SOME* IMPROVEMENT.
AND NOW, IF YOU'LL EXCUSE ME...
WHAT, YOU HAVE AN APPOINTMENT?
LET'S SAY MORE OF A RETURN ENGAGEMENT.
OH, YOU'RE RIGHT ABOUT THAT.
THERE. *THAT* SHOULD PUT AN END TO *"HEF"* HERE. WHAT A START TO--
OH...MY GOD.

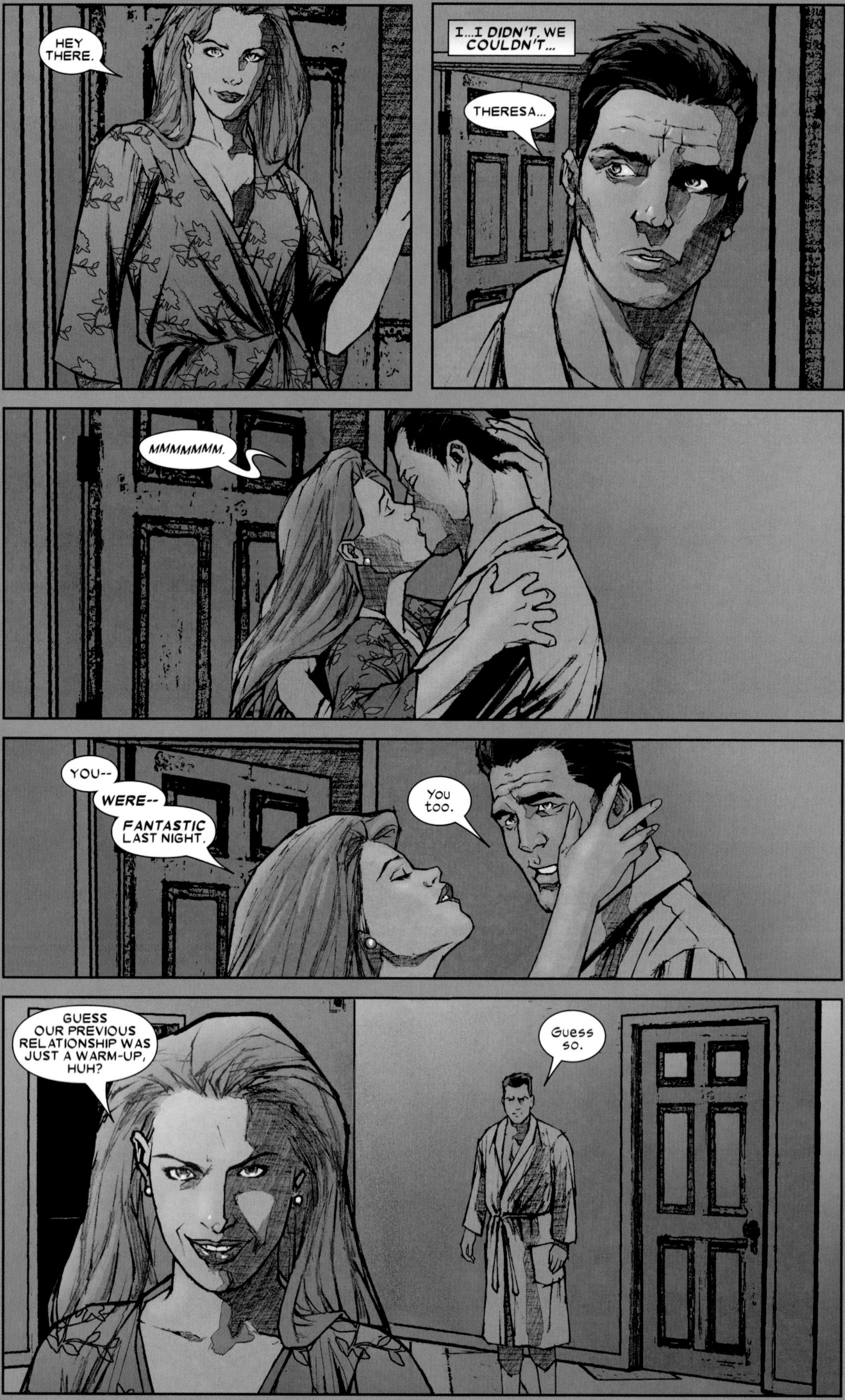
HEY THERE.
I...I DIDN'T. WE COULDN'T...
THERESA...
MMMMMMM.
YOU--
WERE--
FANTASTIC LAST NIGHT.
You too.
GUESS OUR PREVIOUS RELATIONSHIP WAS JUST A WARM-UP, HUH?
Guess so.

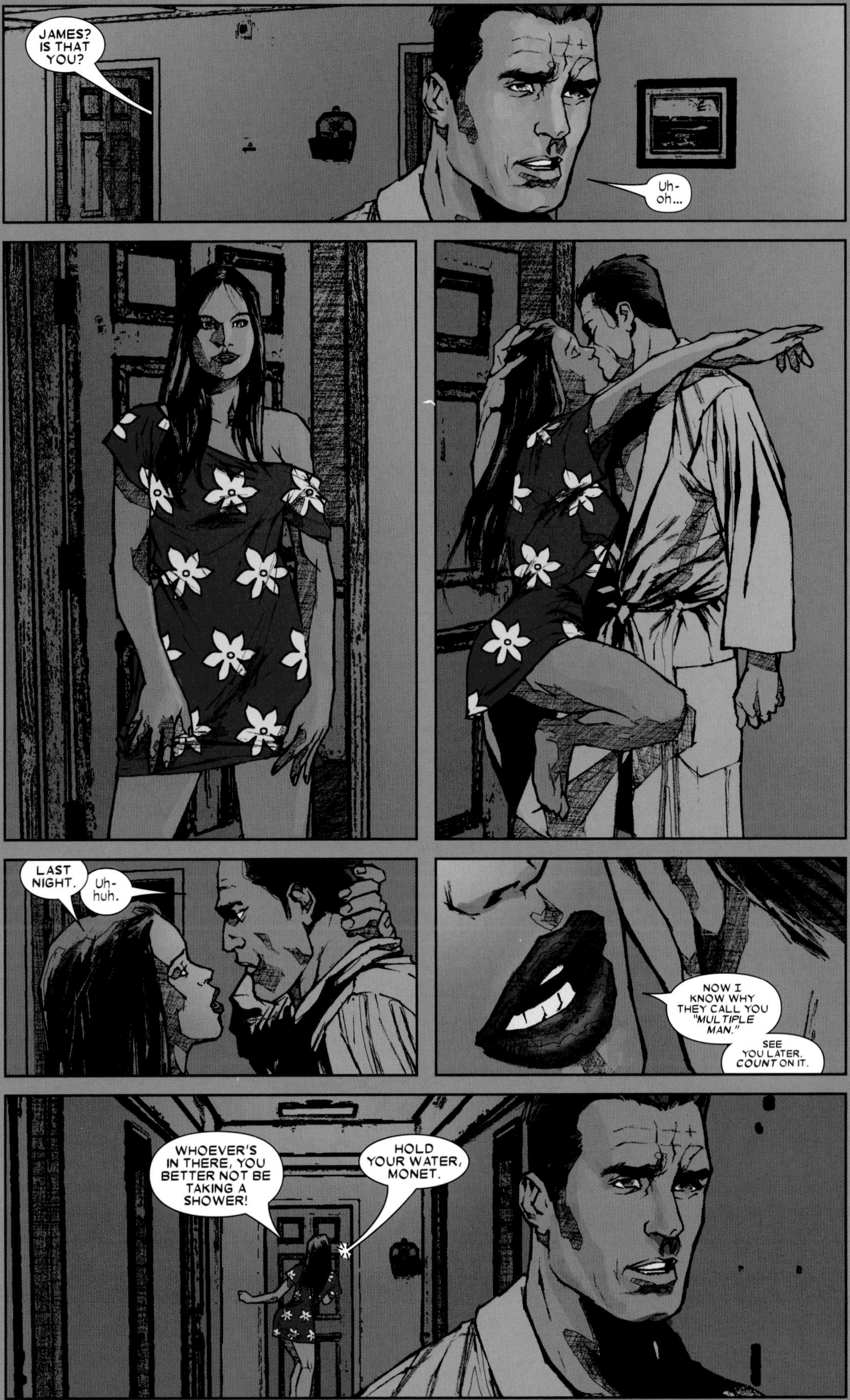
JAMES? IS THAT YOU?
Uh-oh...
LAST NIGHT.
Uh-huh.
NOW I KNOW WHY THEY CALL YOU "MULTIPLE MAN."
SEE YOU LATER. COUNT ON IT.
WHOEVER'S IN THERE, YOU BETTER NOT BE TAKING A SHOWER!
HOLD YOUR WATER, MONET.

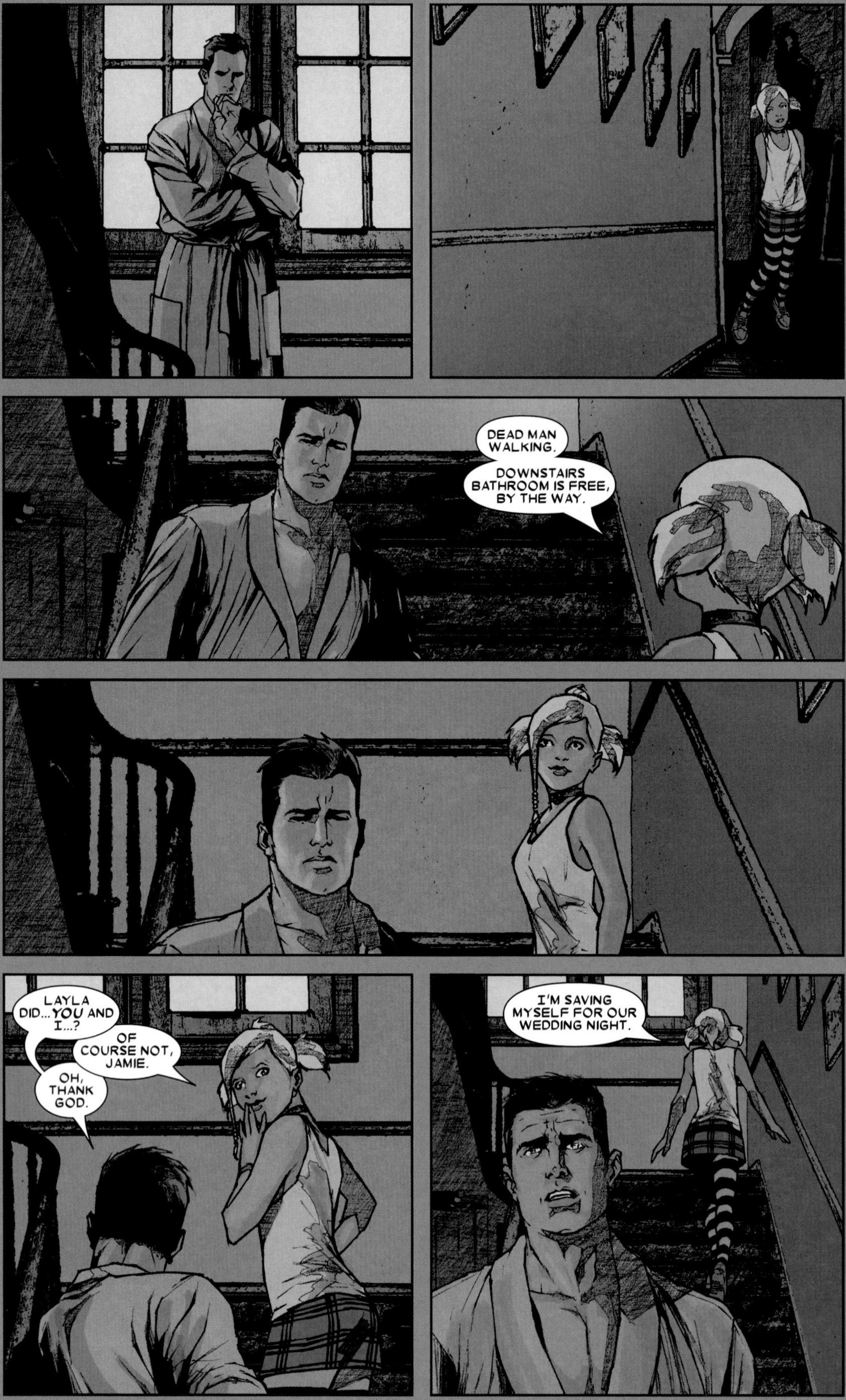
DEAD MAN WALKING.
DOWNSTAIRS BATHROOM IS FREE, BY THE WAY.
LAYLA DID...YOU AND I...?
OF COURSE NOT, JAMIE.
OH, THANK GOD.
I'M SAVING MYSELF FOR OUR WEDDING NIGHT.

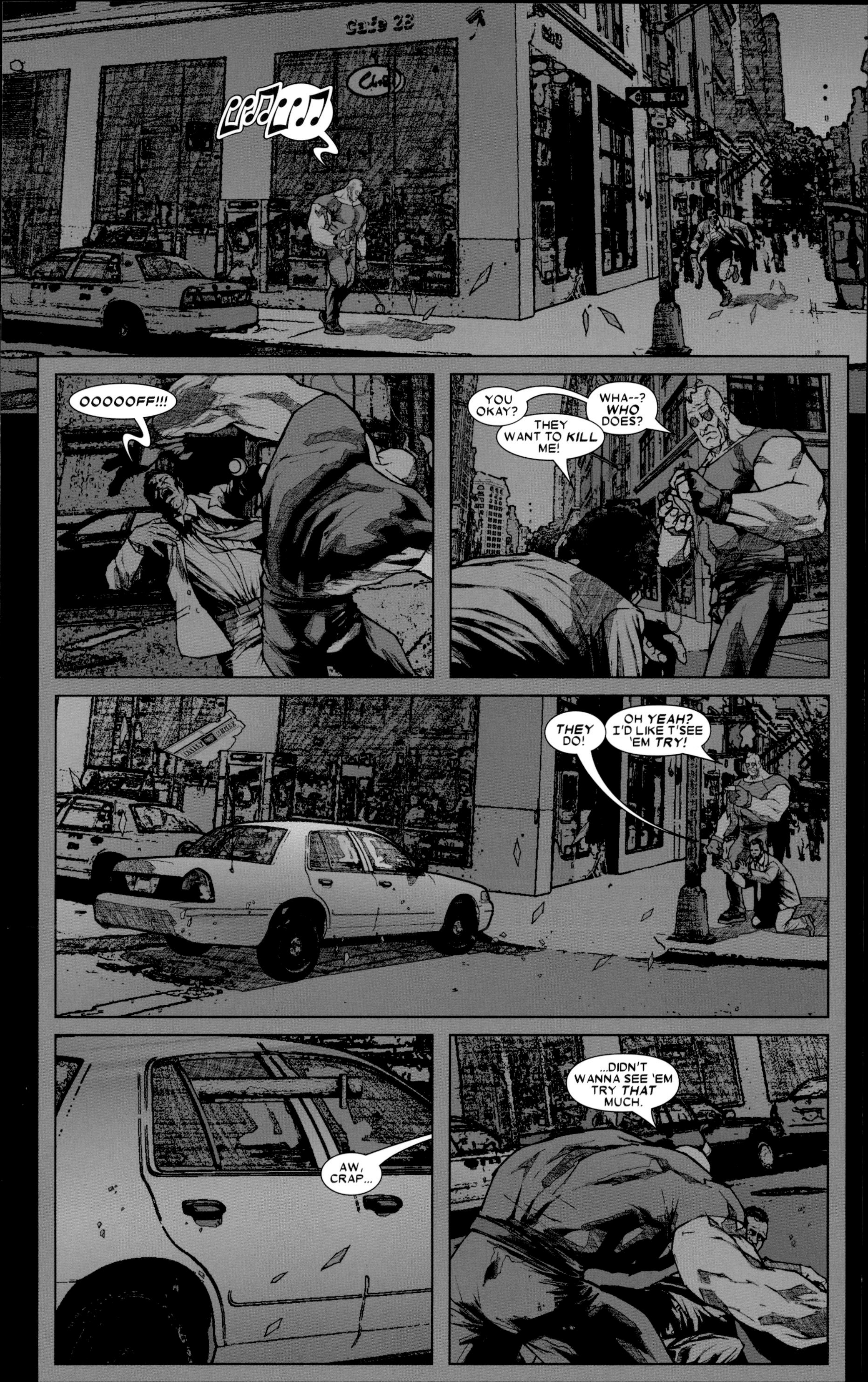
Cafe 28
OOOOOFF!!!
YOU OKAY?
WHA--? WHO DOES?
THEY WANT TO KILL ME!
THEY DO!
OH YEAH? I'D LIKE T'SEE 'EM TRY!
AW, CRAP...
...DIDN'T WANNA SEE 'EM TRY THAT MUCH.

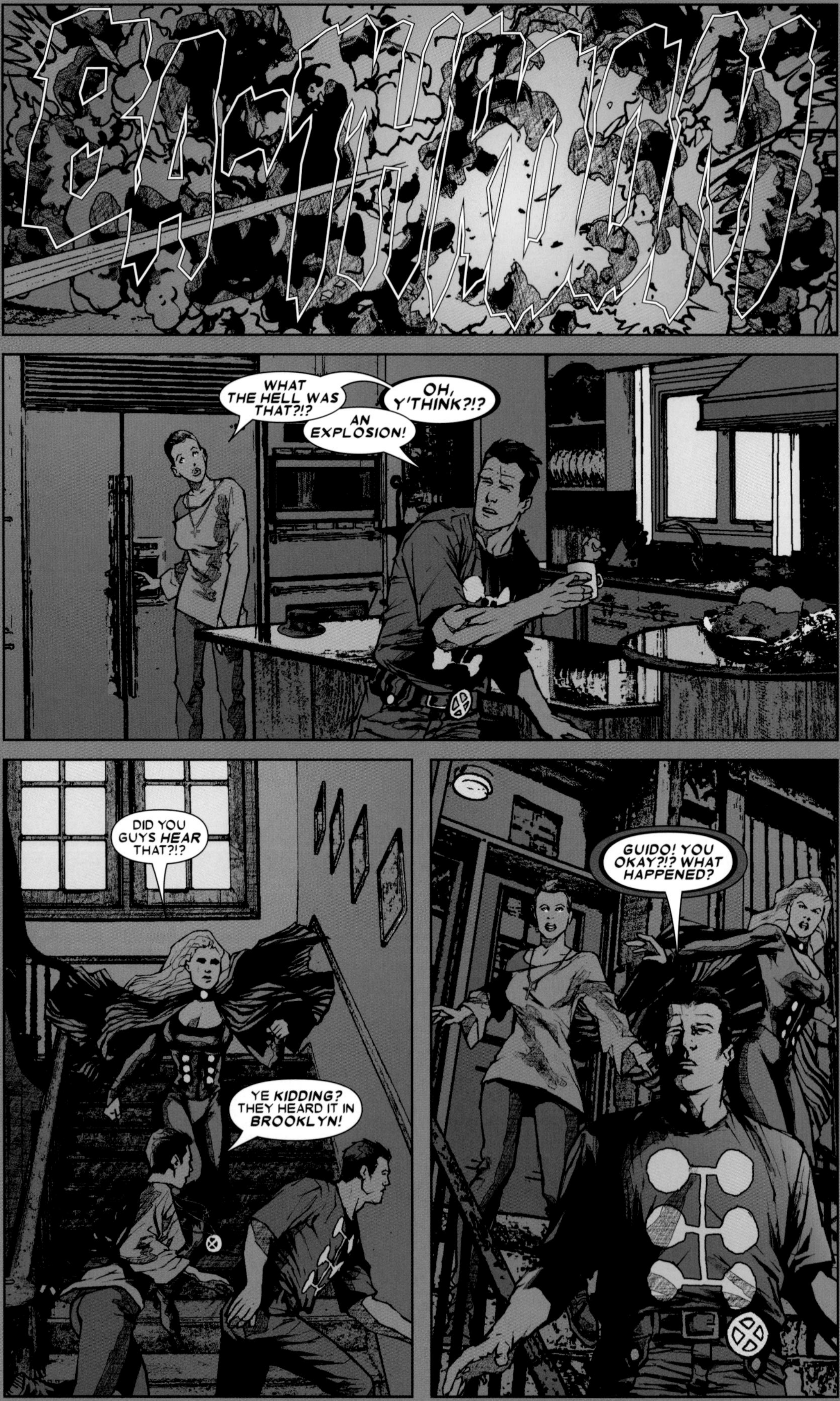
WHAT THE HELL WAS THAT?!?
AN EXPLOSION!
OH, Y'THINK?!?
DID YOU GUYS HEAR THAT?!?
YE KIDDING? THEY HEARD IT IN BROOKLYN!
GUIDO! YOU OKAY?!? WHAT HAPPENED?

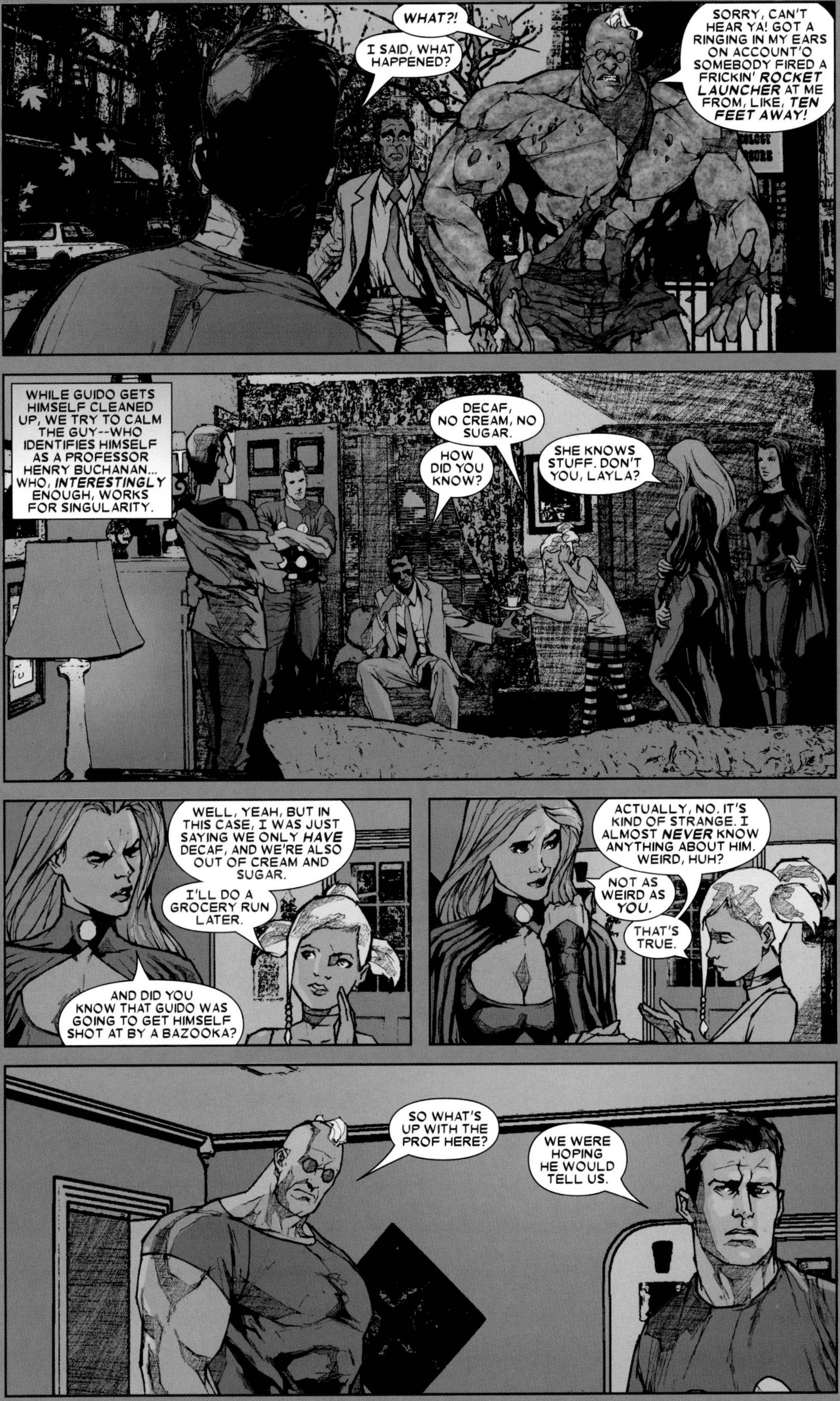
WHAT?!
I SAID, WHAT HAPPENED?
SORRY, CAN'T HEAR YA! GOT A RINGING IN MY EARS ON ACCOUNT'O SOMEBODY FIRED A FRICKIN' ROCKET LAUNCHER AT ME FROM, LIKE, TEN FEET AWAY!
WHILE GUIDO GETS HIMSELF CLEANED UP, WE TRY TO CALM THE GUY--WHO IDENTIFIES HIMSELF AS A PROFESSOR HENRY BUCHANAN... WHO, INTERESTINGLY ENOUGH, WORKS FOR SINGULARITY.
DECAF, NO CREAM, NO SUGAR.
HOW DID YOU KNOW?
SHE KNOWS STUFF. DON'T YOU, LAYLA?
WELL, YEAH, BUT IN THIS CASE, I WAS JUST SAYING WE ONLY HAVE DECAF, AND WE'RE ALSO OUT OF CREAM AND SUGAR.
I'LL DO A GROCERY RUN LATER.
AND DID YOU KNOW THAT GUIDO WAS GOING TO GET HIMSELF SHOT AT BY A BAZOOKA?
ACTUALLY, NO. IT'S KIND OF STRANGE. I ALMOST NEVER KNOW ANYTHING ABOUT HIM. WEIRD, HUH?
NOT AS WEIRD AS YOU.
THAT'S TRUE.
SO WHAT'S UP WITH THE PROF HERE?
WE WERE HOPING HE WOULD TELL US.

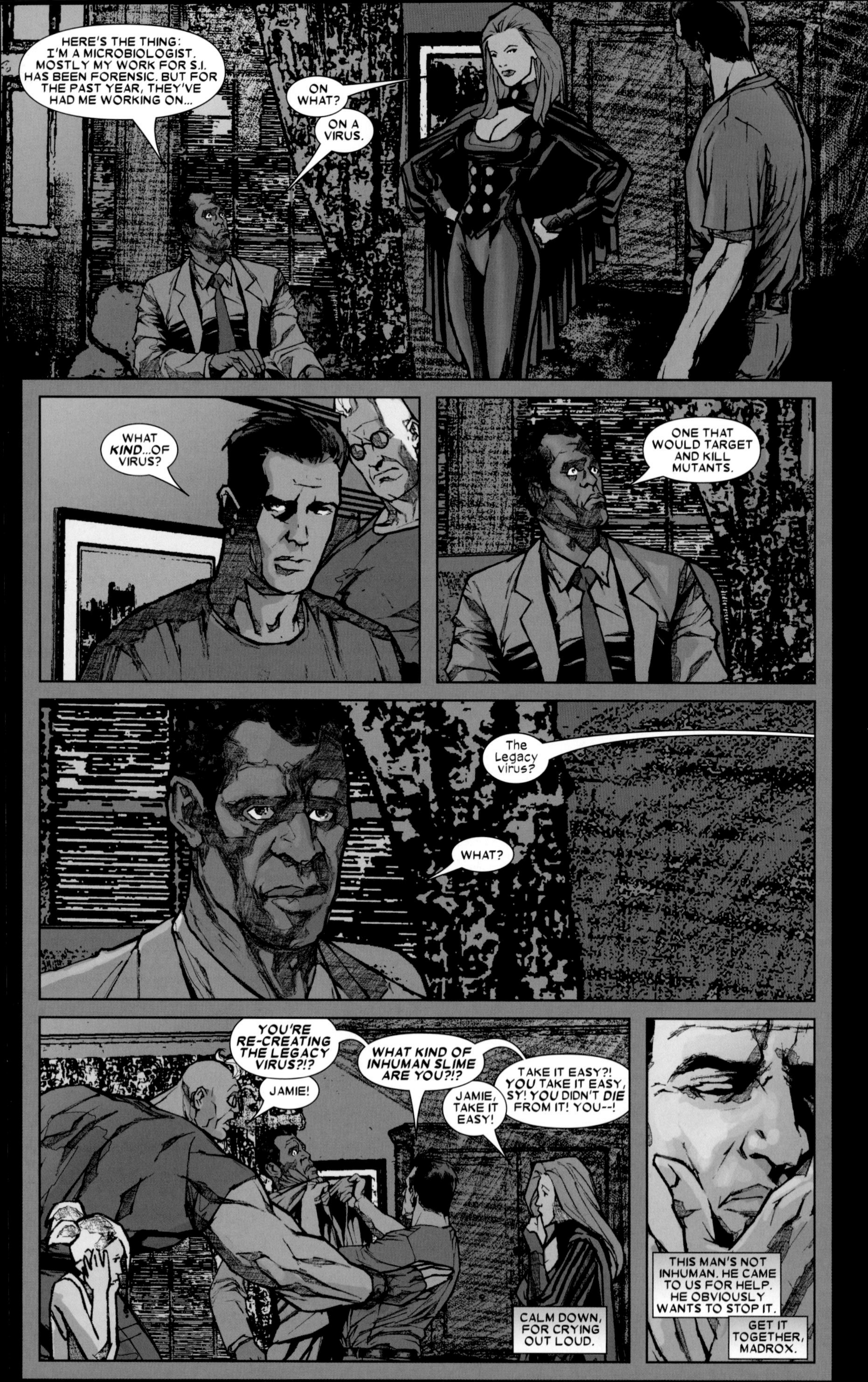
HERE'S THE THING: I'M A MICROBIOLOGIST. MOSTLY MY WORK FOR S.I. HAS BEEN FORENSIC. BUT FOR THE PAST YEAR, THEY'VE HAD ME WORKING ON...
ON WHAT?
ON A VIRUS.
WHAT *KIND*...OF VIRUS?
ONE THAT WOULD TARGET AND KILL MUTANTS.
The Legacy virus?
WHAT?
YOU'RE RE-CREATING THE LEGACY VIRUS?!?
JAMIE!
WHAT KIND OF INHUMAN SLIME ARE YOU?!?
JAMIE, TAKE IT EASY!
TAKE IT EASY?! *YOU* TAKE IT EASY, SY! *YOU* DIDN'T *DIE* FROM IT! YOU--!
CALM DOWN, FOR CRYING OUT LOUD.
THIS MAN'S NOT INHUMAN. HE CAME TO US FOR HELP. HE OBVIOUSLY WANTS TO STOP IT.
GET IT TOGETHER, MADROX.

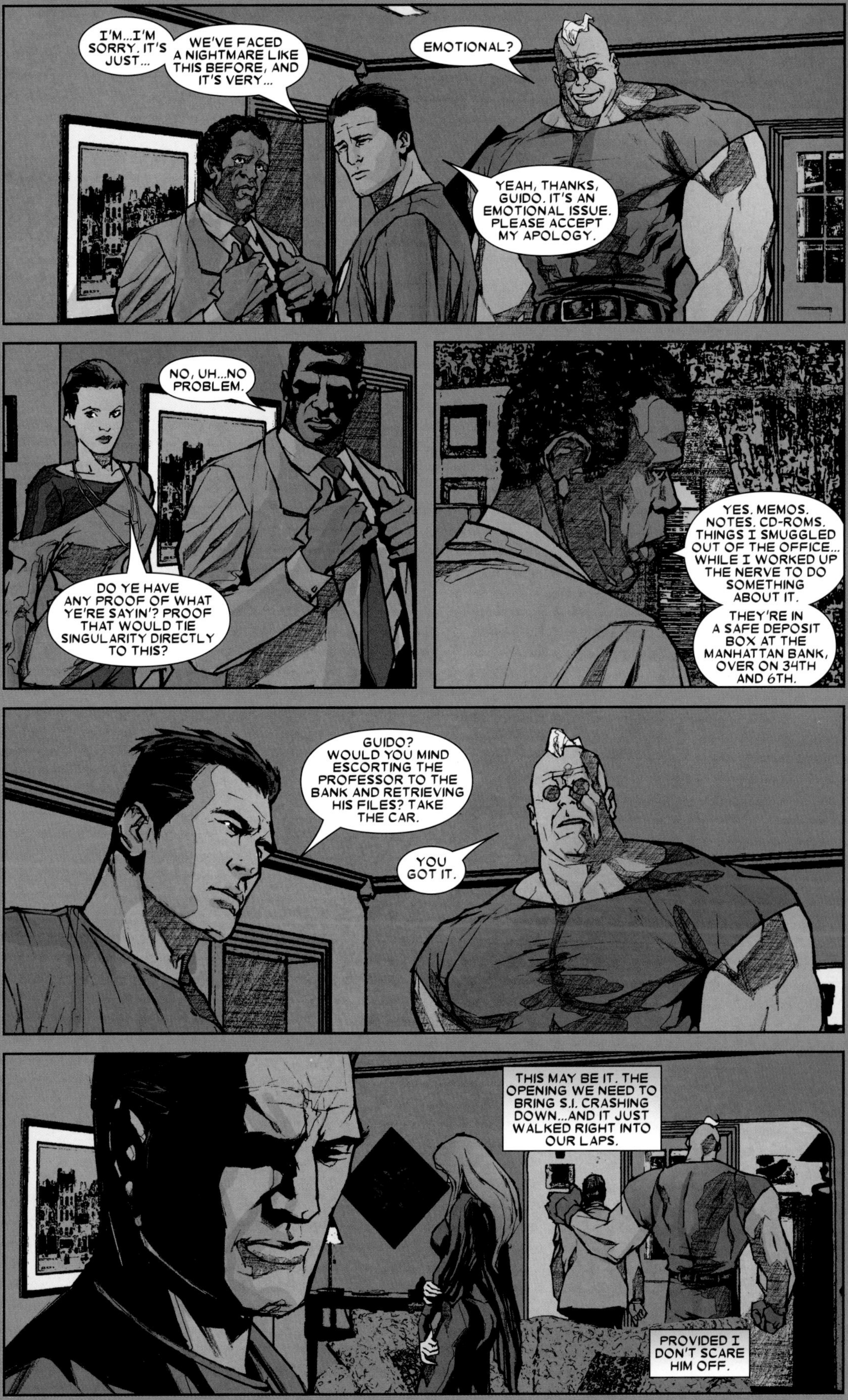
I'M...I'M SORRY. IT'S JUST...
WE'VE FACED A NIGHTMARE LIKE THIS BEFORE, AND IT'S VERY...
EMOTIONAL?
YEAH, THANKS, GUIDO. IT'S AN EMOTIONAL ISSUE. PLEASE ACCEPT MY APOLOGY.
NO, UH...NO PROBLEM.
DO YE HAVE ANY PROOF OF WHAT YE'RE SAYIN'? PROOF THAT WOULD TIE SINGULARITY DIRECTLY TO THIS?
YES. MEMOS. NOTES. CD-ROMS. THINGS I SMUGGLED OUT OF THE OFFICE... WHILE I WORKED UP THE NERVE TO DO SOMETHING ABOUT IT.
THEY'RE IN A SAFE DEPOSIT BOX AT THE MANHATTAN BANK, OVER ON 34TH AND 6TH.
GUIDO? WOULD YOU MIND ESCORTING THE PROFESSOR TO THE BANK AND RETRIEVING HIS FILES? TAKE THE CAR.
YOU GOT IT.
THIS MAY BE IT. THE OPENING WE NEED TO BRING S.I. CRASHING DOWN...AND IT JUST WALKED RIGHT INTO OUR LAPS.
PROVIDED I DON'T SCARE HIM OFF.

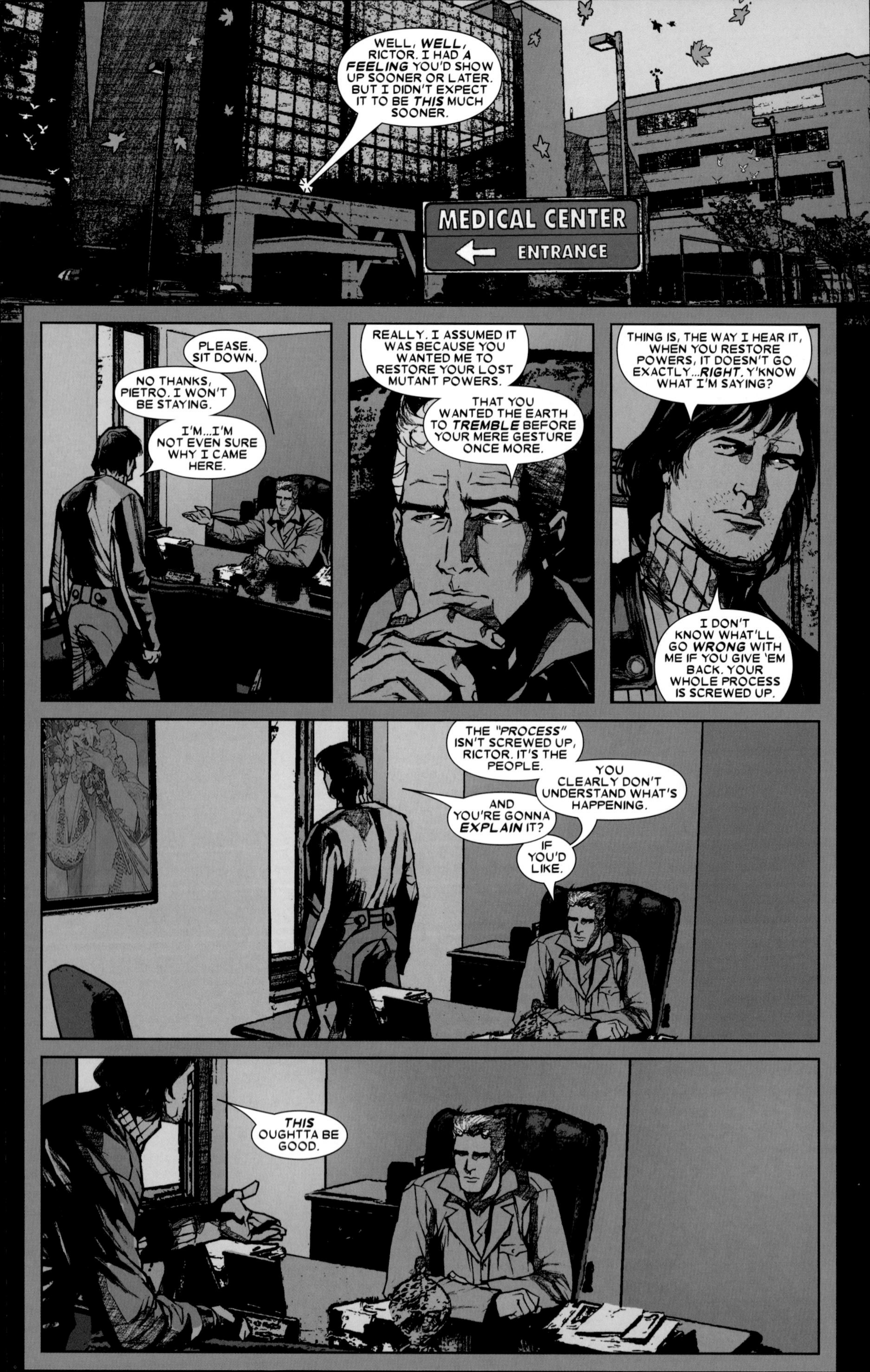
WELL, WELL, RICTOR. I HAD A FEELING YOU'D SHOW UP SOONER OR LATER. BUT I DIDN'T EXPECT IT TO BE THIS MUCH SOONER.
MEDICAL CENTER
ENTRANCE
PLEASE. SIT DOWN.
NO THANKS, PIETRO. I WON'T BE STAYING.
I'M...I'M NOT EVEN SURE WHY I CAME HERE.
REALLY. I ASSUMED IT WAS BECAUSE YOU WANTED ME TO RESTORE YOUR LOST MUTANT POWERS.
THAT YOU WANTED THE EARTH TO TREMBLE BEFORE YOUR MERE GESTURE ONCE MORE.
THING IS, THE WAY I HEAR IT, WHEN YOU RESTORE POWERS, IT DOESN'T GO EXACTLY...RIGHT, Y'KNOW WHAT I'M SAYING?
I DON'T KNOW WHAT'LL GO WRONG WITH ME IF YOU GIVE 'EM BACK. YOUR WHOLE PROCESS IS SCREWED UP.
THE "PROCESS" ISN'T SCREWED UP, RICTOR. IT'S THE PEOPLE.
YOU CLEARLY DON'T UNDERSTAND WHAT'S HAPPENING.
AND YOU'RE GONNA EXPLAIN IT?
IF YOU'D LIKE.
THIS OUGHTTA BE GOOD.

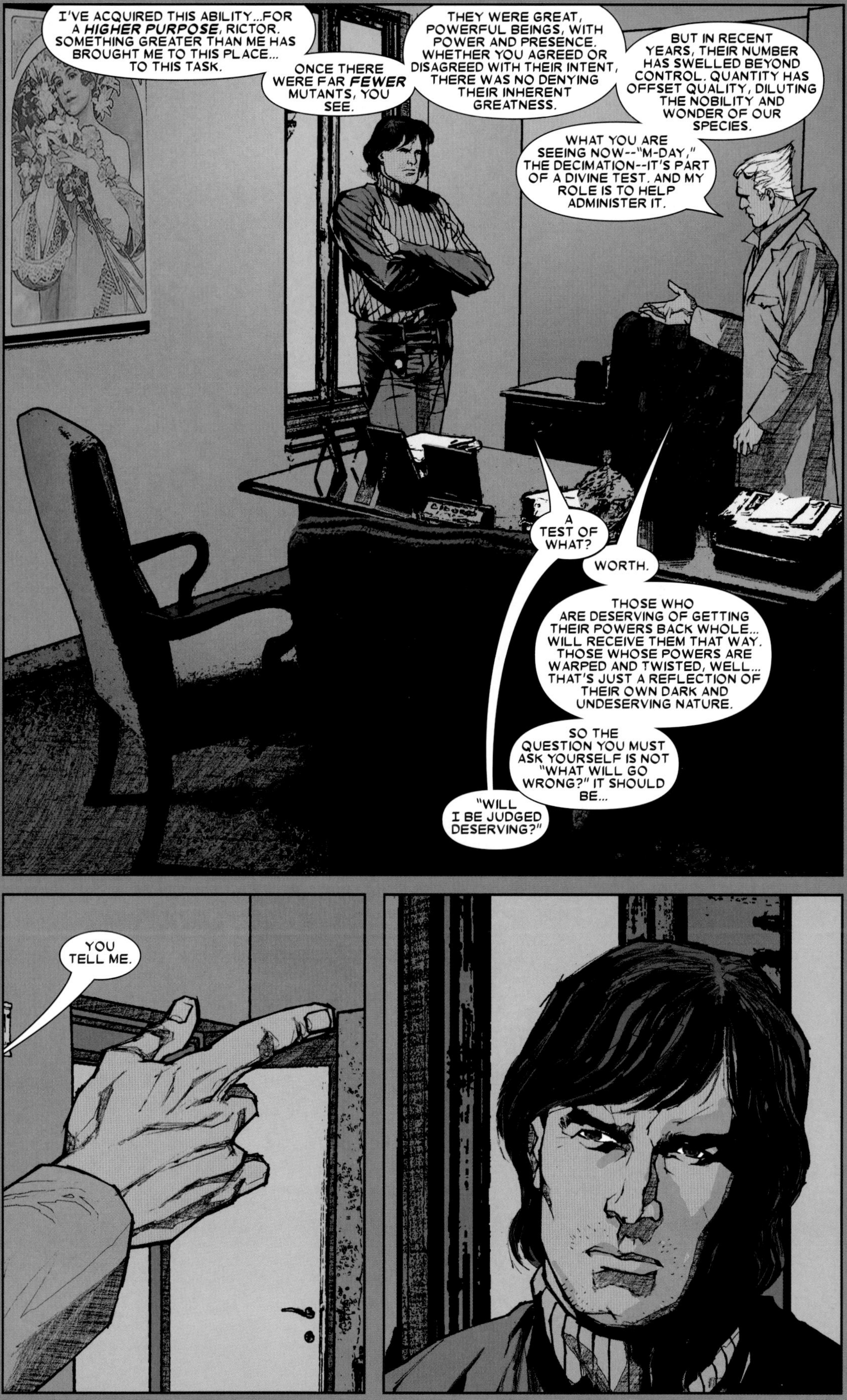
I'VE ACQUIRED THIS ABILITY...FOR A *HIGHER PURPOSE*, RICTOR. SOMETHING GREATER THAN ME HAS BROUGHT ME TO THIS PLACE... TO THIS TASK.
ONCE THERE WERE FAR *FEWER* MUTANTS, YOU SEE.
THEY WERE GREAT, POWERFUL BEINGS, WITH POWER AND PRESENCE. WHETHER YOU AGREED OR DISAGREED WITH THEIR INTENT, THERE WAS NO DENYING THEIR INHERENT GREATNESS.
BUT IN RECENT YEARS, THEIR NUMBER HAS SWELLED BEYOND CONTROL. QUANTITY HAS OFFSET QUALITY, DILUTING THE NOBILITY AND WONDER OF OUR SPECIES.
WHAT YOU ARE SEEING NOW--"M-DAY," THE DECIMATION--IT'S PART OF A DIVINE TEST. AND MY ROLE IS TO HELP ADMINISTER IT.
A TEST OF WHAT?
WORTH.
THOSE WHO ARE DESERVING OF GETTING THEIR POWERS BACK WHOLE... WILL RECEIVE THEM THAT WAY. THOSE WHOSE POWERS ARE WARPED AND TWISTED, WELL... THAT'S JUST A REFLECTION OF THEIR OWN DARK AND UNDESERVING NATURE.
SO THE QUESTION YOU MUST ASK YOURSELF IS NOT "WHAT WILL GO WRONG?" IT SHOULD BE...
"WILL I BE JUDGED DESERVING?"
YOU TELL ME.

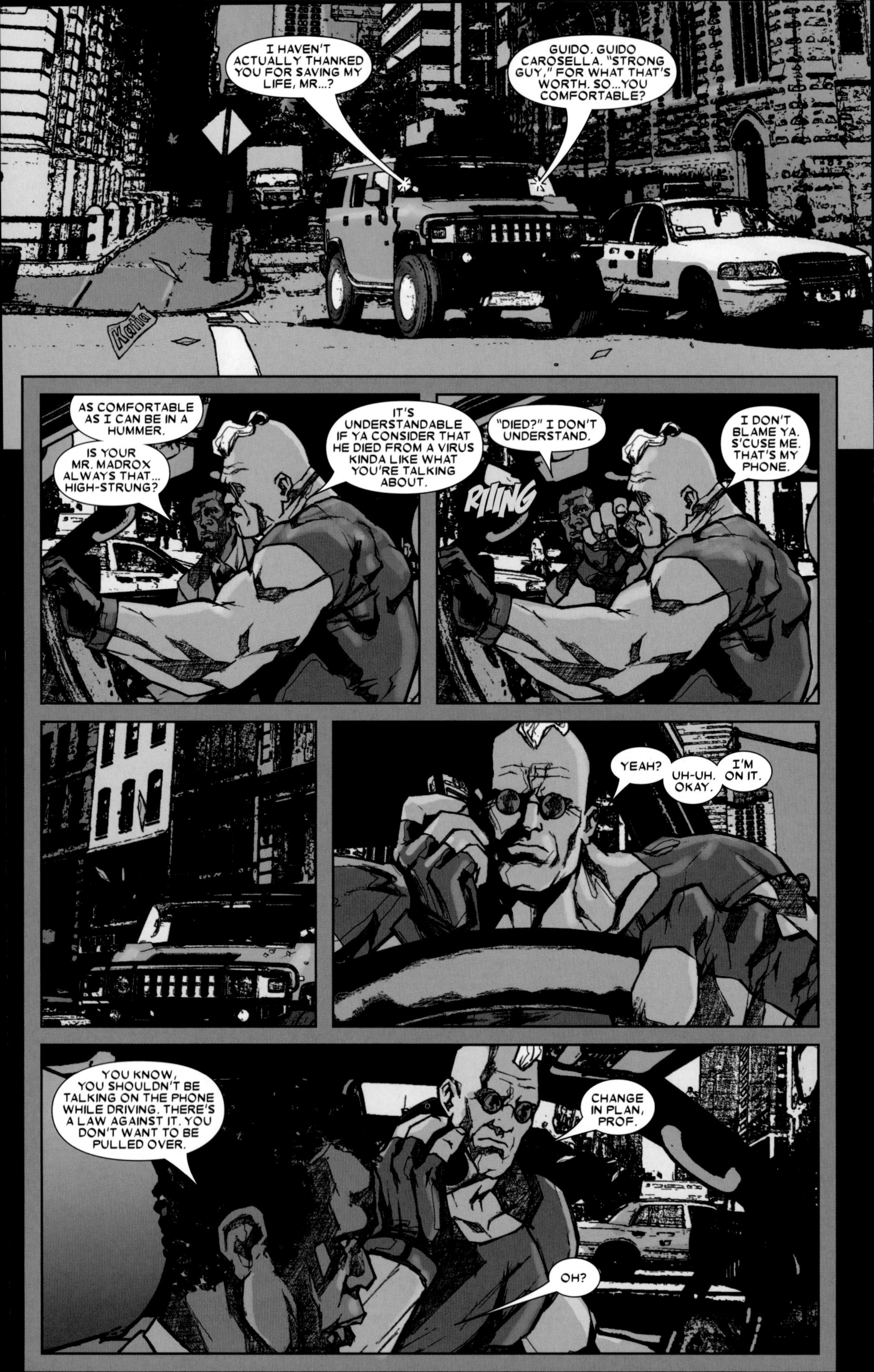
I HAVEN'T ACTUALLY THANKED YOU FOR SAVING MY LIFE, MR...?
GUIDO. GUIDO CAROSELLA. "STRONG GUY," FOR WHAT THAT'S WORTH. SO...YOU COMFORTABLE?
AS COMFORTABLE AS I CAN BE IN A HUMMER.
IS YOUR MR. MADROX ALWAYS THAT... HIGH-STRUNG?
IT'S UNDERSTANDABLE IF YA CONSIDER THAT HE DIED FROM A VIRUS KINDA LIKE WHAT YOU'RE TALKING ABOUT.
"DIED?" I DON'T UNDERSTAND.
RIIING
I DON'T BLAME YA. S'CUSE ME. THAT'S MY PHONE.
YEAH?
UH-UH. OKAY.
I'M ON IT.
YOU KNOW, YOU SHOULDN'T BE TALKING ON THE PHONE WHILE DRIVING. THERE'S A LAW AGAINST IT. YOU DON'T WANT TO BE PULLED OVER.
CHANGE IN PLAN, PROF.
OH?

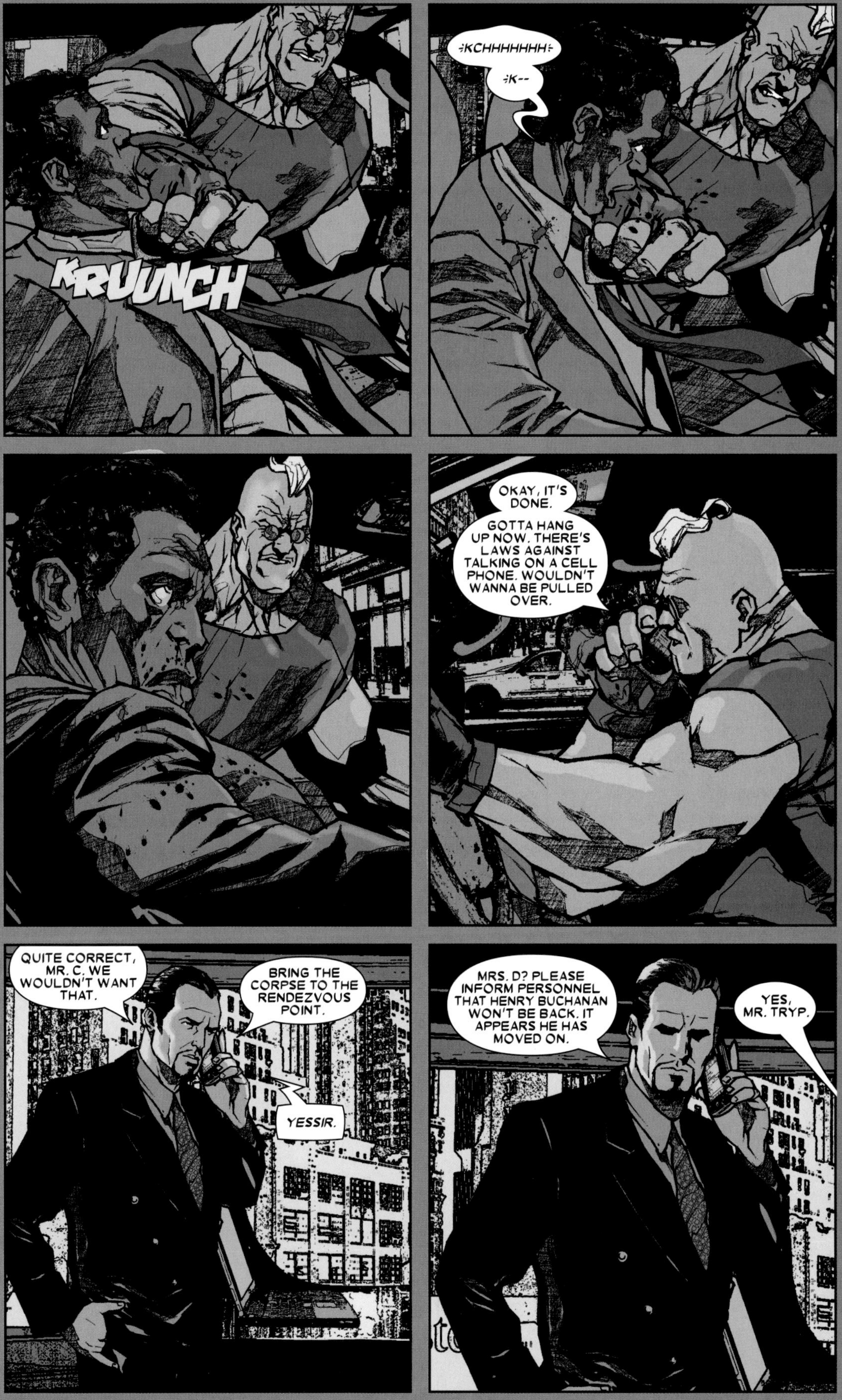
KRUUNCH
-KCHHHHHHH-
-K--
OKAY, IT'S DONE.
GOTTA HANG UP NOW. THERE'S LAWS AGAINST TALKING ON A CELL PHONE. WOULDN'T WANNA BE PULLED OVER.
QUITE CORRECT, MR. C. WE WOULDN'T WANT THAT.
BRING THE CORPSE TO THE RENDEZVOUS POINT.
YESSIR.
MRS. D? PLEASE INFORM PERSONNEL THAT HENRY BUCHANAN WON'T BE BACK. IT APPEARS HE HAS MOVED ON.
YES, MR. TRYP.

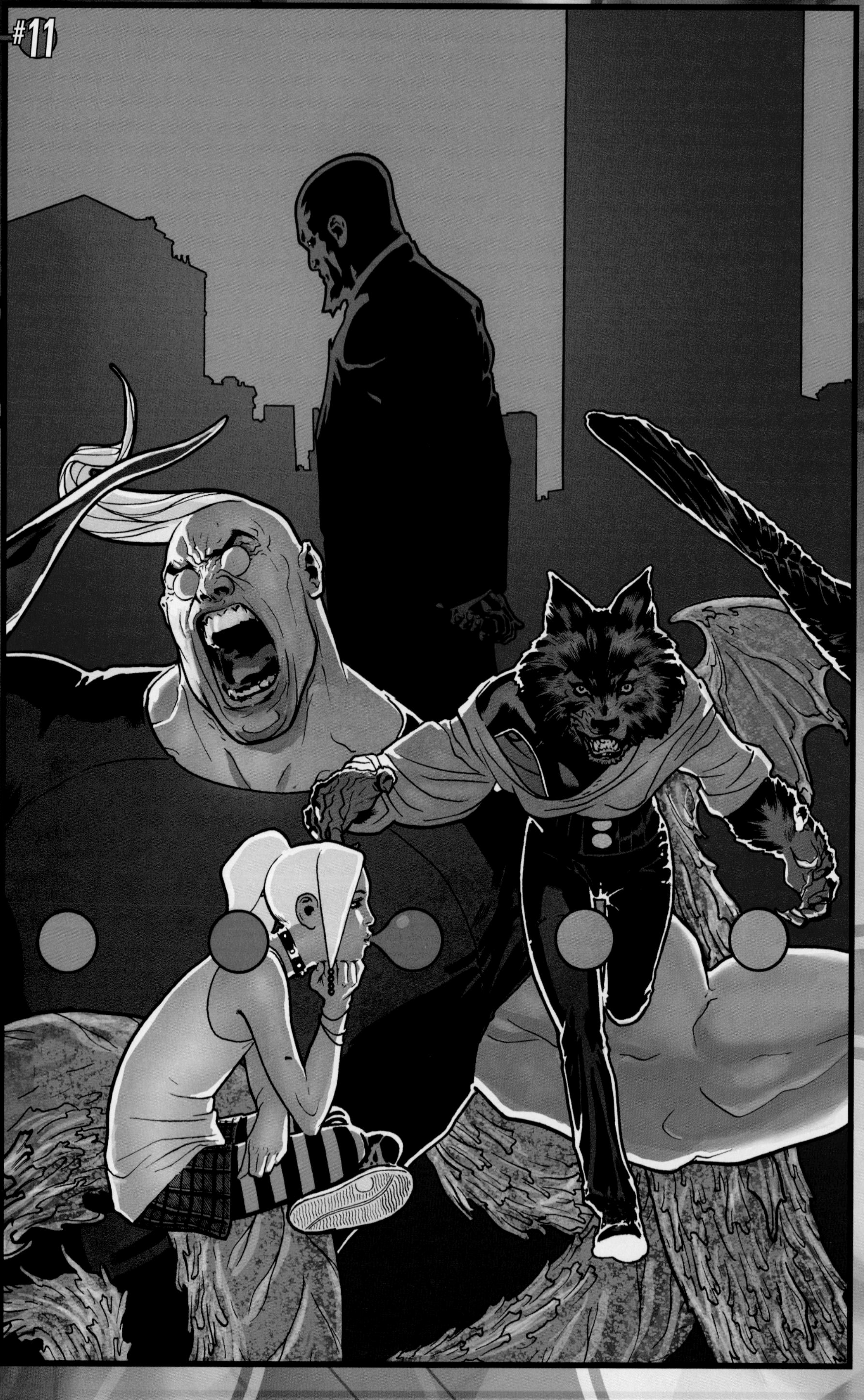
#11

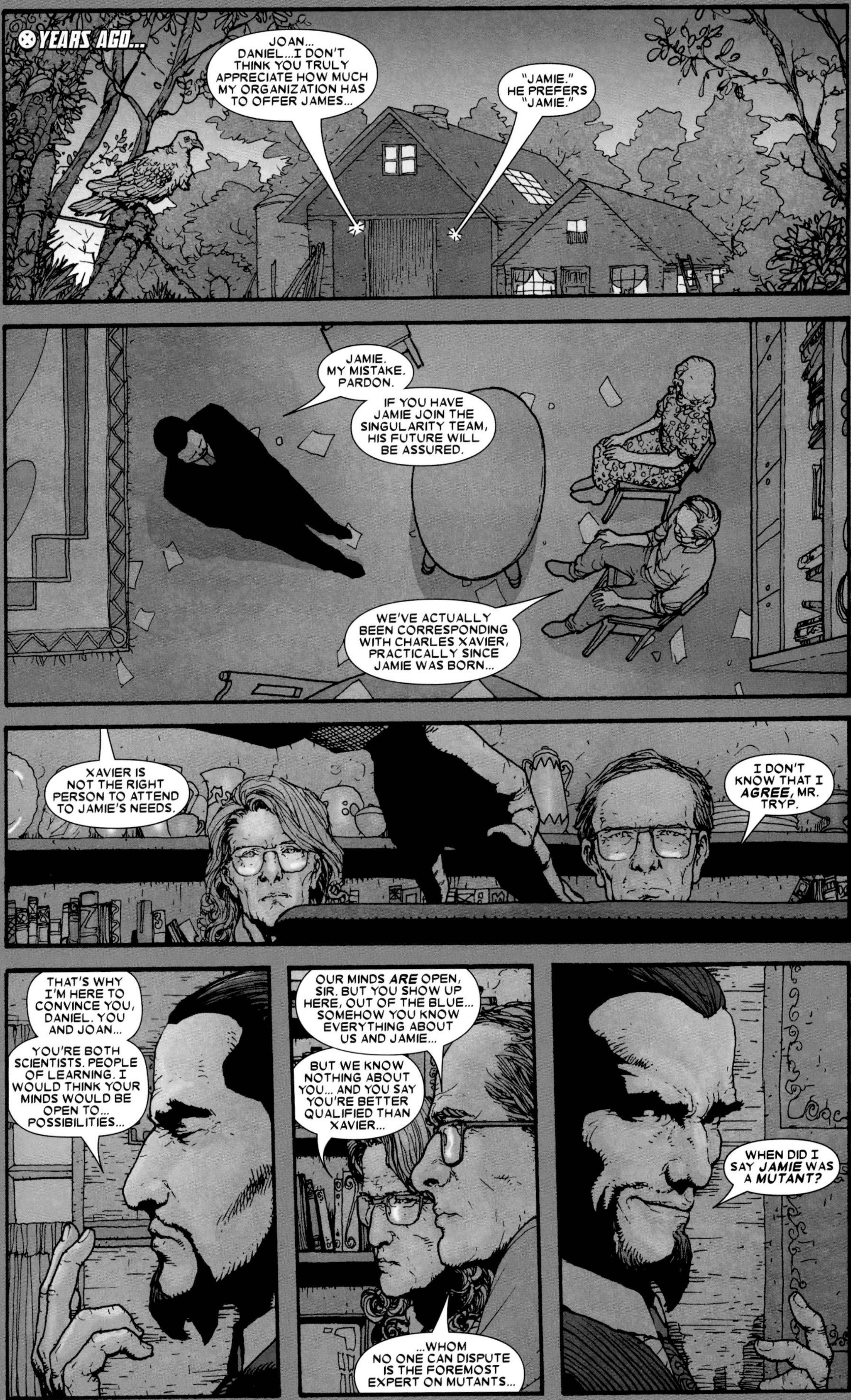
YEARS AGO...
JOAN... DANIEL...I DON'T THINK YOU TRULY APPRECIATE HOW MUCH MY ORGANIZATION HAS TO OFFER JAMES...
"JAMIE." HE PREFERS "JAMIE."
JAMIE. MY MISTAKE. PARDON.
IF YOU HAVE JAMIE JOIN THE SINGULARITY TEAM, HIS FUTURE WILL BE ASSURED.
WE'VE ACTUALLY BEEN CORRESPONDING WITH CHARLES XAVIER, PRACTICALLY SINCE JAMIE WAS BORN...
XAVIER IS NOT THE RIGHT PERSON TO ATTEND TO JAMIE'S NEEDS.
I DON'T KNOW THAT I *AGREE*, MR. TRYP.
THAT'S WHY I'M HERE TO CONVINCE YOU, DANIEL. YOU AND JOAN...
YOU'RE BOTH SCIENTISTS. PEOPLE OF LEARNING. I WOULD THINK YOUR MINDS WOULD BE OPEN TO... POSSIBILITIES...
OUR MINDS *ARE* OPEN, SIR. BUT YOU SHOW UP HERE, OUT OF THE BLUE... SOMEHOW YOU KNOW EVERYTHING ABOUT US AND JAMIE...
BUT WE KNOW NOTHING ABOUT YOU... AND YOU SAY YOU'RE BETTER QUALIFIED THAN XAVIER...
...WHOM NO ONE CAN DISPUTE IS THE FOREMOST EXPERT ON MUTANTS...
WHEN DID I SAY *JAMIE* WAS A *MUTANT?*

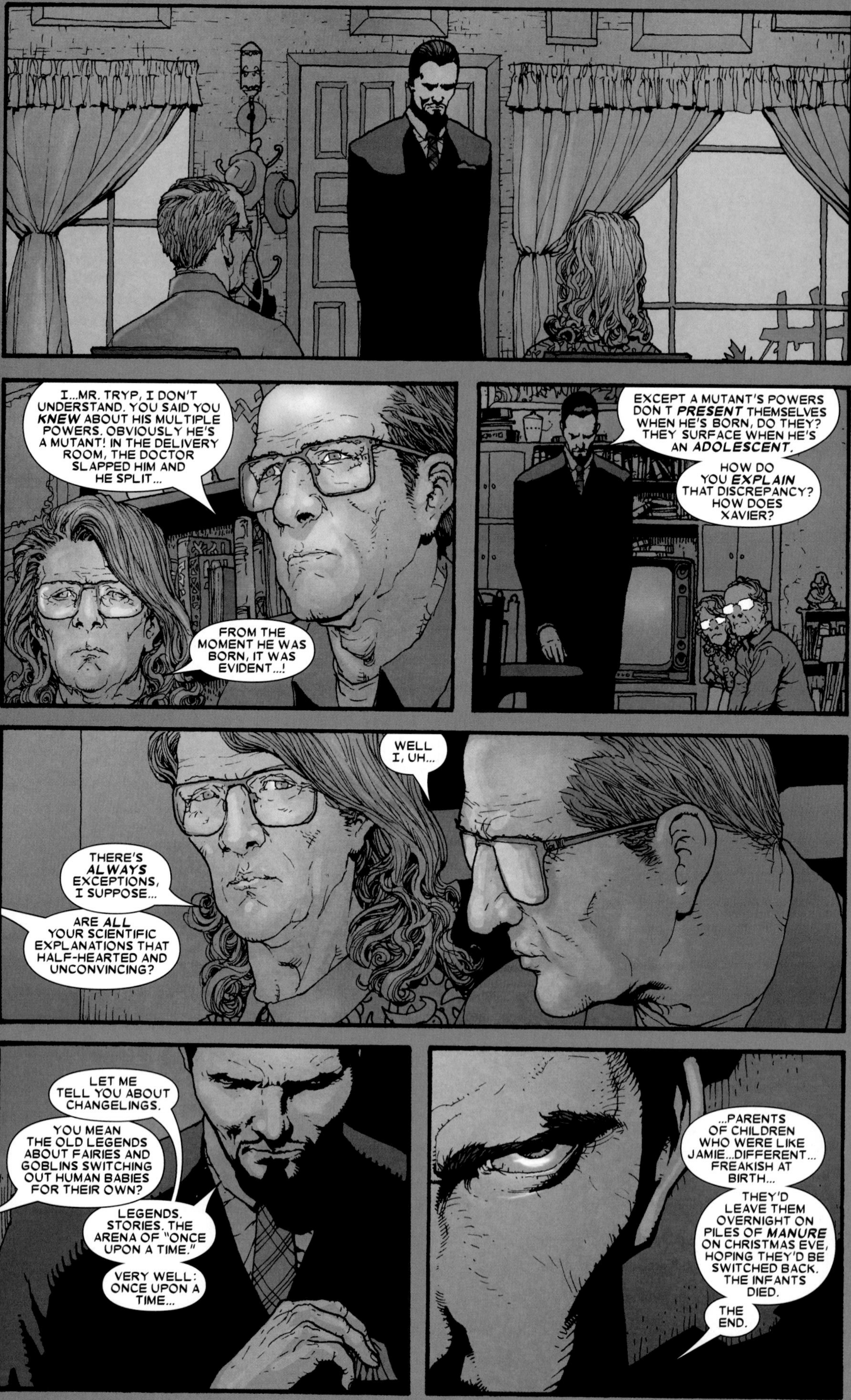
I...MR. TRYP, I DON'T UNDERSTAND. YOU SAID YOU *KNEW* ABOUT HIS MULTIPLE POWERS. OBVIOUSLY HE'S A MUTANT! IN THE DELIVERY ROOM, THE DOCTOR SLAPPED HIM AND HE SPLIT...
FROM THE MOMENT HE WAS BORN, IT WAS EVIDENT...!
EXCEPT A MUTANT'S POWERS DON T *PRESENT* THEMSELVES WHEN HE'S BORN, DO THEY? THEY SURFACE WHEN HE'S AN *ADOLESCENT*.
HOW DO YOU *EXPLAIN* THAT DISCREPANCY? HOW DOES XAVIER?
WELL I, UH...
THERE'S *ALWAYS* EXCEPTIONS, I SUPPOSE...
ARE *ALL* YOUR SCIENTIFIC EXPLANATIONS THAT HALF-HEARTED AND UNCONVINCING?
LET ME TELL YOU ABOUT CHANGELINGS.
YOU MEAN THE OLD LEGENDS ABOUT FAIRIES AND GOBLINS SWITCHING OUT HUMAN BABIES FOR THEIR OWN?
LEGENDS. STORIES. THE ARENA OF "ONCE UPON A TIME."
VERY WELL: ONCE UPON A TIME...
...PARENTS OF CHILDREN WHO WERE LIKE JAMIE...DIFFERENT... FREAKISH AT BIRTH...
THEY'D LEAVE THEM OVERNIGHT ON PILES OF *MANURE* ON CHRISTMAS EVE, HOPING THEY'D BE SWITCHED BACK. THE INFANTS DIED.
THE END.

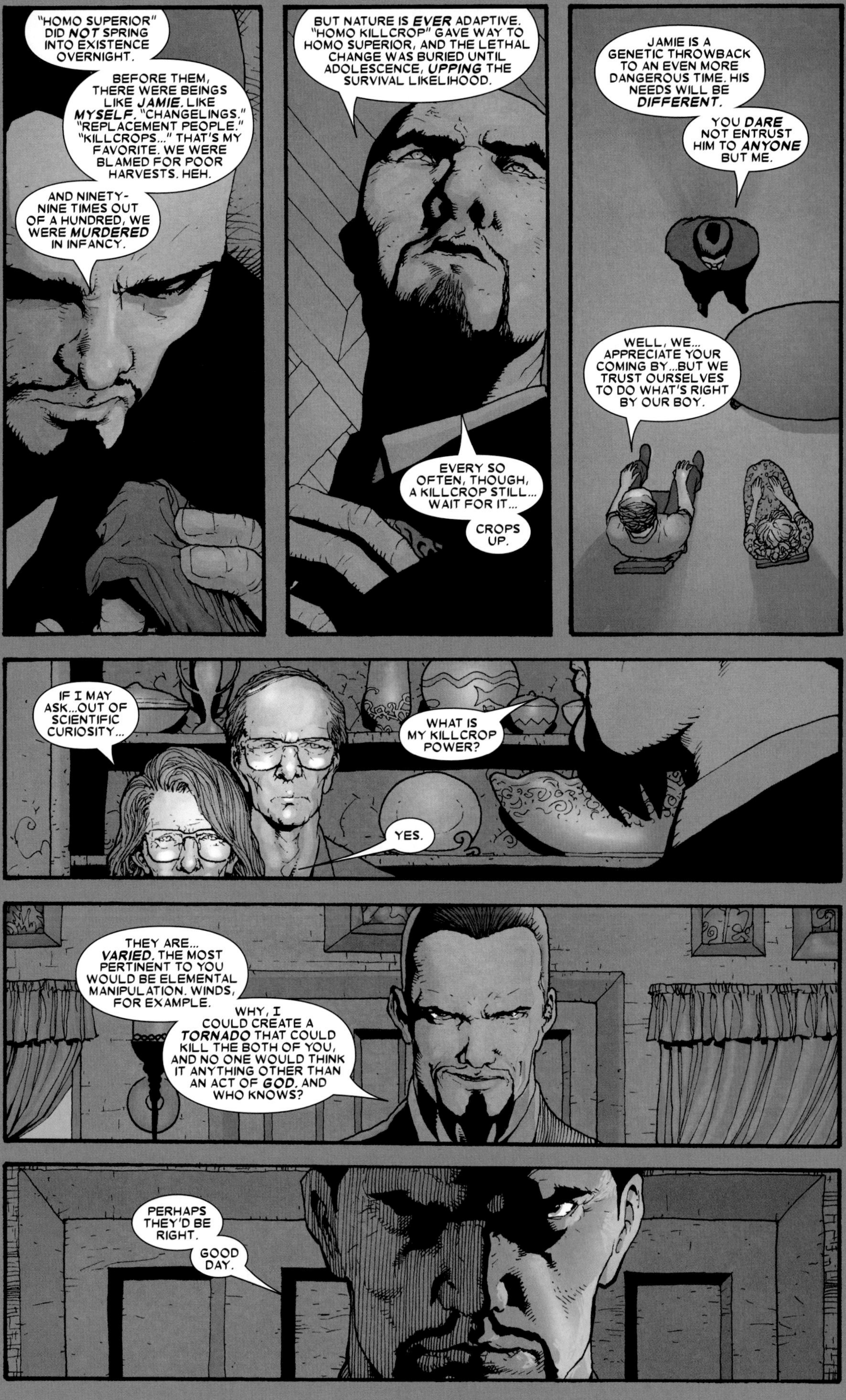
"HOMO SUPERIOR" DID NOT SPRING INTO EXISTENCE OVERNIGHT.
BEFORE THEM, THERE WERE BEINGS LIKE JAMIE. LIKE MYSELF. "CHANGELINGS." "REPLACEMENT PEOPLE." "KILLCROPS..." THAT'S MY FAVORITE. WE WERE BLAMED FOR POOR HARVESTS. HEH.
AND NINETY-NINE TIMES OUT OF A HUNDRED, WE WERE MURDERED IN INFANCY.
BUT NATURE IS EVER ADAPTIVE. "HOMO KILLCROP" GAVE WAY TO HOMO SUPERIOR, AND THE LETHAL CHANGE WAS BURIED UNTIL ADOLESCENCE, UPPING THE SURVIVAL LIKELIHOOD.
EVERY SO OFTEN, THOUGH, A KILLCROP STILL... WAIT FOR IT...
CROPS UP.
JAMIE IS A GENETIC THROWBACK TO AN EVEN MORE DANGEROUS TIME. HIS NEEDS WILL BE DIFFERENT.
YOU DARE NOT ENTRUST HIM TO ANYONE BUT ME.
WELL, WE... APPRECIATE YOUR COMING BY...BUT WE TRUST OURSELVES TO DO WHAT'S RIGHT BY OUR BOY.
IF I MAY ASK...OUT OF SCIENTIFIC CURIOSITY...
WHAT IS MY KILLCROP POWER?
YES.
THEY ARE... VARIED. THE MOST PERTINENT TO YOU WOULD BE ELEMENTAL MANIPULATION. WINDS, FOR EXAMPLE.
WHY, I COULD CREATE A TORNADO THAT COULD KILL THE BOTH OF YOU, AND NO ONE WOULD THINK IT ANYTHING OTHER THAN AN ACT OF GOD. AND WHO KNOWS?
PERHAPS THEY'D BE RIGHT.
GOOD DAY.

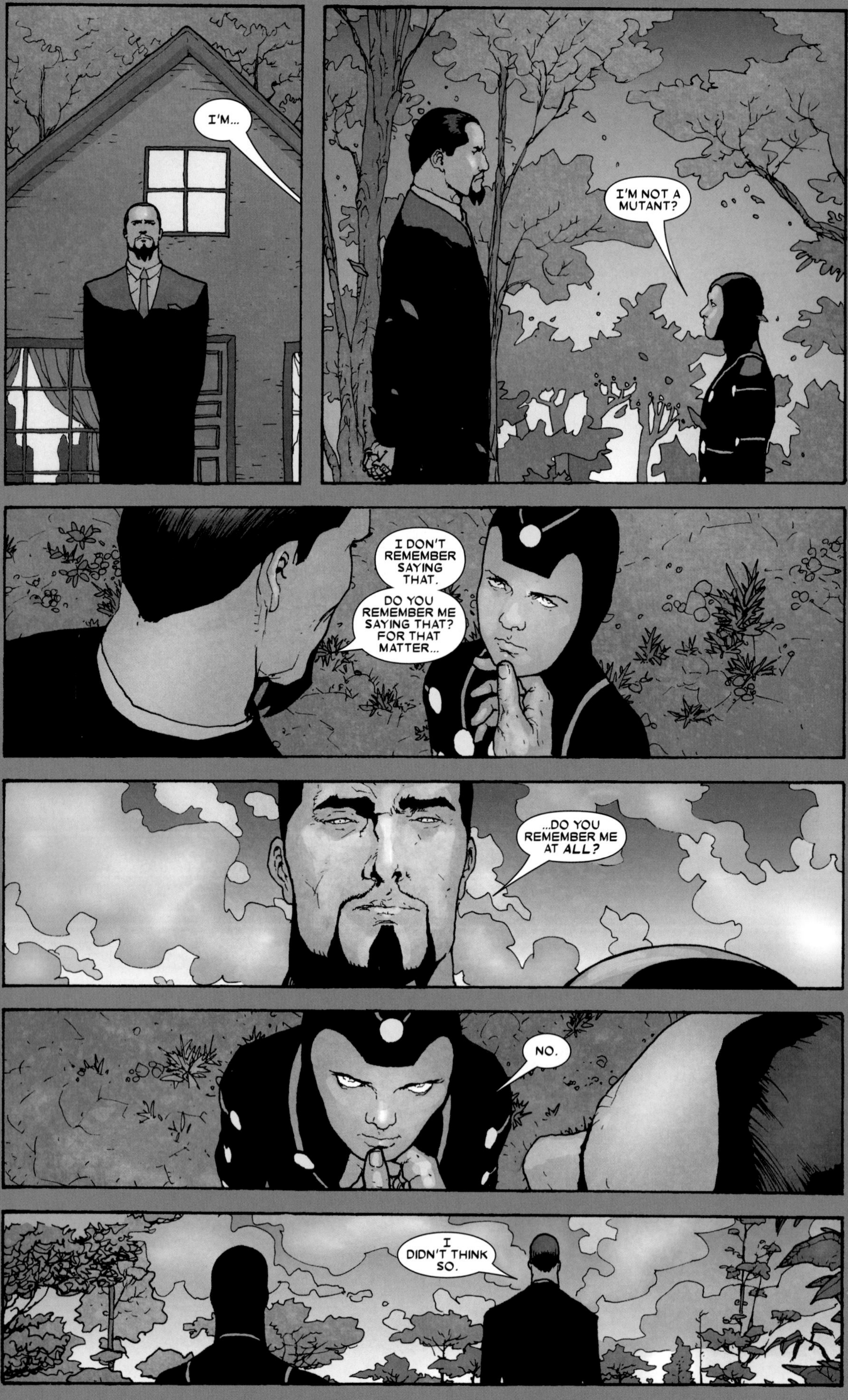
I'M...
I'M NOT A MUTANT?
I DON'T REMEMBER SAYING THAT.
DO YOU REMEMBER ME SAYING THAT? FOR THAT MATTER...
...DO YOU REMEMBER ME AT ALL?
NO.
I DIDN'T THINK SO.

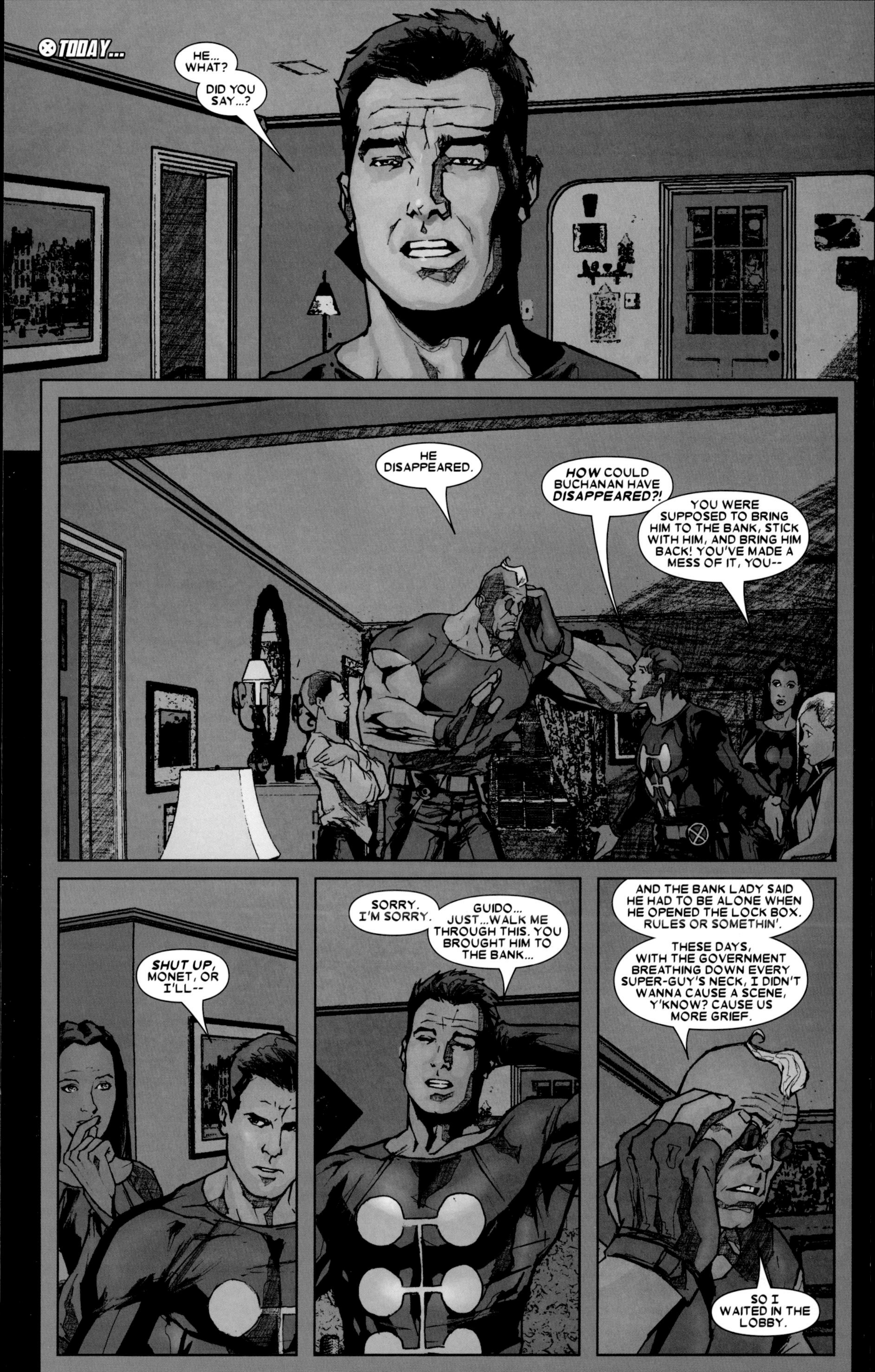
TODAY...
HE... WHAT?
DID YOU SAY...?
HE DISAPPEARED.
HOW COULD BUCHANAN HAVE DISAPPEARED?!
YOU WERE SUPPOSED TO BRING HIM TO THE BANK, STICK WITH HIM, AND BRING HIM BACK! YOU'VE MADE A MESS OF IT, YOU--
SHUT UP, MONET, OR I'LL--
SORRY. I'M SORRY.
GUIDO... JUST...WALK ME THROUGH THIS. YOU BROUGHT HIM TO THE BANK...
AND THE BANK LADY SAID HE HAD TO BE ALONE WHEN HE OPENED THE LOCK BOX. RULES OR SOMETHIN'.
THESE DAYS, WITH THE GOVERNMENT BREATHING DOWN EVERY SUPER-GUY'S NECK, I DIDN'T WANNA CAUSE A SCENE, Y'KNOW? CAUSE US MORE GRIEF.
SO I WAITED IN THE LOBBY.

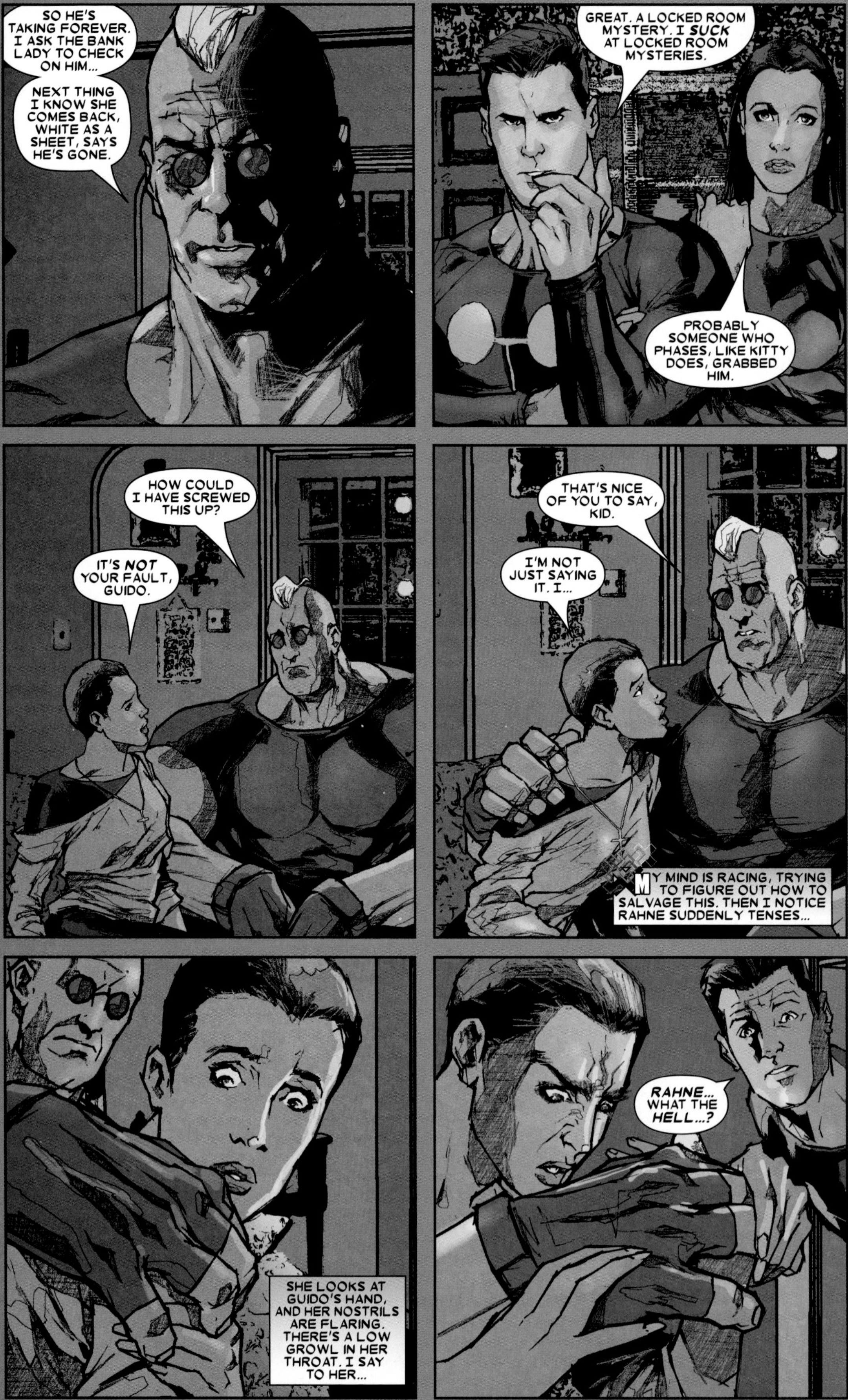

SO HE'S TAKING FOREVER. I ASK THE BANK LADY TO CHECK ON HIM...
NEXT THING I KNOW SHE COMES BACK, WHITE AS A SHEET, SAYS HE'S GONE.
GREAT. A LOCKED ROOM MYSTERY. I *SUCK* AT LOCKED ROOM MYSTERIES.
PROBABLY SOMEONE WHO PHASES, LIKE KITTY DOES, GRABBED HIM.
HOW COULD I HAVE SCREWED THIS UP?
IT'S *NOT* YOUR FAULT, GUIDO.
THAT'S NICE OF YOU TO SAY, KID.
I'M NOT JUST SAYING IT. I...
MY MIND IS RACING, TRYING TO FIGURE OUT HOW TO SALVAGE THIS. THEN I NOTICE RAHNE SUDDENLY TENSES...
SHE LOOKS AT GUIDO'S HAND, AND HER NOSTRILS ARE FLARING. THERE'S A LOW GROWL IN HER THROAT. I SAY TO HER...
RAHNE... WHAT THE *HELL*...?

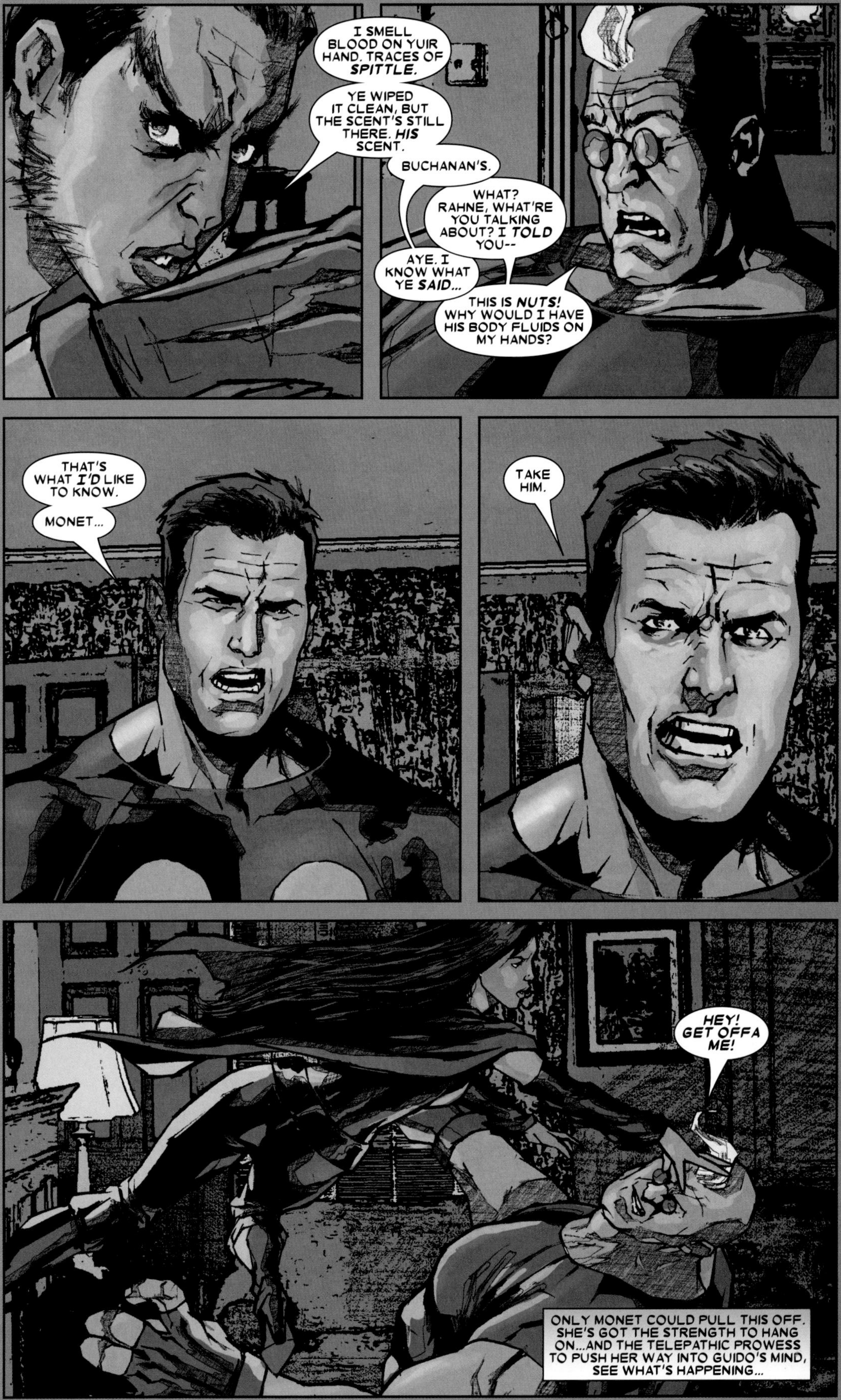
I SMELL BLOOD ON YUIR HAND. TRACES OF SPITTLE.
YE WIPED IT CLEAN, BUT THE SCENT'S STILL THERE. HIS SCENT.
BUCHANAN'S.
WHAT? RAHNE, WHAT'RE YOU TALKING ABOUT? I TOLD YOU--
AYE. I KNOW WHAT YE SAID...
THIS IS NUTS! WHY WOULD I HAVE HIS BODY FLUIDS ON MY HANDS?
THAT'S WHAT I'D LIKE TO KNOW.
MONET...
TAKE HIM.
HEY! GET OFFA ME!
ONLY MONET COULD PULL THIS OFF. SHE'S GOT THE STRENGTH TO HANG ON...AND THE TELEPATHIC PROWESS TO PUSH HER WAY INTO GUIDO'S MIND, SEE WHAT'S HAPPENING...

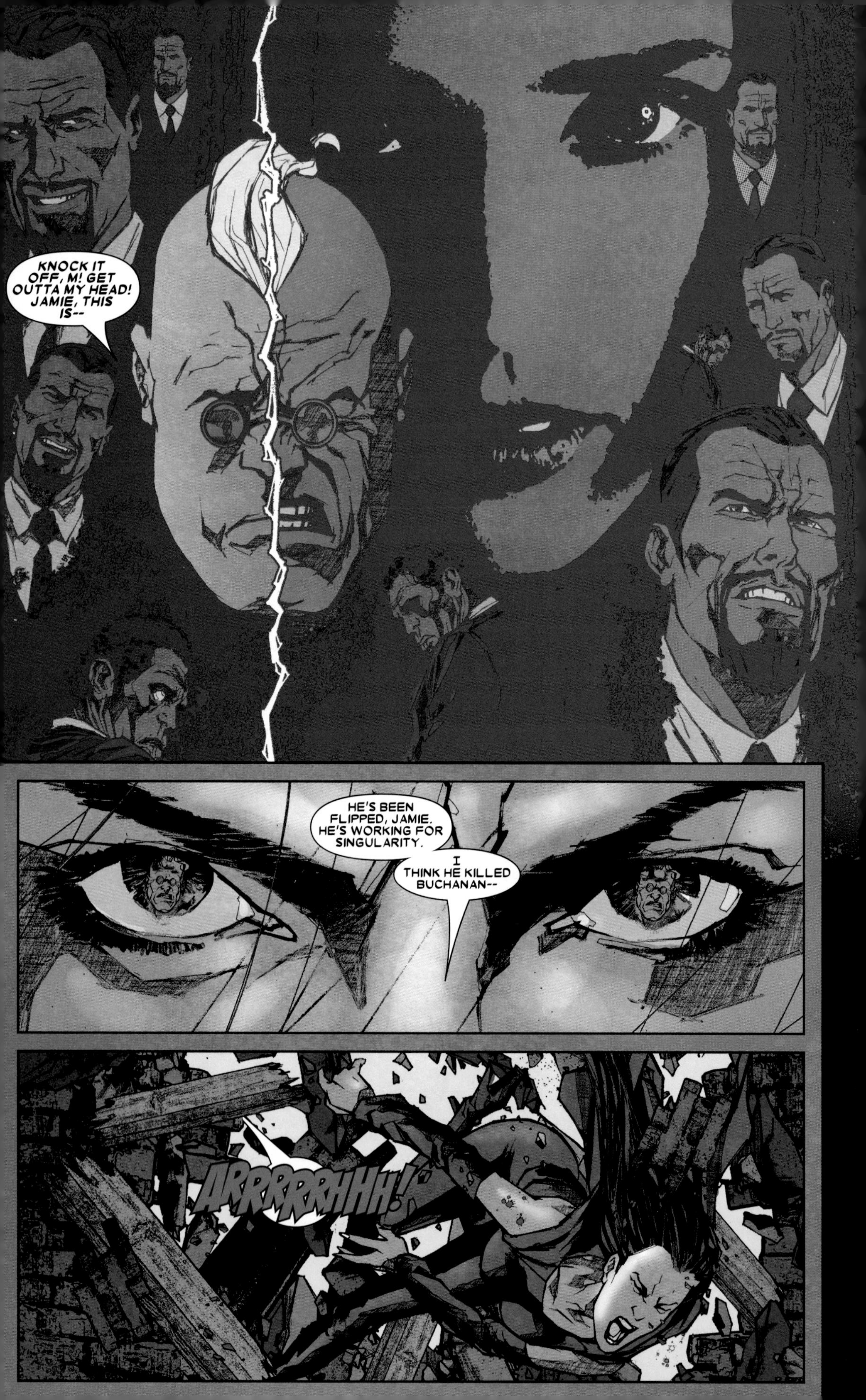
KNOCK IT OFF, M! GET OUTTA MY HEAD! JAMIE, THIS IS--
HE'S BEEN FLIPPED, JAMIE. HE'S WORKING FOR SINGULARITY.
I THINK HE KILLED BUCHANAN--
ARRRRRHHH!

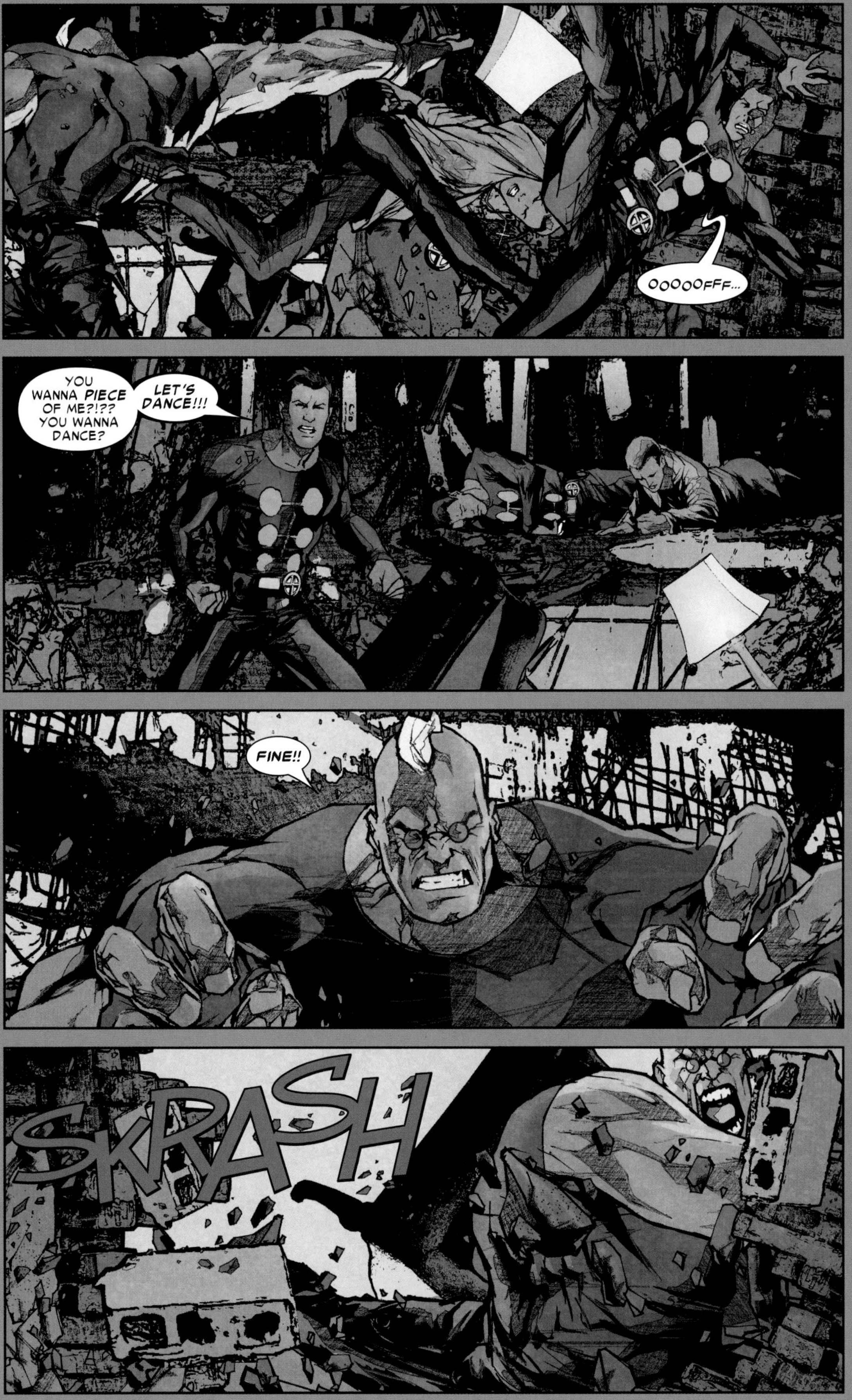
OOOOOFFF...
YOU WANNA PIECE OF ME?!?? YOU WANNA DANCE?
LET'S DANCE!!!
FINE!!
SKRASH

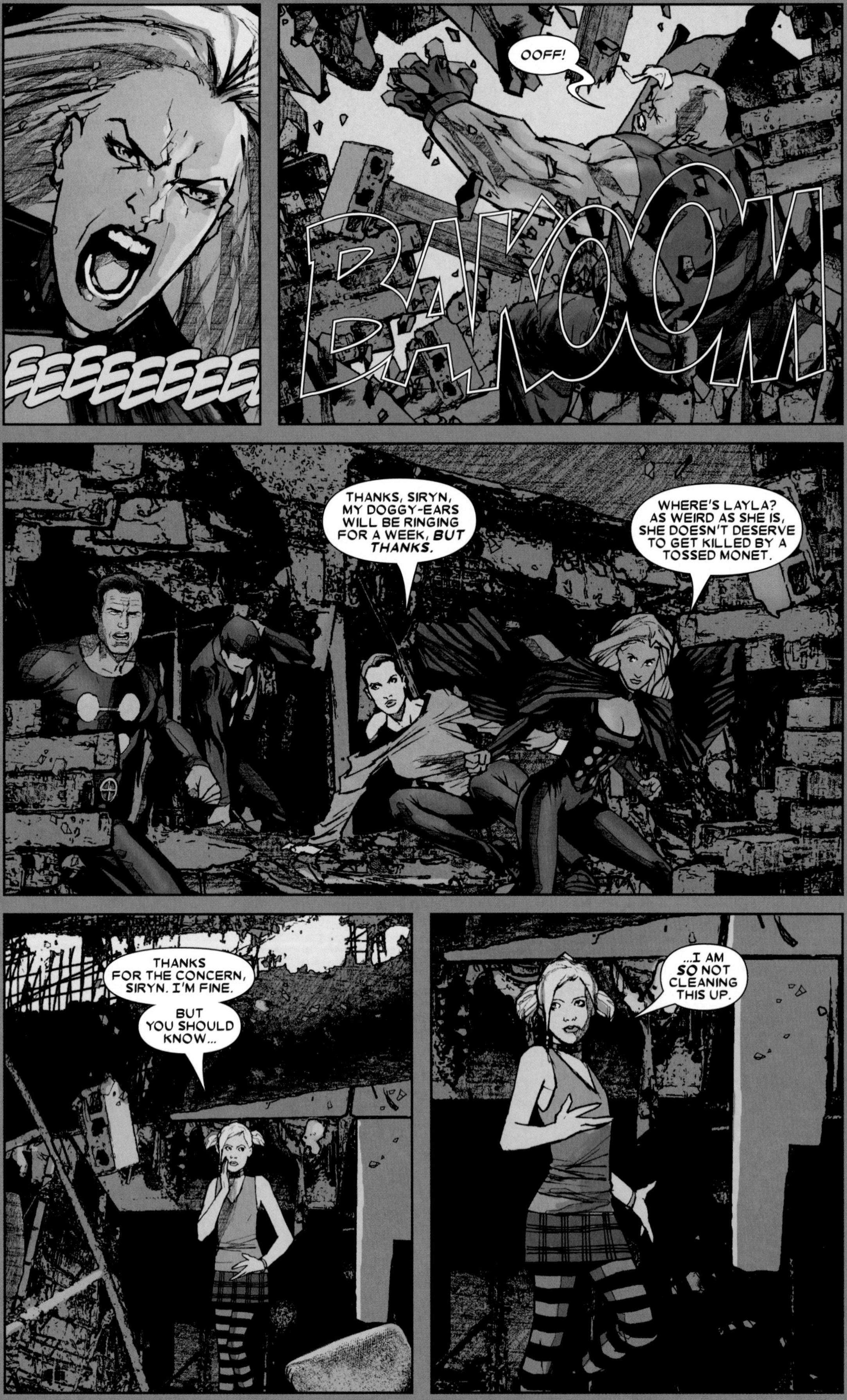
EEEEEEEEE
OOFF!
BAKOOM
THANKS, SIRYN, MY DOGGY-EARS WILL BE RINGING FOR A WEEK, BUT THANKS.
WHERE'S LAYLA? AS WEIRD AS SHE IS, SHE DOESN'T DESERVE TO GET KILLED BY A TOSSED MONET.
THANKS FOR THE CONCERN, SIRYN. I'M FINE.
BUT YOU SHOULD KNOW...
...I AM SO NOT CLEANING THIS UP.

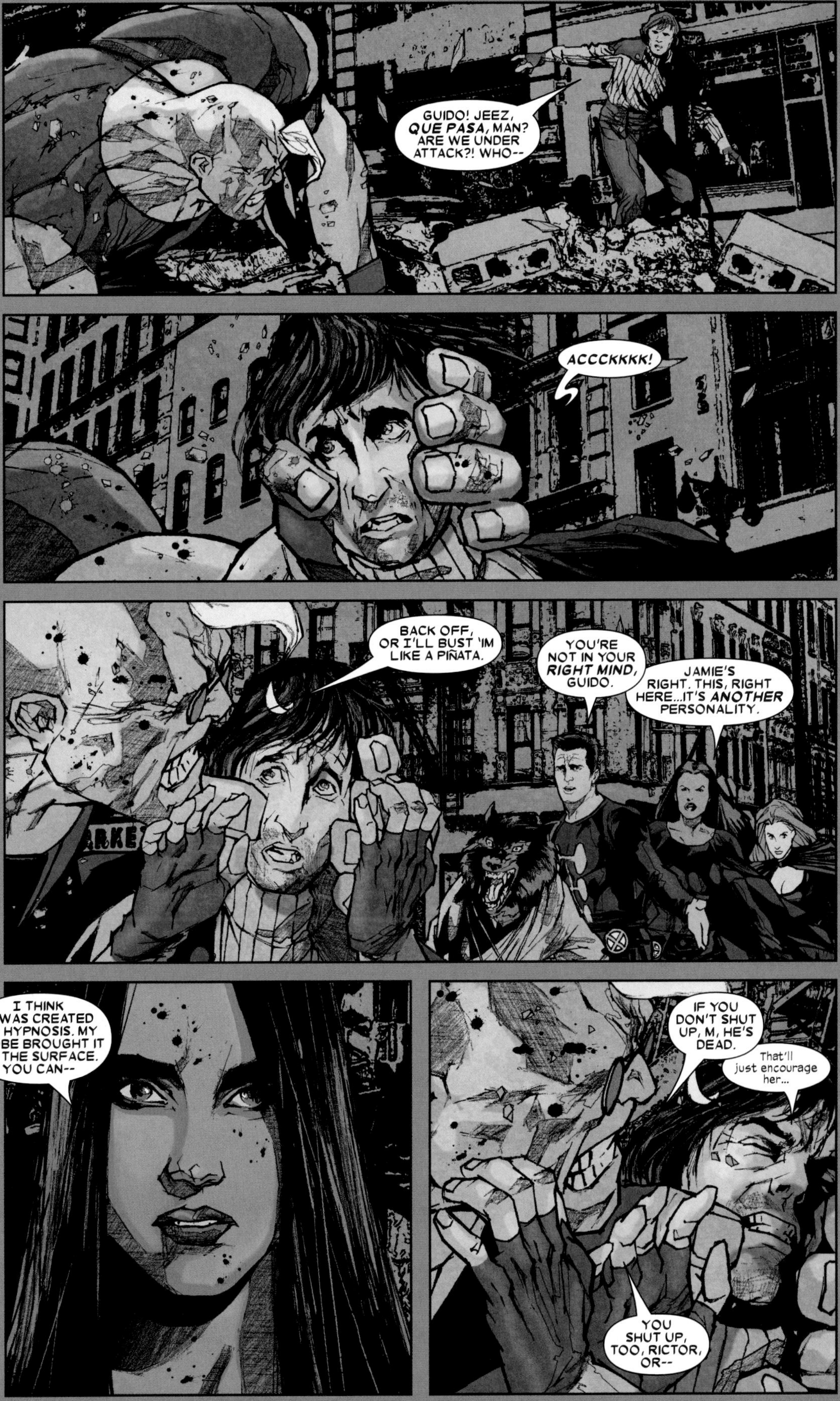
GUIDO! JEEZ, *QUE PASA,* MAN? ARE WE UNDER ATTACK?! WHO--
ACCCKKKK!
BACK OFF, OR I'LL BUST 'IM LIKE A PIÑATA.
YOU'RE NOT IN YOUR *RIGHT MIND,* GUIDO.
JAMIE'S RIGHT. THIS, RIGHT HERE...IT'S *ANOTHER* PERSONALITY.
I THINK T WAS CREATED IA HYPNOSIS. MY OBE BROUGHT IT O THE SURFACE. YOU CAN--
IF YOU DON'T SHUT UP, M, HE'S DEAD.
That'll just encourage her...
YOU SHUT UP, TOO, RICTOR, OR--

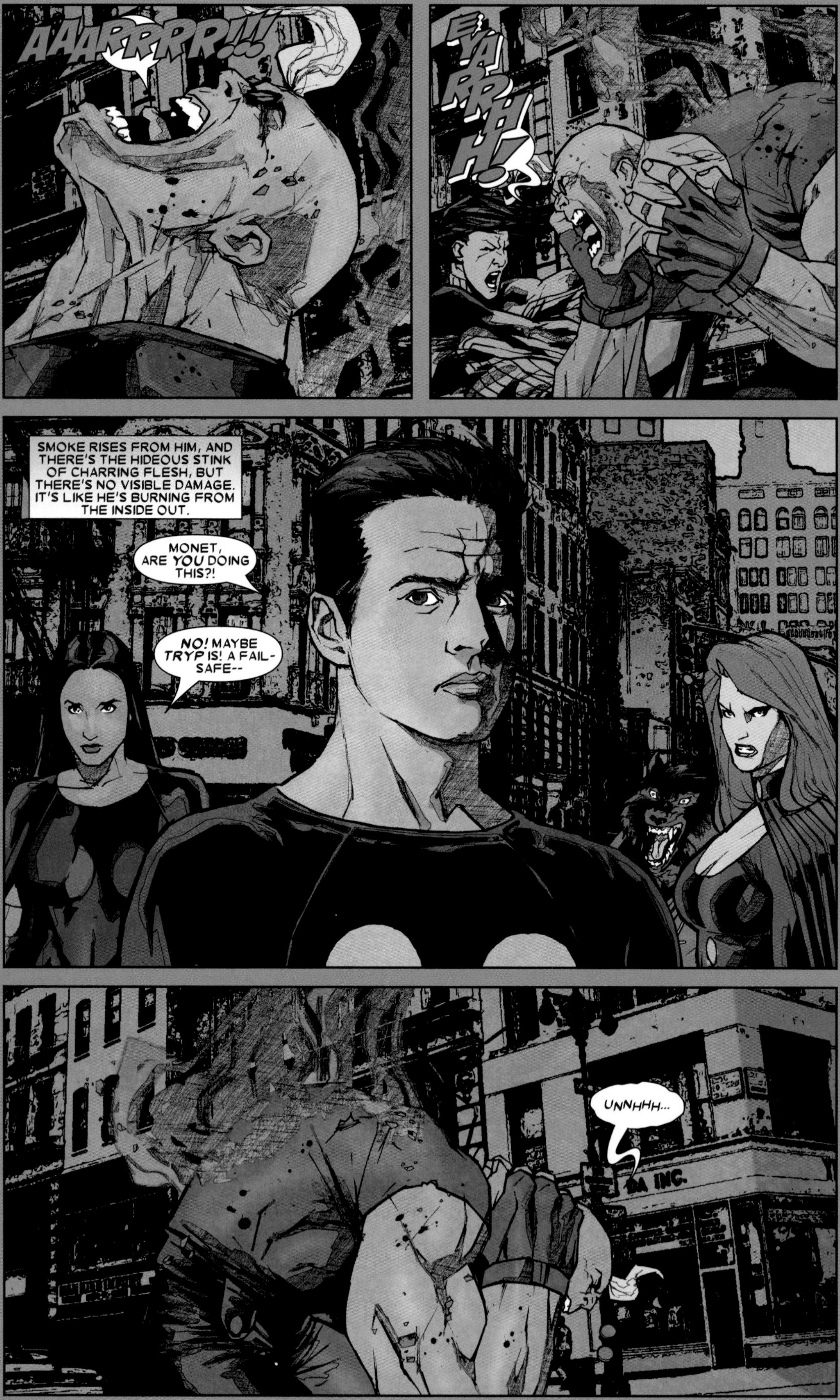
AAARRRR!!!
EYAARRHHH!
SMOKE RISES FROM HIM, AND THERE'S THE HIDEOUS STINK OF CHARRING FLESH, BUT THERE'S NO VISIBLE DAMAGE. IT'S LIKE HE'S BURNING FROM THE INSIDE OUT.
MONET, ARE YOU DOING THIS?!
NO! MAYBE TRYP IS! A FAIL-SAFE--
UNNHHH...
SA INC.

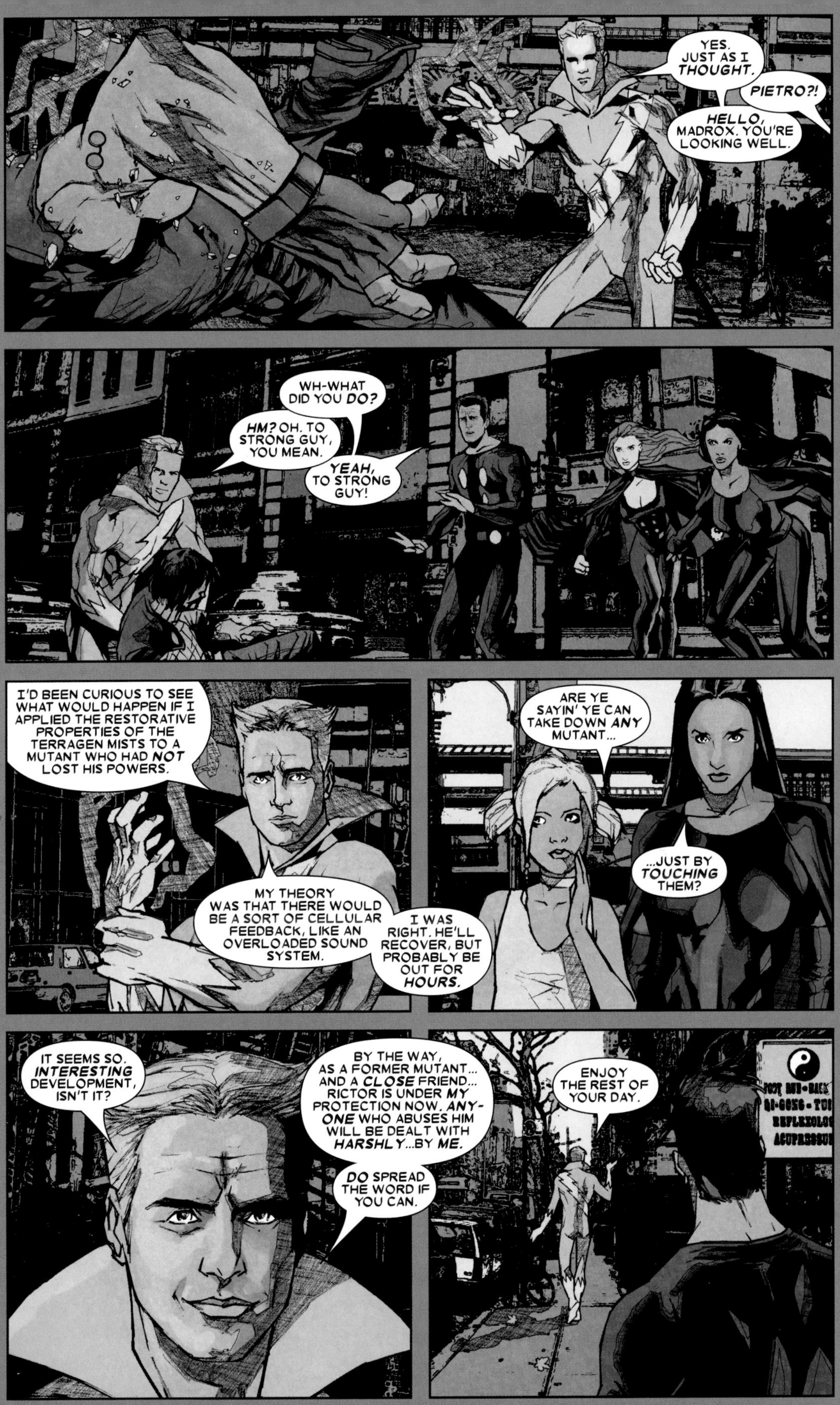
YES. JUST AS I THOUGHT.
PIETRO?!
HELLO, MADROX. YOU'RE LOOKING WELL.
WH-WHAT DID YOU DO?
HM? OH. TO STRONG GUY, YOU MEAN.
YEAH, TO STRONG GUY!
I'D BEEN CURIOUS TO SEE WHAT WOULD HAPPEN IF I APPLIED THE RESTORATIVE PROPERTIES OF THE TERRAGEN MISTS TO A MUTANT WHO HAD NOT LOST HIS POWERS.
MY THEORY WAS THAT THERE WOULD BE A SORT OF CELLULAR FEEDBACK, LIKE AN OVERLOADED SOUND SYSTEM.
I WAS RIGHT. HE'LL RECOVER, BUT PROBABLY BE OUT FOR HOURS.
ARE YE SAYIN' YE CAN TAKE DOWN ANY MUTANT...
...JUST BY TOUCHING THEM?
IT SEEMS SO. INTERESTING DEVELOPMENT, ISN'T IT?
BY THE WAY, AS A FORMER MUTANT... AND A CLOSE FRIEND... RICTOR IS UNDER MY PROTECTION NOW. ANYONE WHO ABUSES HIM WILL BE DEALT WITH HARSHLY...BY ME.
DO SPREAD THE WORD IF YOU CAN.
ENJOY THE REST OF YOUR DAY.

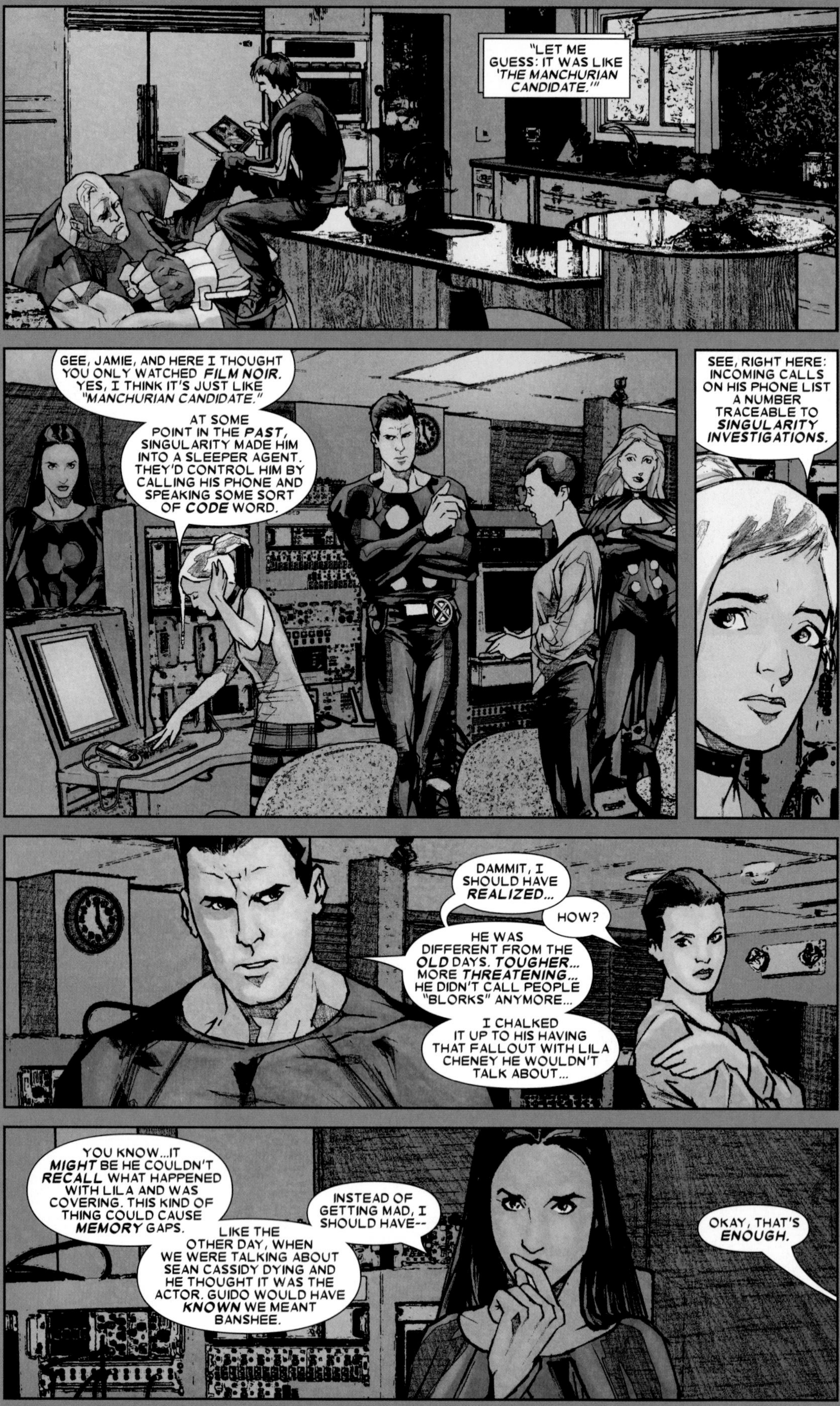
"LET ME GUESS: IT WAS LIKE 'THE MANCHURIAN CANDIDATE.'"
GEE, JAMIE, AND HERE I THOUGHT YOU ONLY WATCHED FILM NOIR. YES, I THINK IT'S JUST LIKE "MANCHURIAN CANDIDATE."
AT SOME POINT IN THE PAST, SINGULARITY MADE HIM INTO A SLEEPER AGENT. THEY'D CONTROL HIM BY CALLING HIS PHONE AND SPEAKING SOME SORT OF CODE WORD.
SEE, RIGHT HERE: INCOMING CALLS ON HIS PHONE LIST A NUMBER TRACEABLE TO SINGULARITY INVESTIGATIONS.
DAMMIT, I SHOULD HAVE REALIZED...
HOW?
HE WAS DIFFERENT FROM THE OLD DAYS. TOUGHER... MORE THREATENING... HE DIDN'T CALL PEOPLE "BLORKS" ANYMORE...
I CHALKED IT UP TO HIS HAVING THAT FALLOUT WITH LILA CHENEY HE WOULDN'T TALK ABOUT...
YOU KNOW...IT MIGHT BE HE COULDN'T RECALL WHAT HAPPENED WITH LILA AND WAS COVERING. THIS KIND OF THING COULD CAUSE MEMORY GAPS.
LIKE THE OTHER DAY, WHEN WE WERE TALKING ABOUT SEAN CASSIDY DYING AND HE THOUGHT IT WAS THE ACTOR. GUIDO WOULD HAVE KNOWN WE MEANT BANSHEE.
INSTEAD OF GETTING MAD, I SHOULD HAVE--
OKAY, THAT'S ENOUGH.

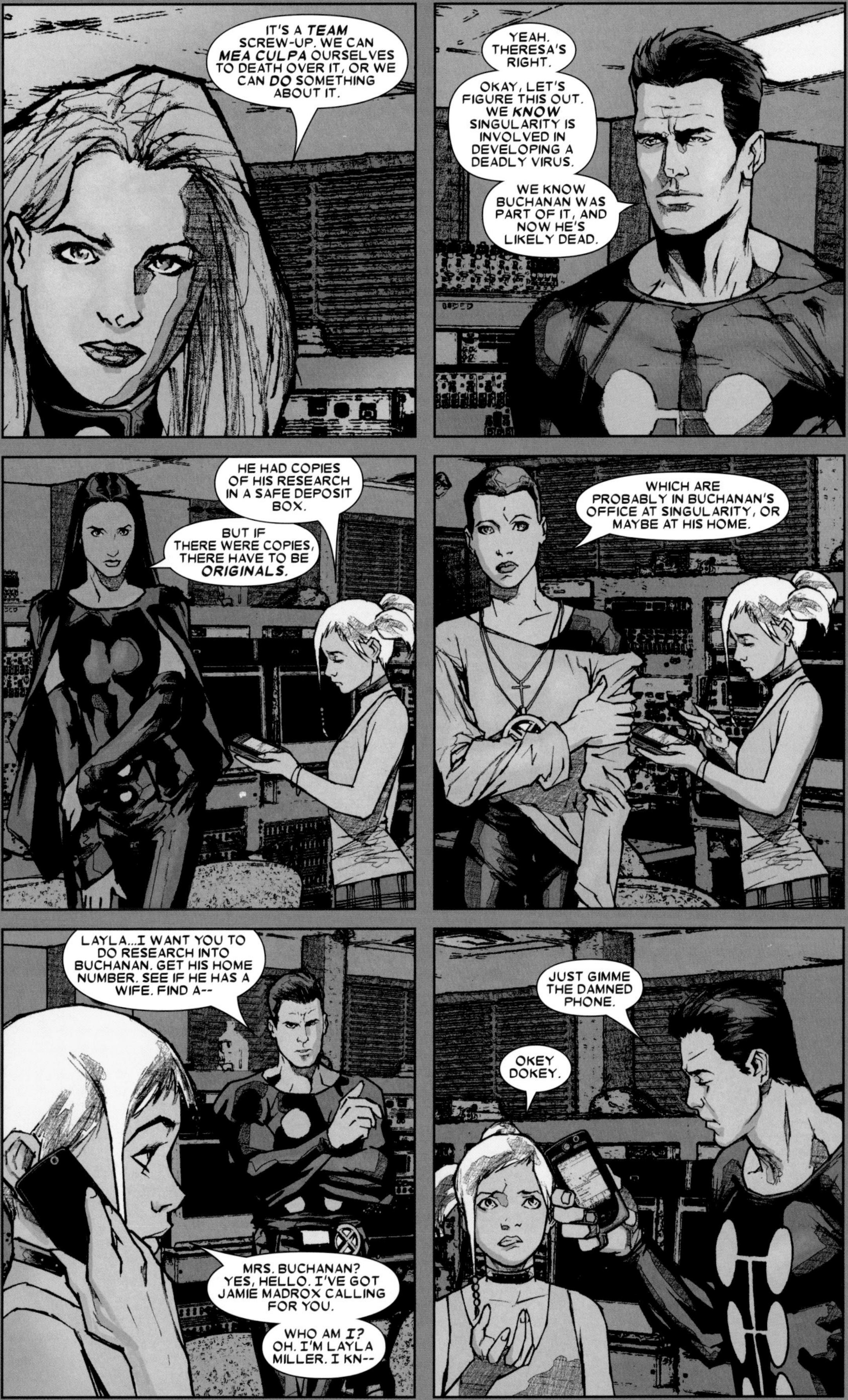
IT'S A TEAM SCREW-UP. WE CAN MEA CULPA OURSELVES TO DEATH OVER IT, OR WE CAN DO SOMETHING ABOUT IT.
YEAH. THERESA'S RIGHT.
OKAY, LET'S FIGURE THIS OUT. WE KNOW SINGULARITY IS INVOLVED IN DEVELOPING A DEADLY VIRUS.
WE KNOW BUCHANAN WAS PART OF IT, AND NOW HE'S LIKELY DEAD.
HE HAD COPIES OF HIS RESEARCH IN A SAFE DEPOSIT BOX.
BUT IF THERE WERE COPIES, THERE HAVE TO BE ORIGINALS.
WHICH ARE PROBABLY IN BUCHANAN'S OFFICE AT SINGULARITY, OR MAYBE AT HIS HOME.
LAYLA...I WANT YOU TO DO RESEARCH INTO BUCHANAN. GET HIS HOME NUMBER. SEE IF HE HAS A WIFE. FIND A--
MRS. BUCHANAN? YES, HELLO. I'VE GOT JAMIE MADROX CALLING FOR YOU.
WHO AM I? OH. I'M LAYLA MILLER. I KN--
JUST GIMME THE DAMNED PHONE.
OKEY DOKEY.

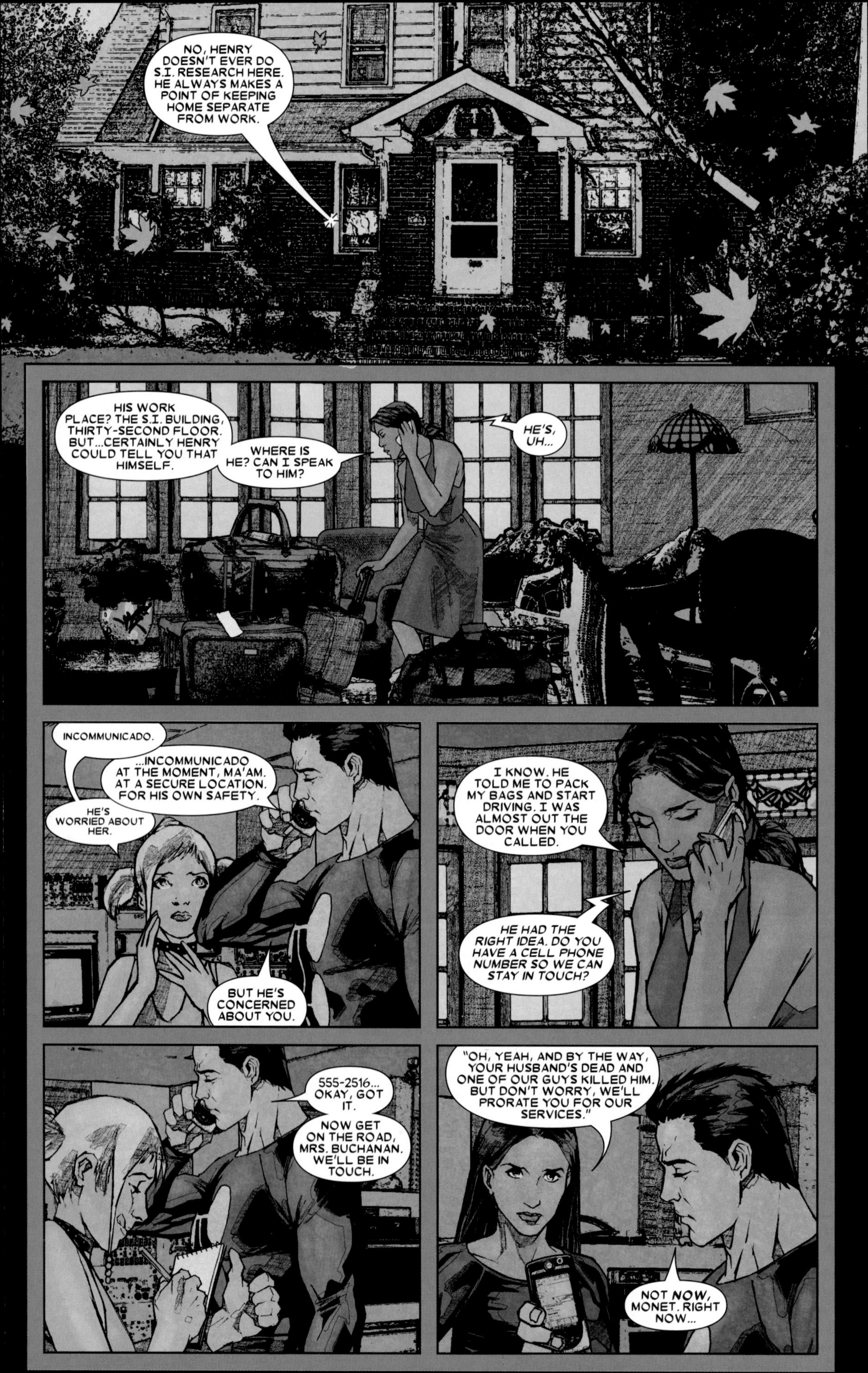
NO, HENRY DOESN'T EVER DO S.I. RESEARCH HERE. HE ALWAYS MAKES A POINT OF KEEPING HOME SEPARATE FROM WORK.
HIS WORK PLACE? THE S.I. BUILDING, THIRTY-SECOND FLOOR. BUT...CERTAINLY HENRY COULD TELL YOU THAT HIMSELF.
WHERE IS HE? CAN I SPEAK TO HIM?
HE'S, UH...
INCOMMUNICADO.
...INCOMMUNICADO AT THE MOMENT, MA'AM. AT A SECURE LOCATION. FOR HIS OWN SAFETY.
HE'S WORRIED ABOUT HER.
BUT HE'S CONCERNED ABOUT YOU.
I KNOW. HE TOLD ME TO PACK MY BAGS AND START DRIVING. I WAS ALMOST OUT THE DOOR WHEN YOU CALLED.
HE HAD THE RIGHT IDEA. DO YOU HAVE A CELL PHONE NUMBER SO WE CAN STAY IN TOUCH?
555-2516... OKAY, GOT IT.
NOW GET ON THE ROAD, MRS. BUCHANAN. WE'LL BE IN TOUCH.
"OH, YEAH, AND BY THE WAY, YOUR HUSBAND'S DEAD AND ONE OF OUR GUYS KILLED HIM. BUT DON'T WORRY, WE'LL PRORATE YOU FOR OUR SERVICES."
NOT NOW, MONET. RIGHT NOW...

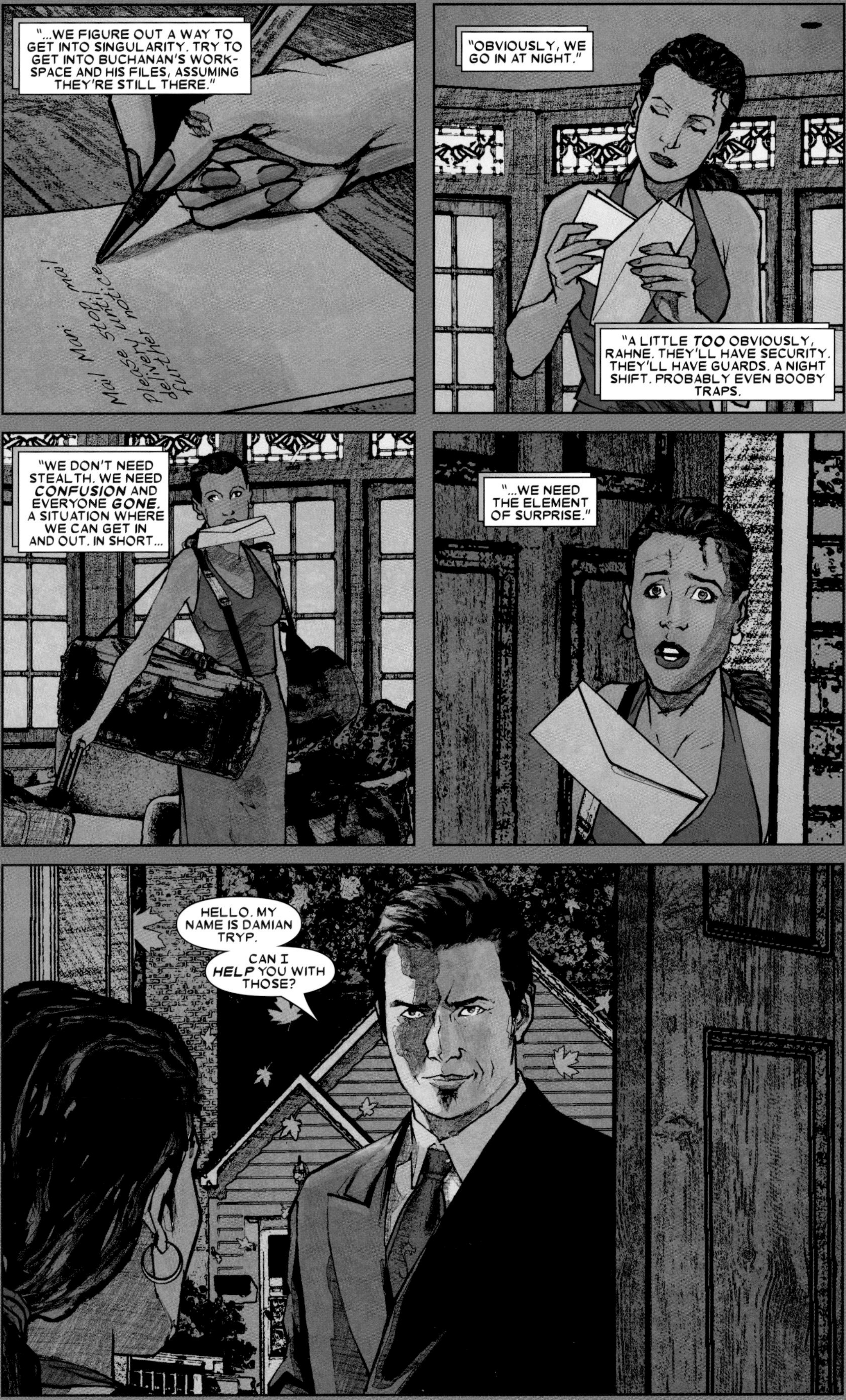
"...WE FIGURE OUT A WAY TO GET INTO SINGULARITY. TRY TO GET INTO BUCHANAN'S WORK-SPACE AND HIS FILES, ASSUMING THEY'RE STILL THERE."
Mail Man: Please stop mail delivery until further notice!
"OBVIOUSLY, WE GO IN AT NIGHT."
"A LITTLE TOO OBVIOUSLY, RAHNE. THEY'LL HAVE SECURITY. THEY'LL HAVE GUARDS. A NIGHT SHIFT. PROBABLY EVEN BOOBY TRAPS.
"WE DON'T NEED STEALTH. WE NEED CONFUSION AND EVERYONE GONE. A SITUATION WHERE WE CAN GET IN AND OUT. IN SHORT...
"...WE NEED THE ELEMENT OF SURPRISE."
HELLO. MY NAME IS DAMIAN TRYP.
CAN I HELP YOU WITH THOSE?

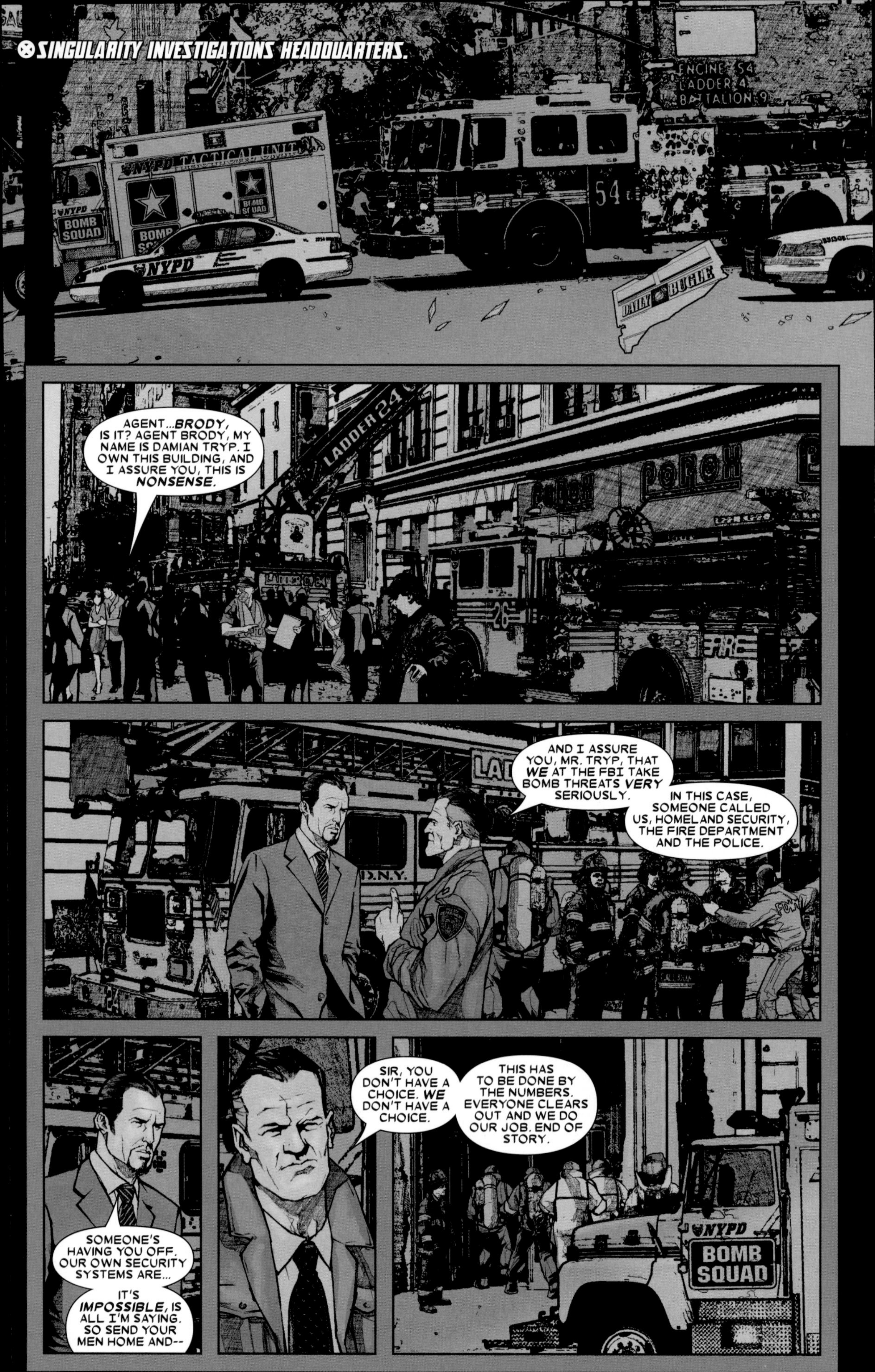
SINGULARITY INVESTIGATIONS HEADQUARTERS.
ENGINE 54
LADDER 4
BATTALION 9
NYPD TACTICAL UNIT
BOMB SQUAD
NYPD
DAILY BUGLE
AGENT...BRODY, IS IT? AGENT BRODY, MY NAME IS DAMIAN TRYP. I OWN THIS BUILDING, AND I ASSURE YOU, THIS IS NONSENSE.
LADDER 24
AND I ASSURE YOU, MR. TRYP, THAT WE AT THE FBI TAKE BOMB THREATS VERY SERIOUSLY.
IN THIS CASE, SOMEONE CALLED US, HOMELAND SECURITY, THE FIRE DEPARTMENT AND THE POLICE.
SOMEONE'S HAVING YOU OFF. OUR OWN SECURITY SYSTEMS ARE...
IT'S IMPOSSIBLE, IS ALL I'M SAYING. SO SEND YOUR MEN HOME AND--
SIR, YOU DON'T HAVE A CHOICE. WE DON'T HAVE A CHOICE.
THIS HAS TO BE DONE BY THE NUMBERS. EVERYONE CLEARS OUT AND WE DO OUR JOB. END OF STORY.
NYPD
BOMB SQUAD

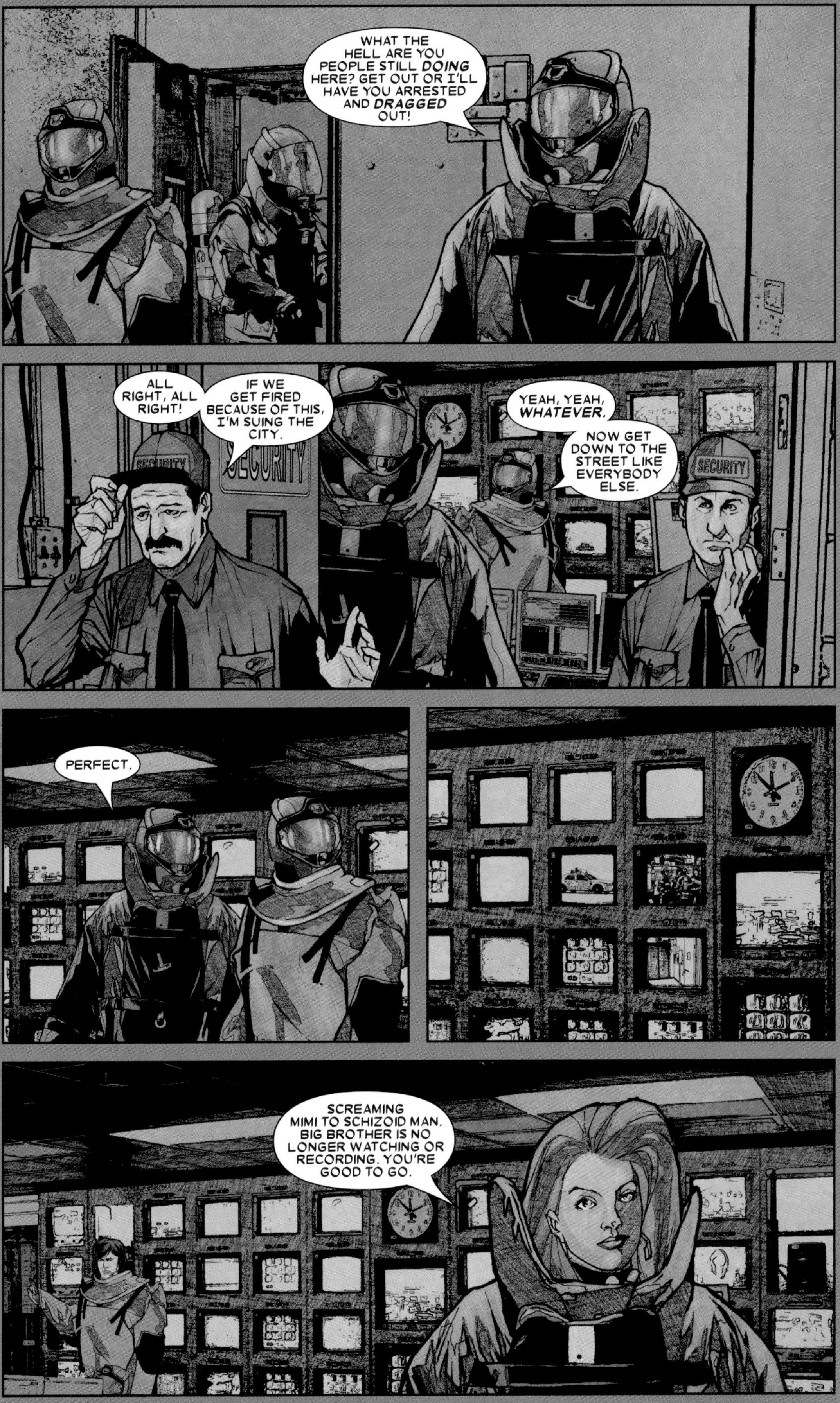
WHAT THE HELL ARE YOU PEOPLE STILL DOING HERE? GET OUT OR I'LL HAVE YOU ARRESTED AND DRAGGED OUT!
ALL RIGHT, ALL RIGHT!
IF WE GET FIRED BECAUSE OF THIS, I'M SUING THE CITY.
SECURITY
YEAH, YEAH, WHATEVER.
NOW GET DOWN TO THE STREET LIKE EVERYBODY ELSE.
SECURITY
SECURITY
PERFECT.
SCREAMING MIMI TO SCHIZOID MAN. BIG BROTHER IS NO LONGER WATCHING OR RECORDING. YOU'RE GOOD TO GO.

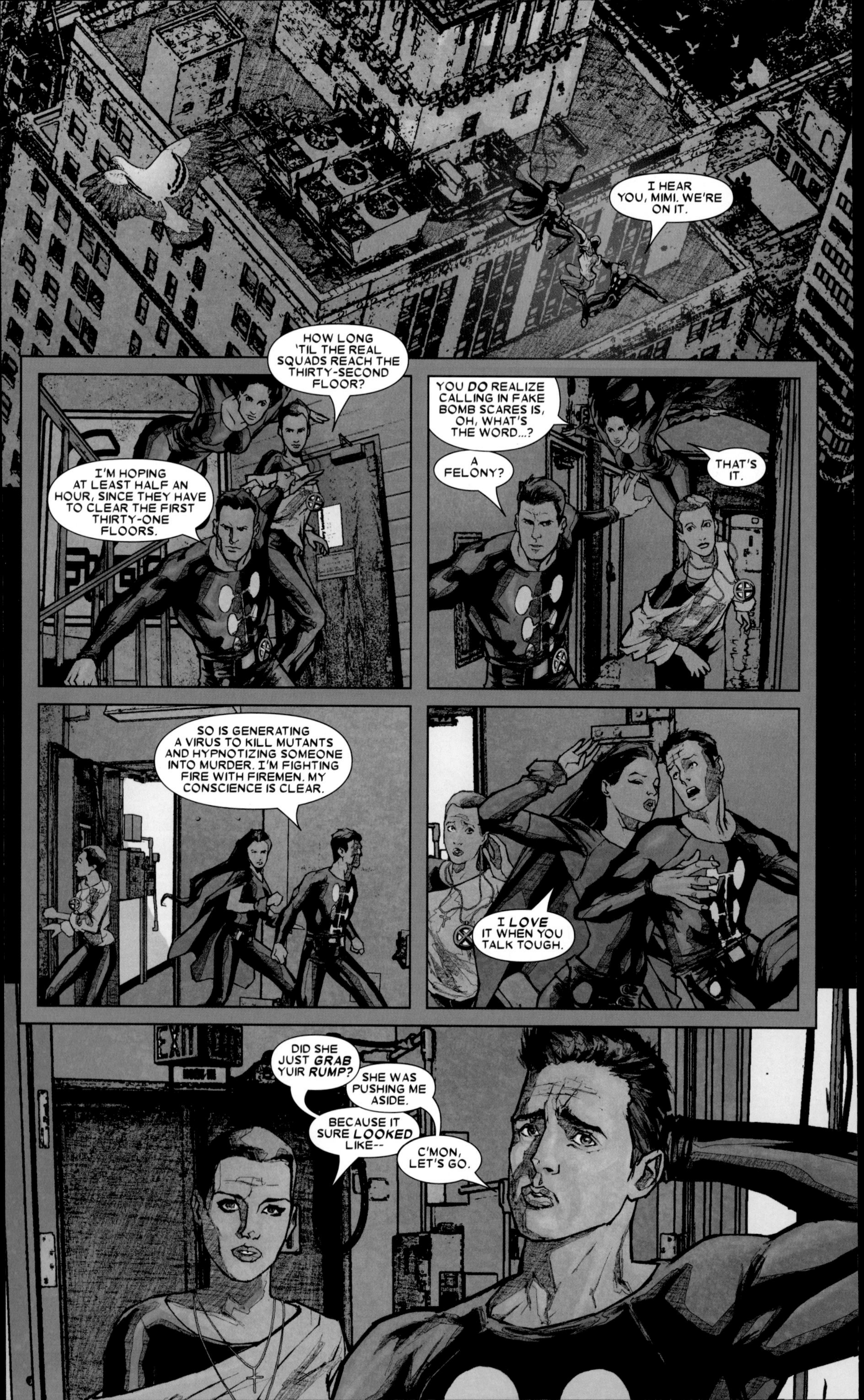
I HEAR YOU, MIMI. WE'RE ON IT.
HOW LONG 'TIL THE REAL SQUADS REACH THE THIRTY-SECOND FLOOR?
I'M HOPING AT LEAST HALF AN HOUR, SINCE THEY HAVE TO CLEAR THE FIRST THIRTY-ONE FLOORS.
YOU *DO* REALIZE CALLING IN FAKE BOMB SCARES IS, OH, WHAT'S THE WORD...?
A FELONY?
THAT'S IT.
SO IS GENERATING A VIRUS TO KILL MUTANTS AND HYPNOTIZING SOMEONE INTO MURDER. I'M FIGHTING FIRE WITH FIREMEN. MY CONSCIENCE IS CLEAR.
I *LOVE* IT WHEN YOU TALK TOUGH.
DID SHE JUST *GRAB* YUIR *RUMP*?
SHE WAS PUSHING ME ASIDE.
BECAUSE IT SURE *LOOKED* LIKE--
C'MON, LET'S GO.

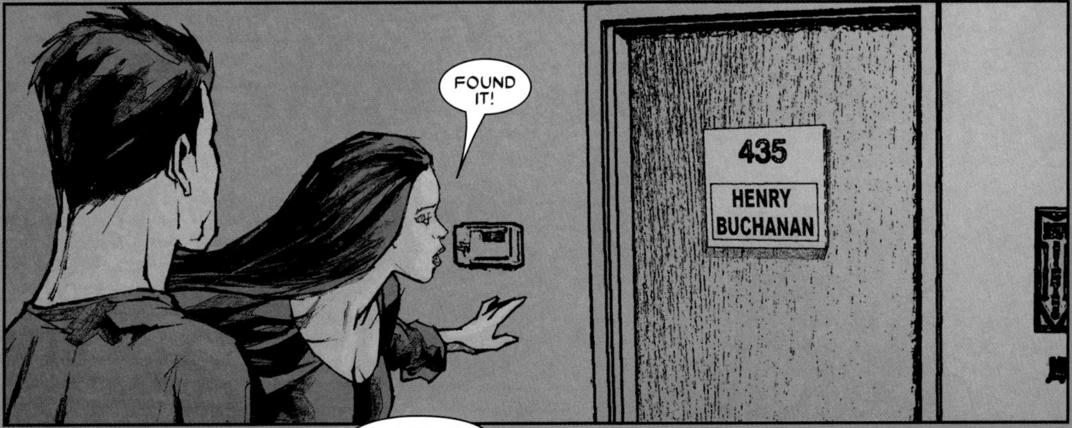
FOUND IT!
435
HENRY BUCHANAN

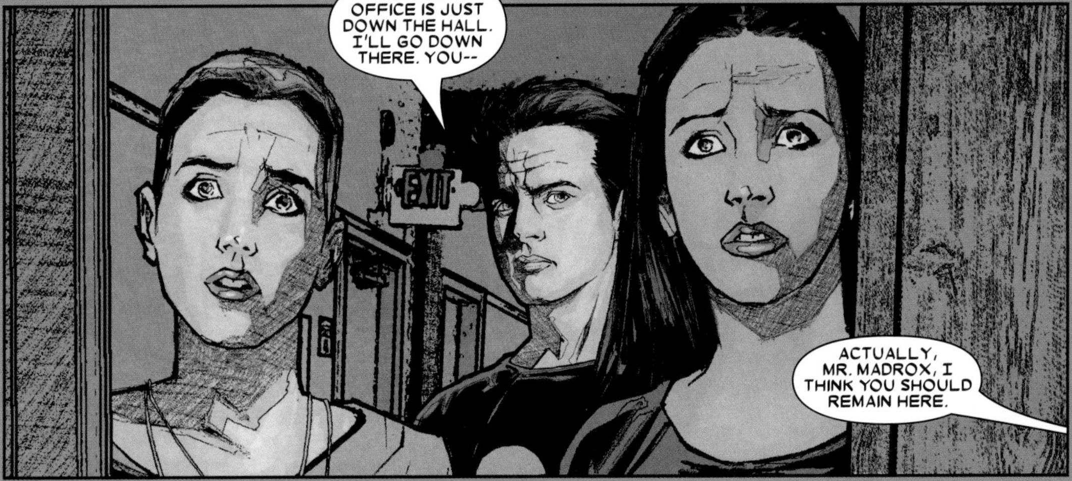
AND TRYP'S OFFICE IS JUST DOWN THE HALL. I'LL GO DOWN THERE. YOU--
EXIT
ACTUALLY, MR. MADROX, I THINK YOU SHOULD REMAIN HERE.

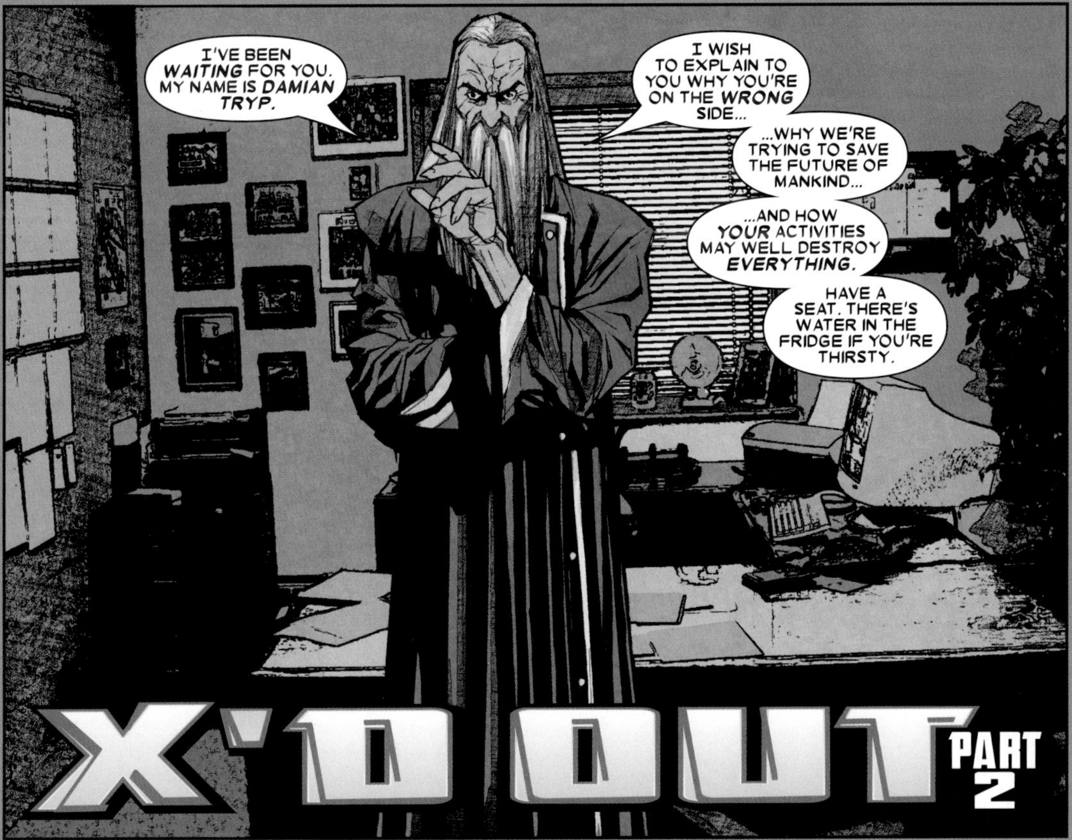
I'VE BEEN *WAITING* FOR YOU. MY NAME IS *DAMIAN TRYP.*
I WISH TO EXPLAIN TO YOU WHY YOU'RE ON THE *WRONG* SIDE...
...WHY WE'RE TRYING TO SAVE THE FUTURE OF MANKIND...
...AND HOW *YOUR* ACTIVITIES MAY WELL DESTROY *EVERYTHING.*
HAVE A SEAT. THERE'S WATER IN THE FRIDGE IF YOU'RE THIRSTY.
X'D OUT PART 2

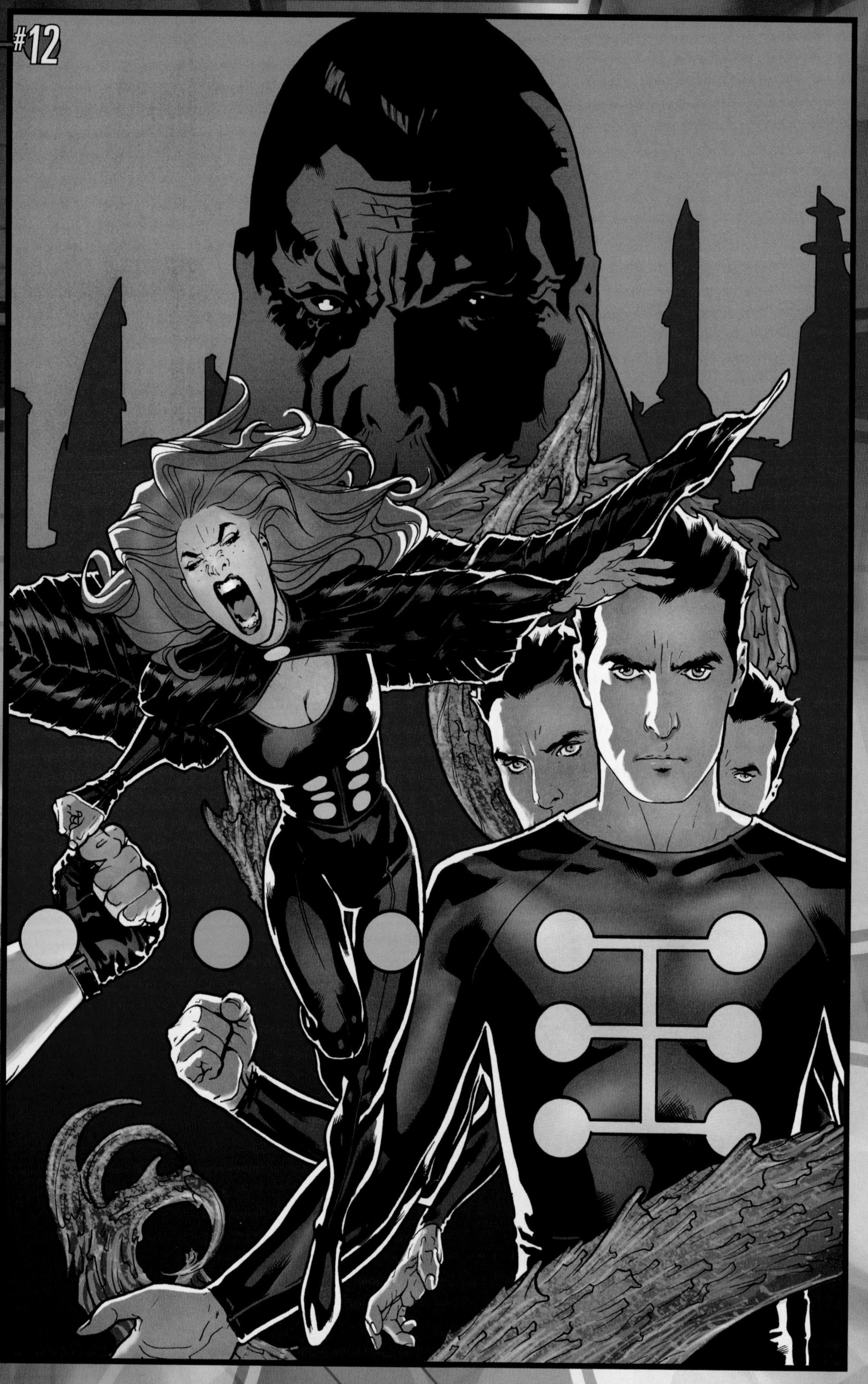
#12

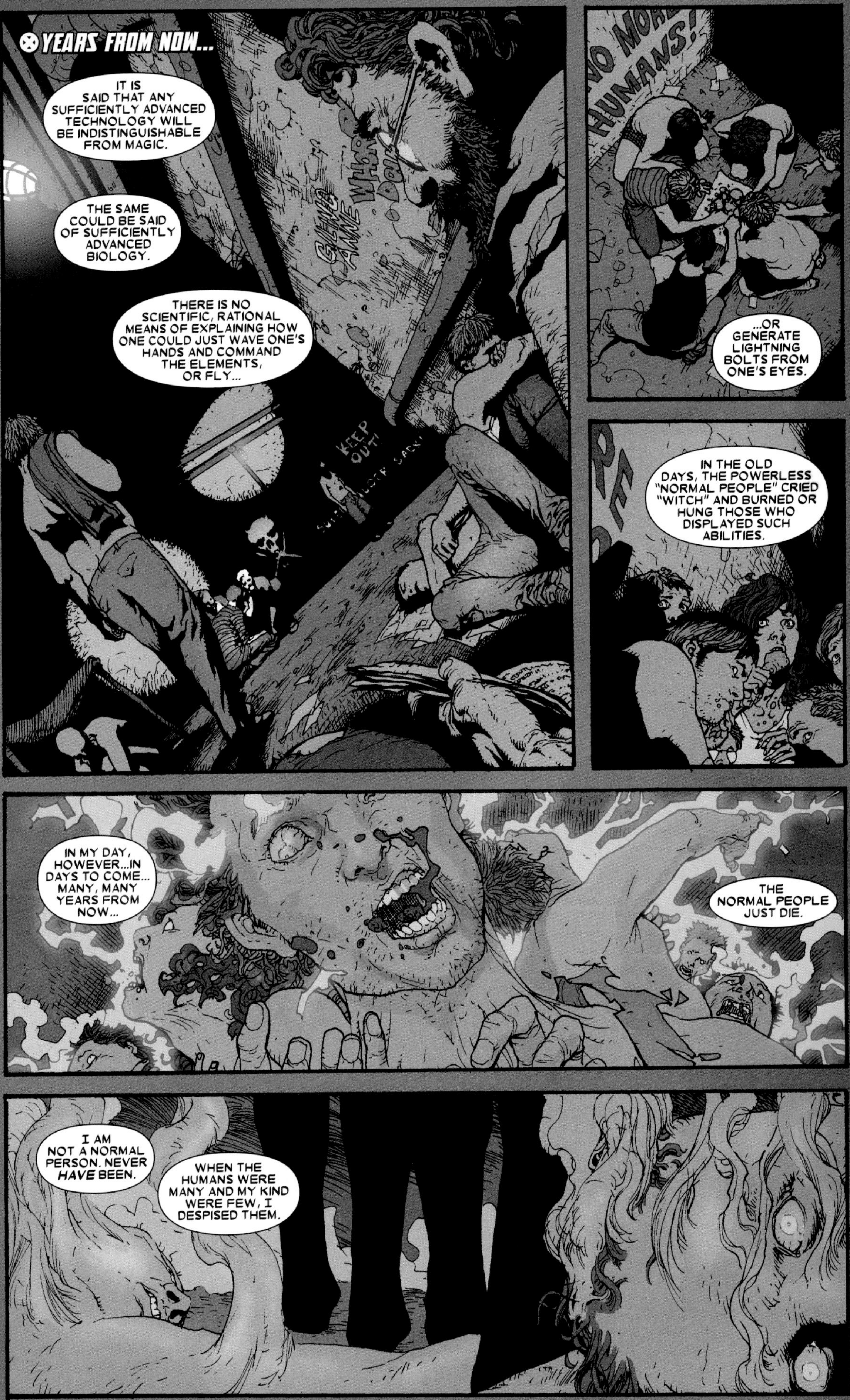
YEARS FROM NOW...
IT IS SAID THAT ANY SUFFICIENTLY ADVANCED TECHNOLOGY WILL BE INDISTINGUISHABLE FROM MAGIC.
THE SAME COULD BE SAID OF SUFFICIENTLY ADVANCED BIOLOGY.
THERE IS NO SCIENTIFIC, RATIONAL MEANS OF EXPLAINING HOW ONE COULD JUST WAVE ONE'S HANDS AND COMMAND THE ELEMENTS, OR FLY...
NO MORE HUMANS!
...OR GENERATE LIGHTNING BOLTS FROM ONE'S EYES.
KEEP OUT!
IN THE OLD DAYS, THE POWERLESS "NORMAL PEOPLE" CRIED "WITCH" AND BURNED OR HUNG THOSE WHO DISPLAYED SUCH ABILITIES.
IN MY DAY, HOWEVER...IN DAYS TO COME... MANY, MANY YEARS FROM NOW...
THE NORMAL PEOPLE JUST DIE.
I AM NOT A NORMAL PERSON. NEVER *HAVE* BEEN.
WHEN THE HUMANS WERE MANY AND MY KIND WERE FEW, I DESPISED THEM.

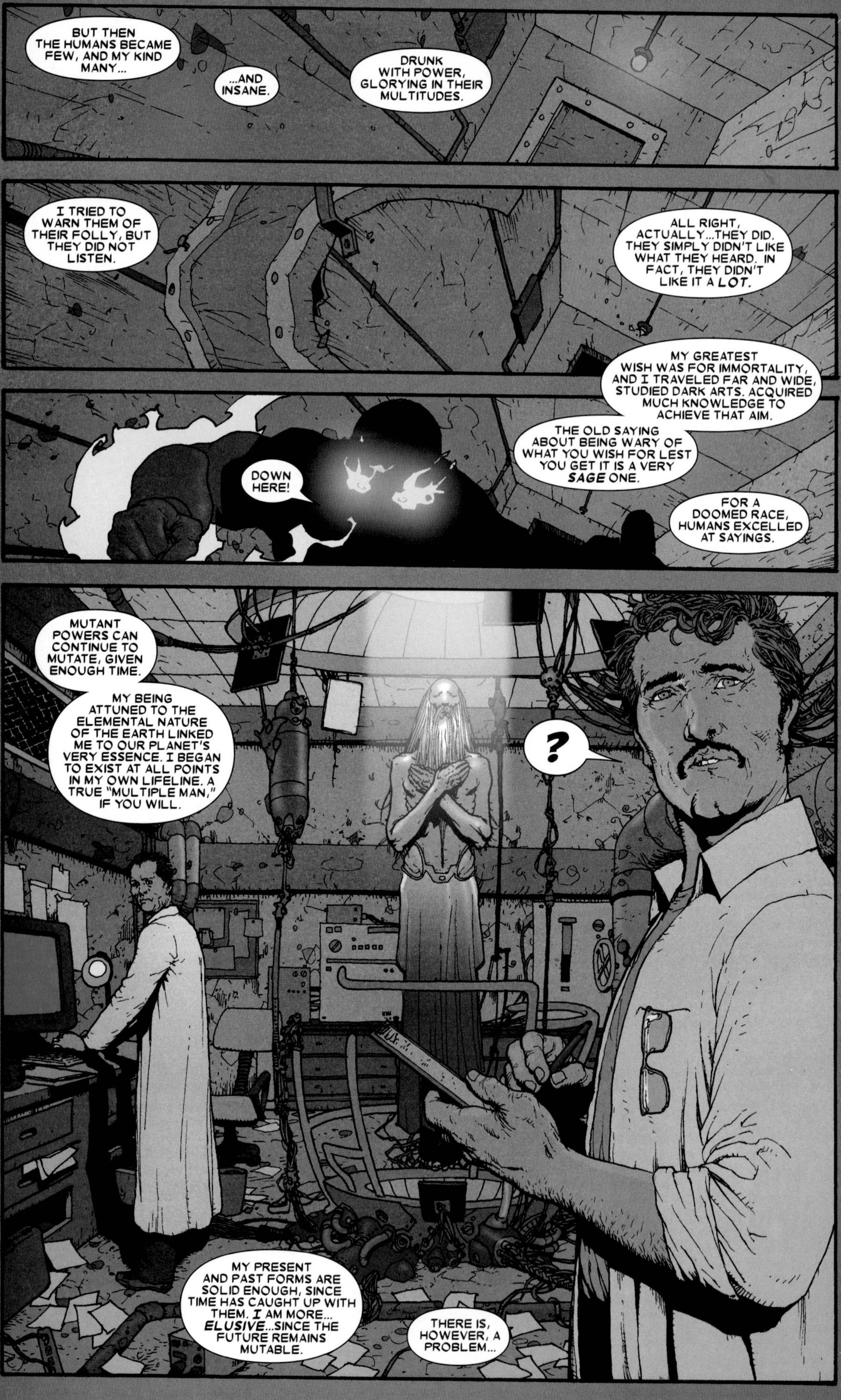
BUT THEN THE HUMANS BECAME FEW, AND MY KIND MANY...
...AND INSANE.
DRUNK WITH POWER, GLORYING IN THEIR MULTITUDES.
I TRIED TO WARN THEM OF THEIR FOLLY, BUT THEY DID NOT LISTEN.
ALL RIGHT, ACTUALLY...THEY DID. THEY SIMPLY DIDN'T LIKE WHAT THEY HEARD. IN FACT, THEY DIDN'T LIKE IT A LOT.
MY GREATEST WISH WAS FOR IMMORTALITY, AND I TRAVELED FAR AND WIDE, STUDIED DARK ARTS. ACQUIRED MUCH KNOWLEDGE TO ACHIEVE THAT AIM.
THE OLD SAYING ABOUT BEING WARY OF WHAT YOU WISH FOR LEST YOU GET IT IS A VERY SAGE ONE.
DOWN HERE!
FOR A DOOMED RACE, HUMANS EXCELLED AT SAYINGS.
MUTANT POWERS CAN CONTINUE TO MUTATE, GIVEN ENOUGH TIME.
MY BEING ATTUNED TO THE ELEMENTAL NATURE OF THE EARTH LINKED ME TO OUR PLANET'S VERY ESSENCE. I BEGAN TO EXIST AT ALL POINTS IN MY OWN LIFELINE. A TRUE "MULTIPLE MAN," IF YOU WILL.
?
MY PRESENT AND PAST FORMS ARE SOLID ENOUGH, SINCE TIME HAS CAUGHT UP WITH THEM. I AM MORE... ELUSIVE...SINCE THE FUTURE REMAINS MUTABLE.
THERE IS, HOWEVER, A PROBLEM...

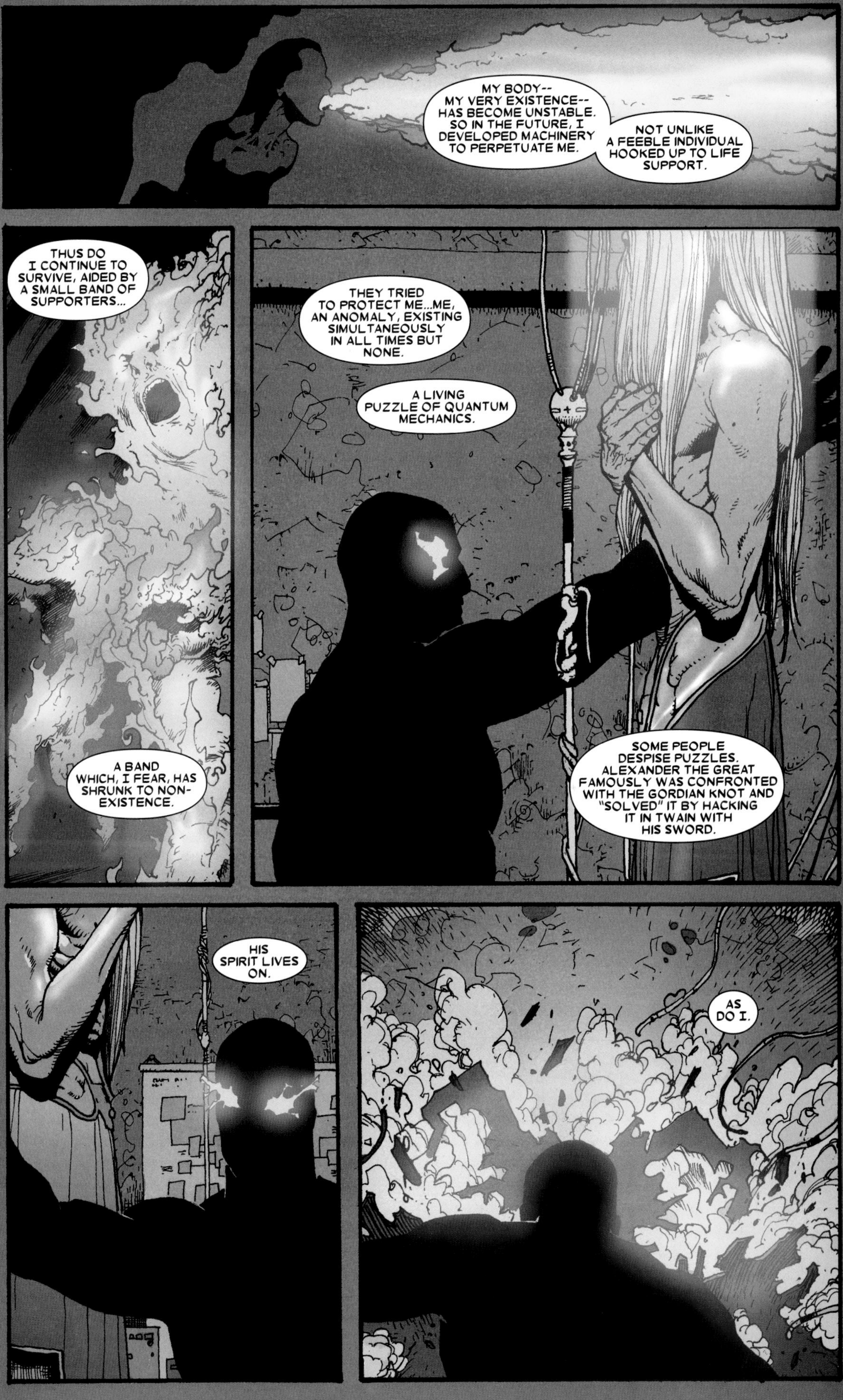
MY BODY-- MY VERY EXISTENCE-- HAS BECOME UNSTABLE. SO IN THE FUTURE, I DEVELOPED MACHINERY TO PERPETUATE ME.
NOT UNLIKE A FEEBLE INDIVIDUAL HOOKED UP TO LIFE SUPPORT.
THUS DO I CONTINUE TO SURVIVE, AIDED BY A SMALL BAND OF SUPPORTERS...
A BAND WHICH, I FEAR, HAS SHRUNK TO NON-EXISTENCE.
THEY TRIED TO PROTECT ME...ME, AN ANOMALY, EXISTING SIMULTANEOUSLY IN ALL TIMES BUT NONE.
A LIVING PUZZLE OF QUANTUM MECHANICS.
SOME PEOPLE DESPISE PUZZLES. ALEXANDER THE GREAT FAMOUSLY WAS CONFRONTED WITH THE GORDIAN KNOT AND "SOLVED" IT BY HACKING IT IN TWAIN WITH HIS SWORD.
HIS SPIRIT LIVES ON.
AS DO I.

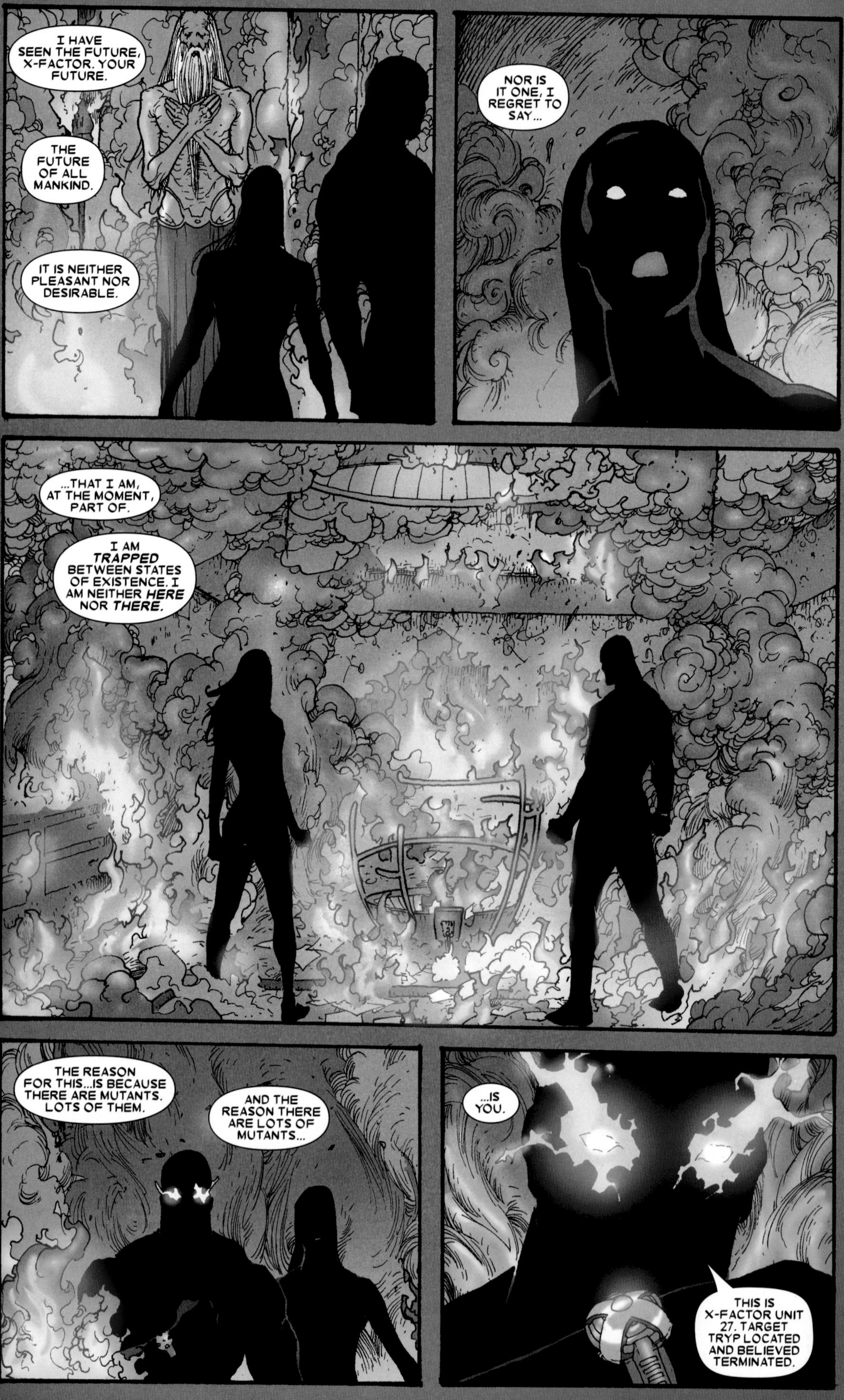
I HAVE SEEN THE FUTURE, X-FACTOR. YOUR FUTURE.
THE FUTURE OF ALL MANKIND.
IT IS NEITHER PLEASANT NOR DESIRABLE.
NOR IS IT ONE, I REGRET TO SAY...
...THAT I AM, AT THE MOMENT, PART OF.
I AM *TRAPPED* BETWEEN STATES OF EXISTENCE. I AM NEITHER *HERE* NOR *THERE.*
THE REASON FOR THIS...IS BECAUSE THERE ARE MUTANTS. LOTS OF THEM.
AND THE REASON THERE ARE LOTS OF MUTANTS...
...IS YOU.
THIS IS X-FACTOR UNIT 27. TARGET TRYP LOCATED AND BELIEVED TERMINATED.

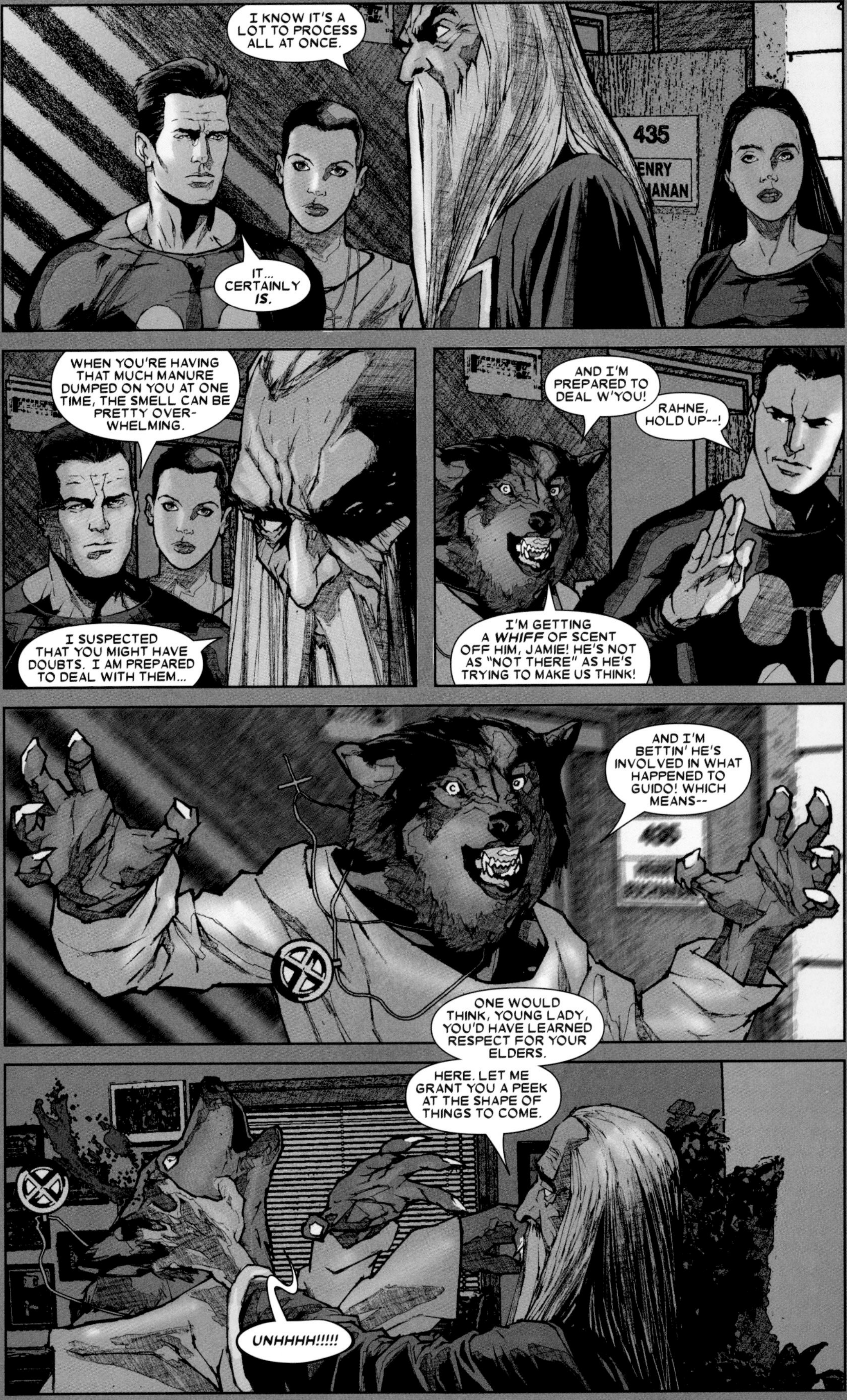
I KNOW IT'S A LOT TO PROCESS ALL AT ONCE.
435
ENRY
HANAN
IT... CERTAINLY *IS.*
WHEN YOU'RE HAVING THAT MUCH MANURE DUMPED ON YOU AT ONE TIME, THE SMELL CAN BE PRETTY OVER-WHELMING.
I SUSPECTED THAT YOU MIGHT HAVE DOUBTS. I AM PREPARED TO DEAL WITH THEM...
AND I'M PREPARED TO DEAL W'YOU!
RAHNE, HOLD UP--!
I'M GETTING A *WHIFF* OF SCENT OFF HIM, JAMIE! HE'S NOT AS "NOT THERE" AS HE'S TRYING TO MAKE US THINK!
AND I'M BETTIN' HE'S INVOLVED IN WHAT HAPPENED TO GUIDO! WHICH MEANS--
ONE WOULD THINK, YOUNG LADY, YOU'D HAVE LEARNED RESPECT FOR YOUR ELDERS.
HERE. LET ME GRANT YOU A PEEK AT THE SHAPE OF THINGS TO COME.
UNHHHH!!!!!

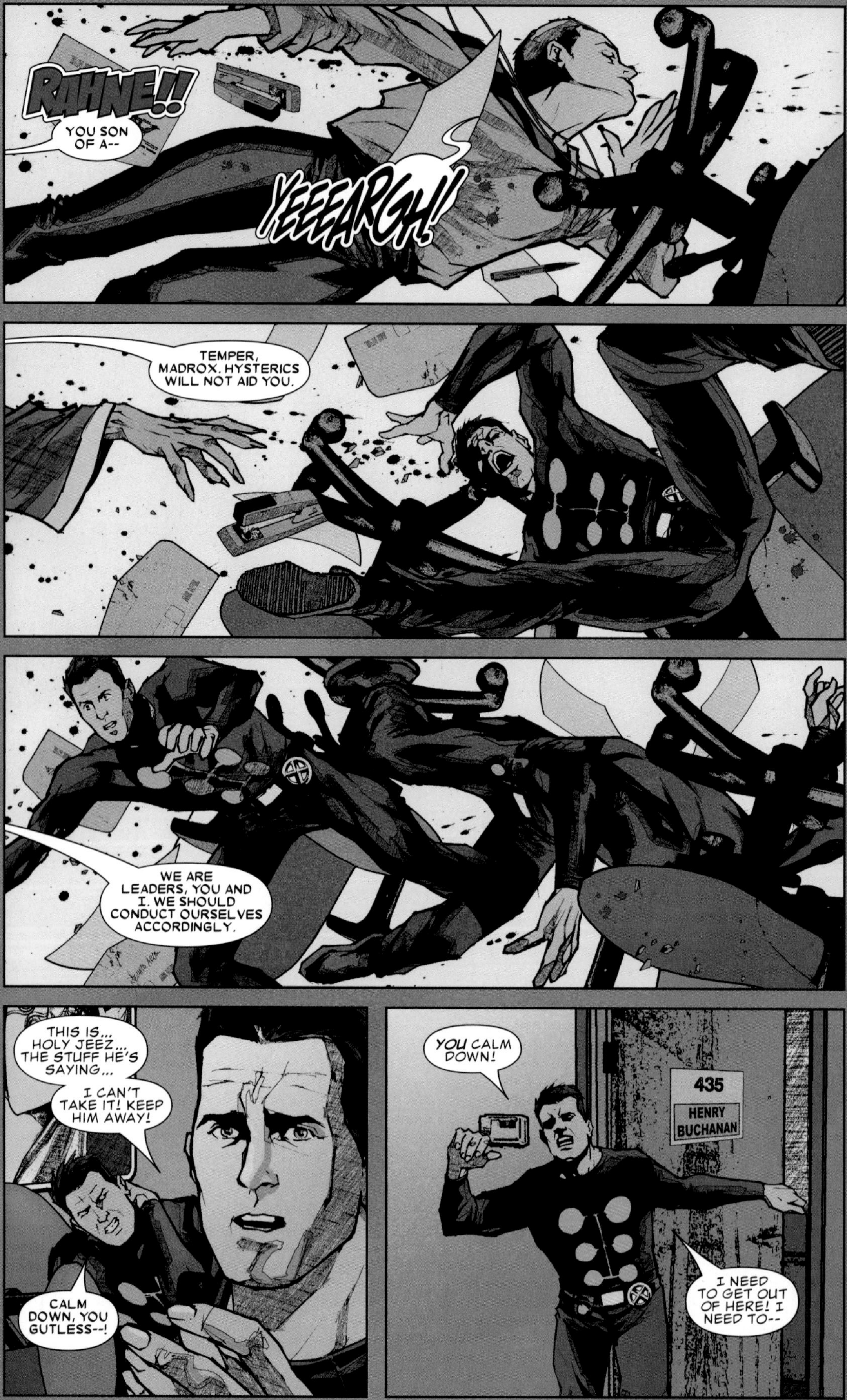
RAHNE!!
YOU SON OF A--
YEEEARGH!
TEMPER, MADROX. HYSTERICS WILL NOT AID YOU.
WE ARE LEADERS, YOU AND I. WE SHOULD CONDUCT OURSELVES ACCORDINGLY.
THIS IS... HOLY JEEZ... THE STUFF HE'S SAYING...
I CAN'T TAKE IT! KEEP HIM AWAY!
CALM DOWN, YOU GUTLESS--!
YOU CALM DOWN!
435
HENRY BUCHANAN
I NEED TO GET OUT OF HERE! I NEED TO--

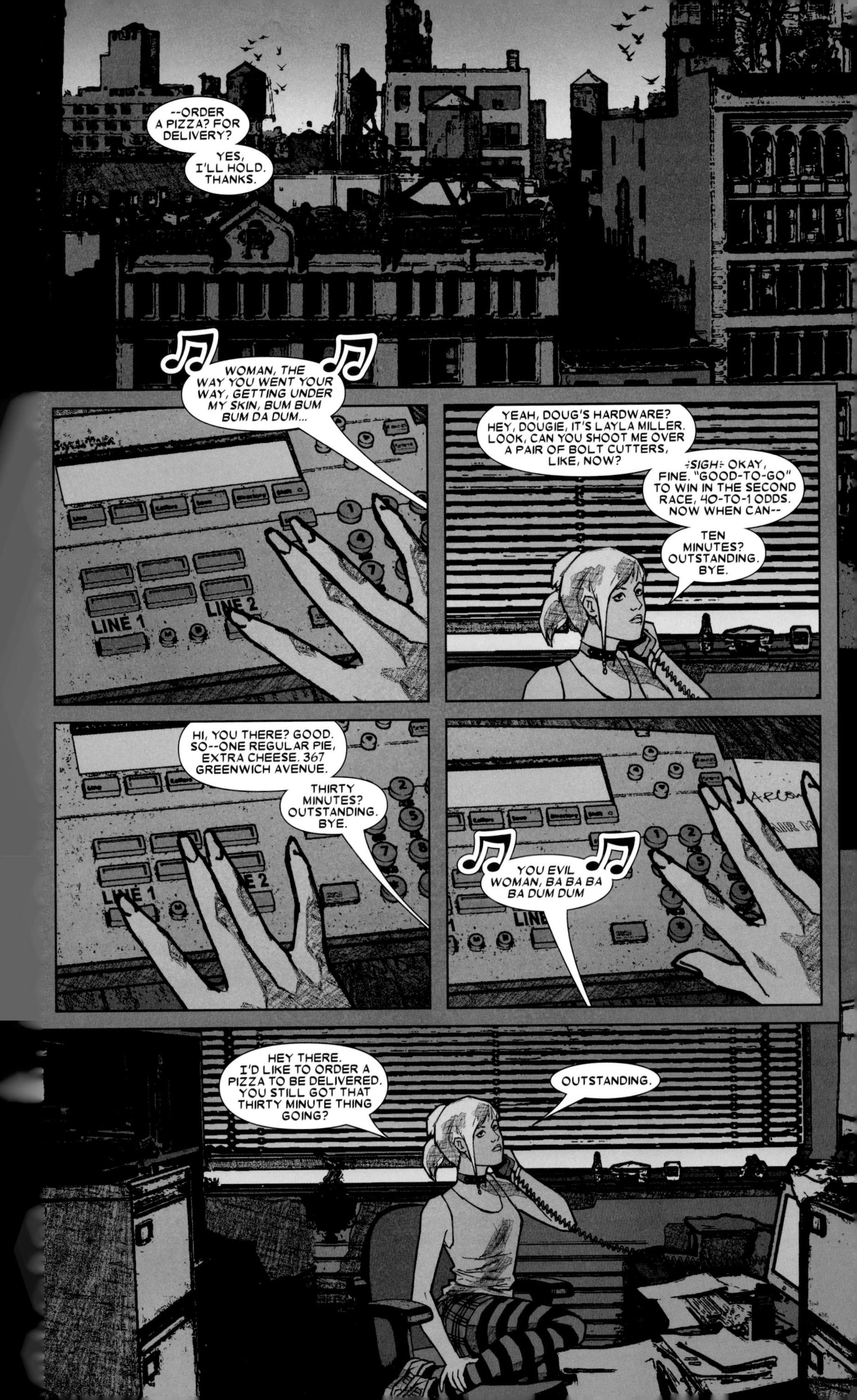
--ORDER A PIZZA? FOR DELIVERY?
YES, I'LL HOLD. THANKS.
WOMAN, THE WAY YOU WENT YOUR WAY, GETTING UNDER MY SKIN, BUM BUM BUM DA DUM...
LINE 1
LINE 2
YEAH, DOUG'S HARDWARE? HEY, DOUGIE, IT'S LAYLA MILLER. LOOK, CAN YOU SHOOT ME OVER A PAIR OF BOLT CUTTERS, LIKE, NOW?
-SIGH- OKAY, FINE. "GOOD-TO-GO" TO WIN IN THE SECOND RACE, 40-TO-1 ODDS. NOW WHEN CAN--
TEN MINUTES? OUTSTANDING. BYE.
HI, YOU THERE? GOOD. SO--ONE REGULAR PIE, EXTRA CHEESE. 367 GREENWICH AVENUE.
THIRTY MINUTES? OUTSTANDING. BYE.
YOU EVIL WOMAN, BA BA BA BA DUM DUM
HEY THERE. I'D LIKE TO ORDER A PIZZA TO BE DELIVERED. YOU STILL GOT THAT THIRTY MINUTE THING GOING?
OUTSTANDING.

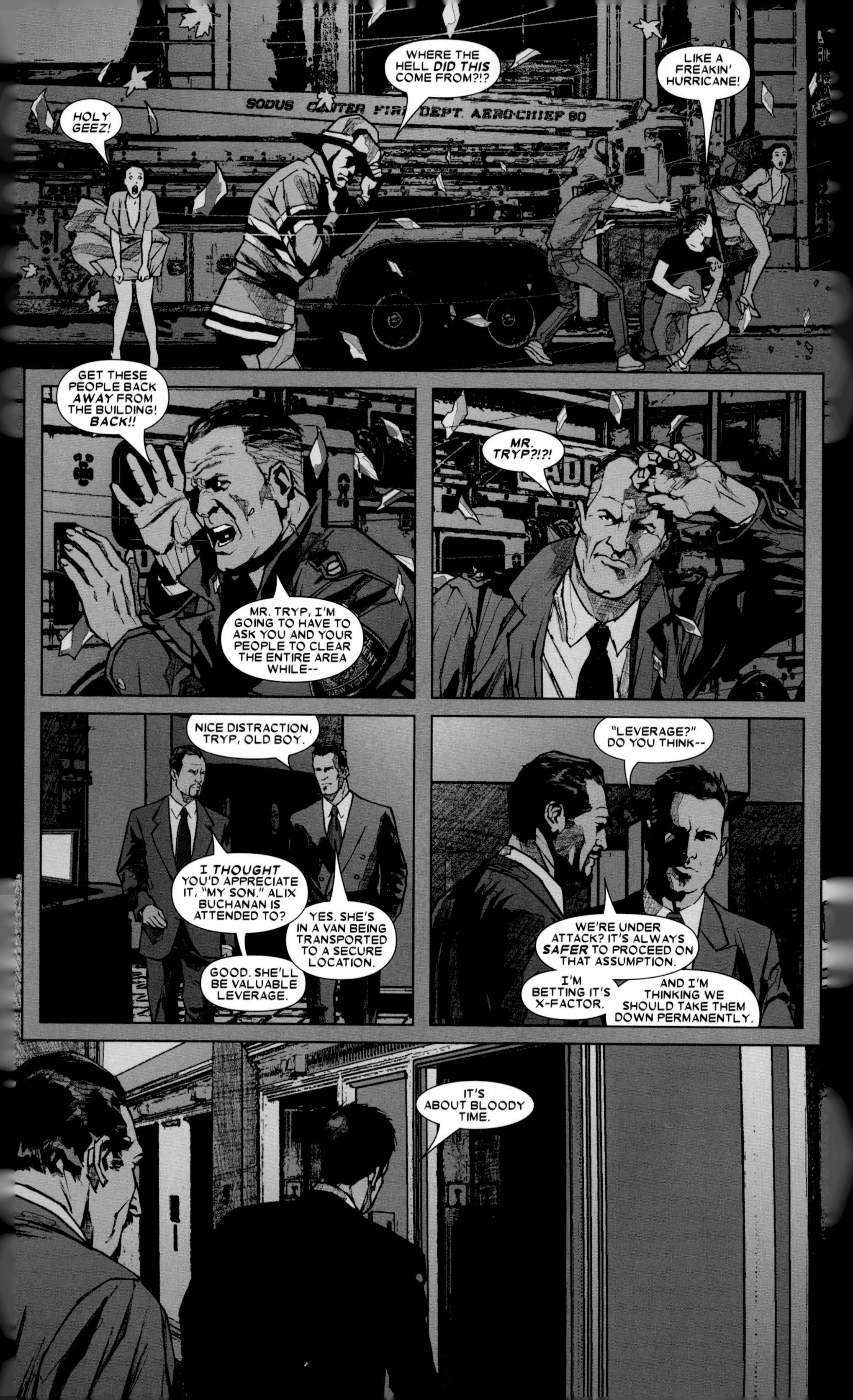
HOLY GEEZ!
WHERE THE HELL DID THIS COME FROM?!?
LIKE A FREAKIN' HURRICANE!
GET THESE PEOPLE BACK AWAY FROM THE BUILDING! BACK!!
MR. TRYP, I'M GOING TO HAVE TO ASK YOU AND YOUR PEOPLE TO CLEAR THE ENTIRE AREA WHILE--
MR. TRYP?!?!
NICE DISTRACTION, TRYP, OLD BOY.
I THOUGHT YOU'D APPRECIATE IT, "MY SON." ALIX BUCHANAN IS ATTENDED TO?
YES. SHE'S IN A VAN BEING TRANSPORTED TO A SECURE LOCATION.
GOOD. SHE'LL BE VALUABLE LEVERAGE.
"LEVERAGE?" DO YOU THINK--
WE'RE UNDER ATTACK? IT'S ALWAYS SAFER TO PROCEED ON THAT ASSUMPTION.
I'M BETTING IT'S X-FACTOR.
AND I'M THINKING WE SHOULD TAKE THEM DOWN PERMANENTLY.
IT'S ABOUT BLOODY TIME.

HEY, THERESA! GET IN HERE! THERE'S SOME STUFF IN HERE YOU SHOULD BE CHECKING OUT...

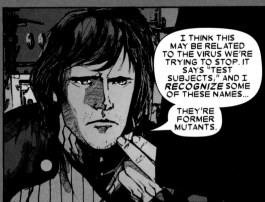

I THINK THIS MAY BE RELATED TO THE VIRUS WE'RE TRYING TO STOP. IT SAYS "TEST SUBJECTS," AND I *RECOGNIZE* SOME OF THESE NAMES...

THEY'RE FORMER MUTANTS.

THERESA! YO, "SCREAMING MIMI?" YOU COPYING THIS...?

I HEAR YOU, *RIC.* I'M JUST...

A LITTLE DISTRACTED.

IT APPEARS SINGULARITY INVESTIGATIONS IS RATHER WELL ARMED.

HOW WELL ARMED?

PRETTY DARNED.

MONET, CAN YOU--?

CALM DOWN, FOR GOD'S SAKE, WILL YOU, JAMIE? I CAN'T SENSE A THING IF YOU'RE THIS FRANTIC...

WHAT YOU WILL SENSE IS THAT THE YOUNG LADY IS IN DEEP SHOCK. SHE WILL RECOVER.

HUMANITY, HOWEVER, WILL NOT, IF YOU PERSIST IN YOUR COURSE TO SAFEGUARD THE FORMER MUTANTS.

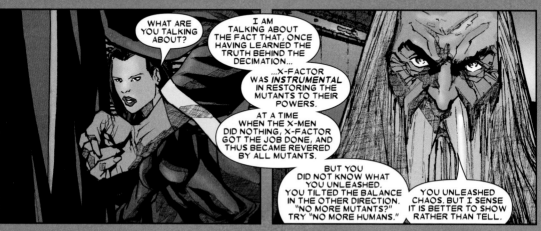

WHAT ARE YOU TALKING ABOUT?

I AM TALKING ABOUT THE FACT THAT, ONCE HAVING LEARNED THE TRUTH BEHIND THE DECIMATION...

...X-FACTOR WAS INSTRUMENTAL IN RESTORING THE MUTANTS TO THEIR POWERS.

AT A TIME WHEN THE X-MEN DID NOTHING, X-FACTOR GOT THE JOB DONE, AND THUS BECAME REVERED BY ALL MUTANTS.

BUT YOU DID NOT KNOW WHAT YOU UNLEASHED. YOU TILTED THE BALANCE IN THE OTHER DIRECTION. "NO MORE MUTANTS?" TRY "NO MORE HUMANS."

YOU UNLEASHED CHAOS. BUT I SENSE IT IS BETTER TO SHOW RATHER THAN TELL.

AND TAPPING YOUR PSYCHIC POWERS WILL ENABLE ME TO...

SORRY, CASPER. YOU'RE NOT GETTING YOUR GHOSTLY HANDS ON ME.

FORTUNATELY ENOUGH...

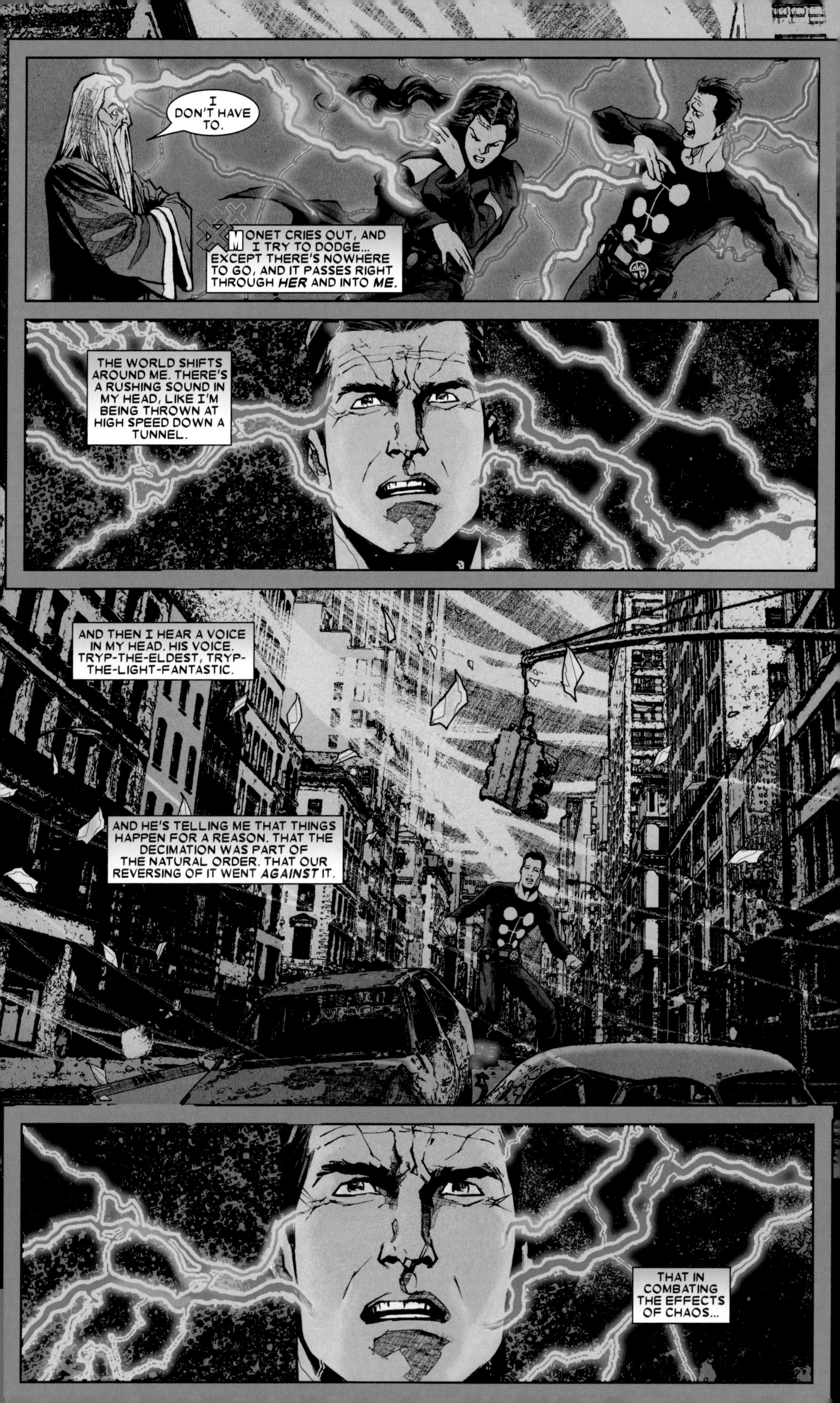
I DON'T HAVE TO.
MONET CRIES OUT, AND I TRY TO DODGE... EXCEPT THERE'S NOWHERE TO GO, AND IT PASSES RIGHT THROUGH *HER* AND INTO *ME.*
THE WORLD SHIFTS AROUND ME. THERE'S A RUSHING SOUND IN MY HEAD, LIKE I'M BEING THROWN AT HIGH SPEED DOWN A TUNNEL.
AND THEN I HEAR A VOICE IN MY HEAD. HIS VOICE. TRYP-THE-ELDEST, TRYP-THE-LIGHT-FANTASTIC.
AND HE'S TELLING ME THAT THINGS HAPPEN FOR A REASON. THAT THE DECIMATION WAS PART OF THE NATURAL ORDER. THAT OUR REVERSING OF IT WENT *AGAINST* IT.
THAT IN COMBATING THE EFFECTS OF CHAOS...

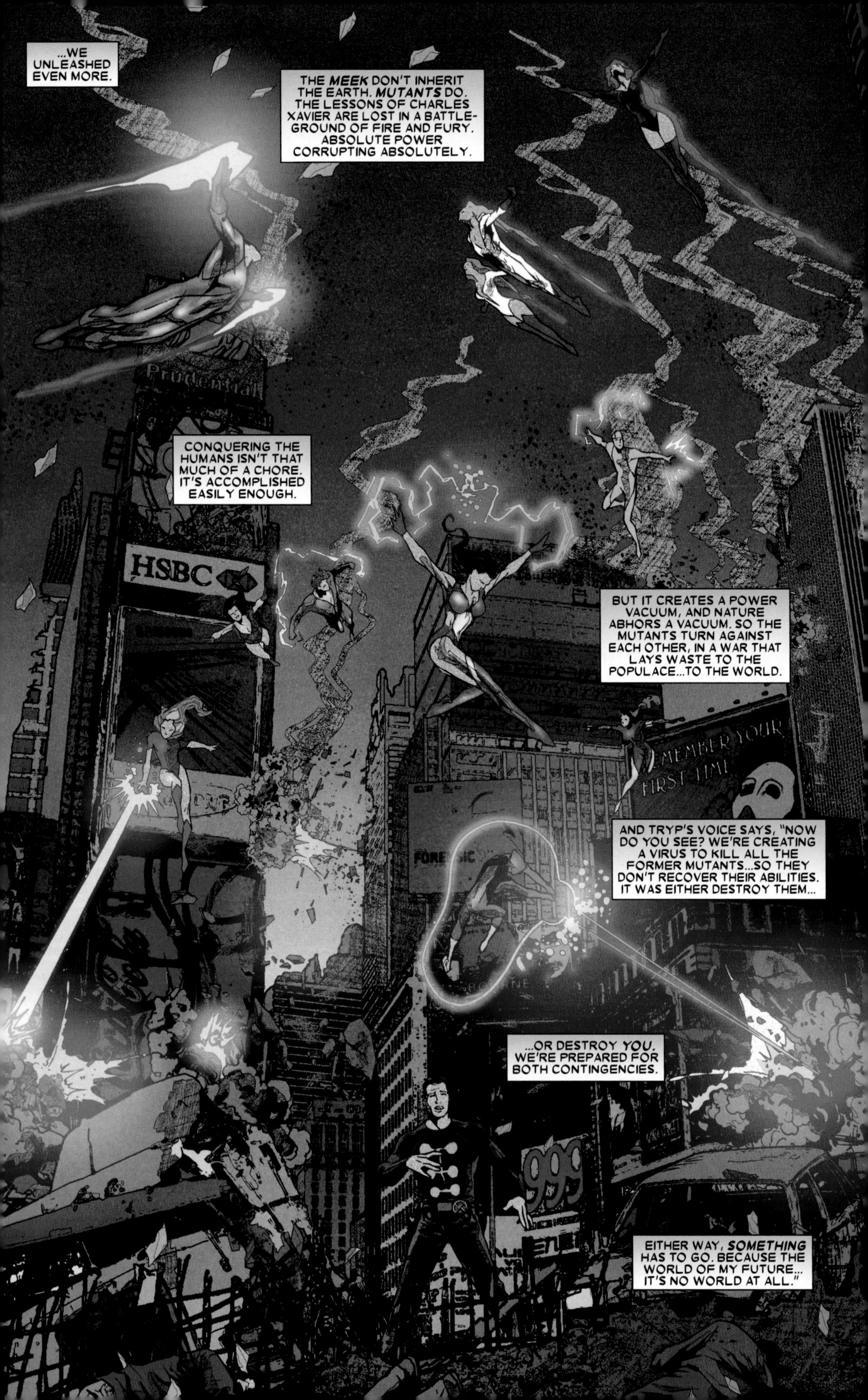
...WE UNLEASHED EVEN MORE.
THE MEEK DON'T INHERIT THE EARTH. MUTANTS DO. THE LESSONS OF CHARLES XAVIER ARE LOST IN A BATTLE-GROUND OF FIRE AND FURY. ABSOLUTE POWER CORRUPTING ABSOLUTELY.
Prudential
CONQUERING THE HUMANS ISN'T THAT MUCH OF A CHORE. IT'S ACCOMPLISHED EASILY ENOUGH.
HSBC
BUT IT CREATES A POWER VACUUM, AND NATURE ABHORS A VACUUM. SO THE MUTANTS TURN AGAINST EACH OTHER, IN A WAR THAT LAYS WASTE TO THE POPULACE...TO THE WORLD.
FIRST TIME
AND TRYP'S VOICE SAYS, "NOW DO YOU SEE? WE'RE CREATING A VIRUS TO KILL ALL THE FORMER MUTANTS...SO THEY DON'T RECOVER THEIR ABILITIES. IT WAS EITHER DESTROY THEM...
...OR DESTROY YOU. WE'RE PREPARED FOR BOTH CONTINGENCIES.
999
EITHER WAY, SOMETHING HAS TO GO. BECAUSE THE WORLD OF MY FUTURE... IT'S NO WORLD AT ALL."

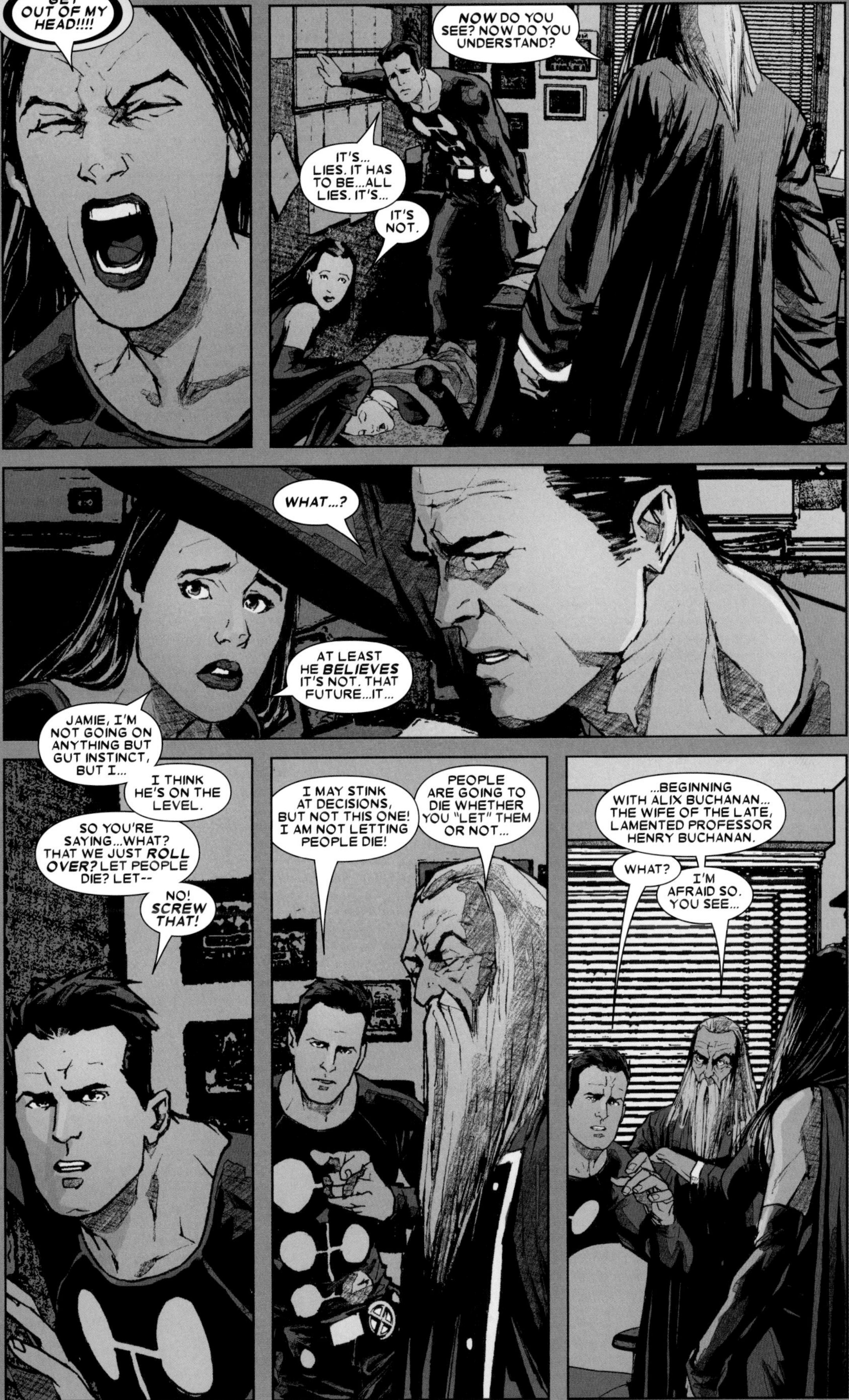
GET OUT OF MY HEAD!!!!
NOW DO YOU SEE? NOW DO YOU UNDERSTAND?
IT'S... LIES. IT HAS TO BE...ALL LIES. IT'S...
IT'S NOT.
WHAT...?
AT LEAST HE BELIEVES IT'S NOT. THAT FUTURE...IT...
JAMIE, I'M NOT GOING ON ANYTHING BUT GUT INSTINCT, BUT I...
I THINK HE'S ON THE LEVEL.
SO YOU'RE SAYING...WHAT? THAT WE JUST ROLL OVER? LET PEOPLE DIE? LET--
NO! SCREW THAT!
I MAY STINK AT DECISIONS, BUT NOT THIS ONE! I AM NOT LETTING PEOPLE DIE!
PEOPLE ARE GOING TO DIE WHETHER YOU "LET" THEM OR NOT...
...BEGINNING WITH ALIX BUCHANAN... THE WIFE OF THE LATE, LAMENTED PROFESSOR HENRY BUCHANAN.
WHAT?
I'M AFRAID SO. YOU SEE...

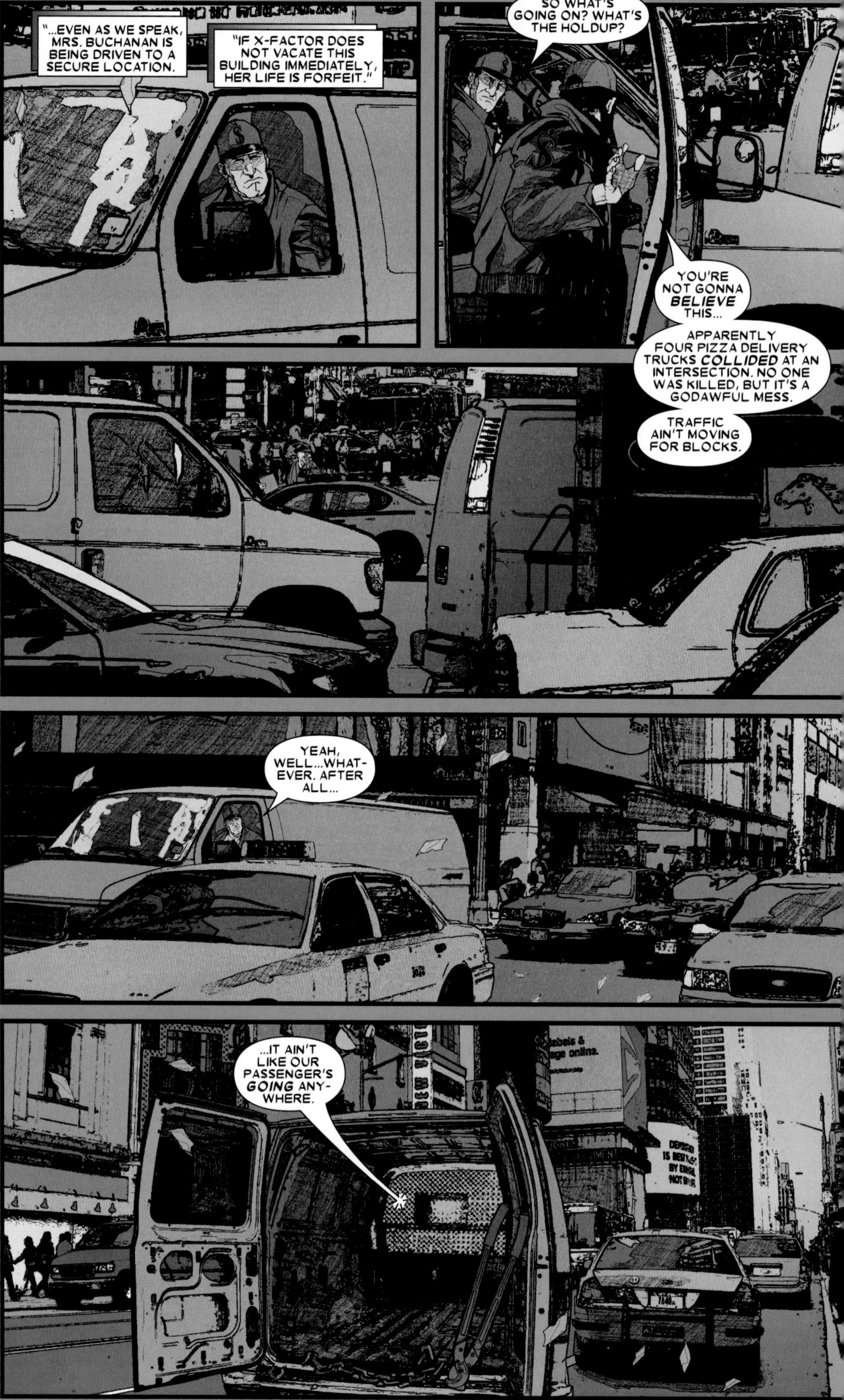
"...EVEN AS WE SPEAK, MRS. BUCHANAN IS BEING DRIVEN TO A SECURE LOCATION.
"IF X-FACTOR DOES NOT VACATE THIS BUILDING IMMEDIATELY, HER LIFE IS FORFEIT."
SO WHAT'S GOING ON? WHAT'S THE HOLDUP?
YOU'RE NOT GONNA *BELIEVE* THIS...
APPARENTLY FOUR PIZZA DELIVERY TRUCKS *COLLIDED* AT AN INTERSECTION. NO ONE WAS KILLED, BUT IT'S A GODAWFUL MESS.
TRAFFIC AIN'T MOVING FOR BLOCKS.
YEAH, WELL...WHAT-EVER. AFTER ALL...
...IT AIN'T LIKE OUR PASSENGER'S *GOING* ANY-WHERE.

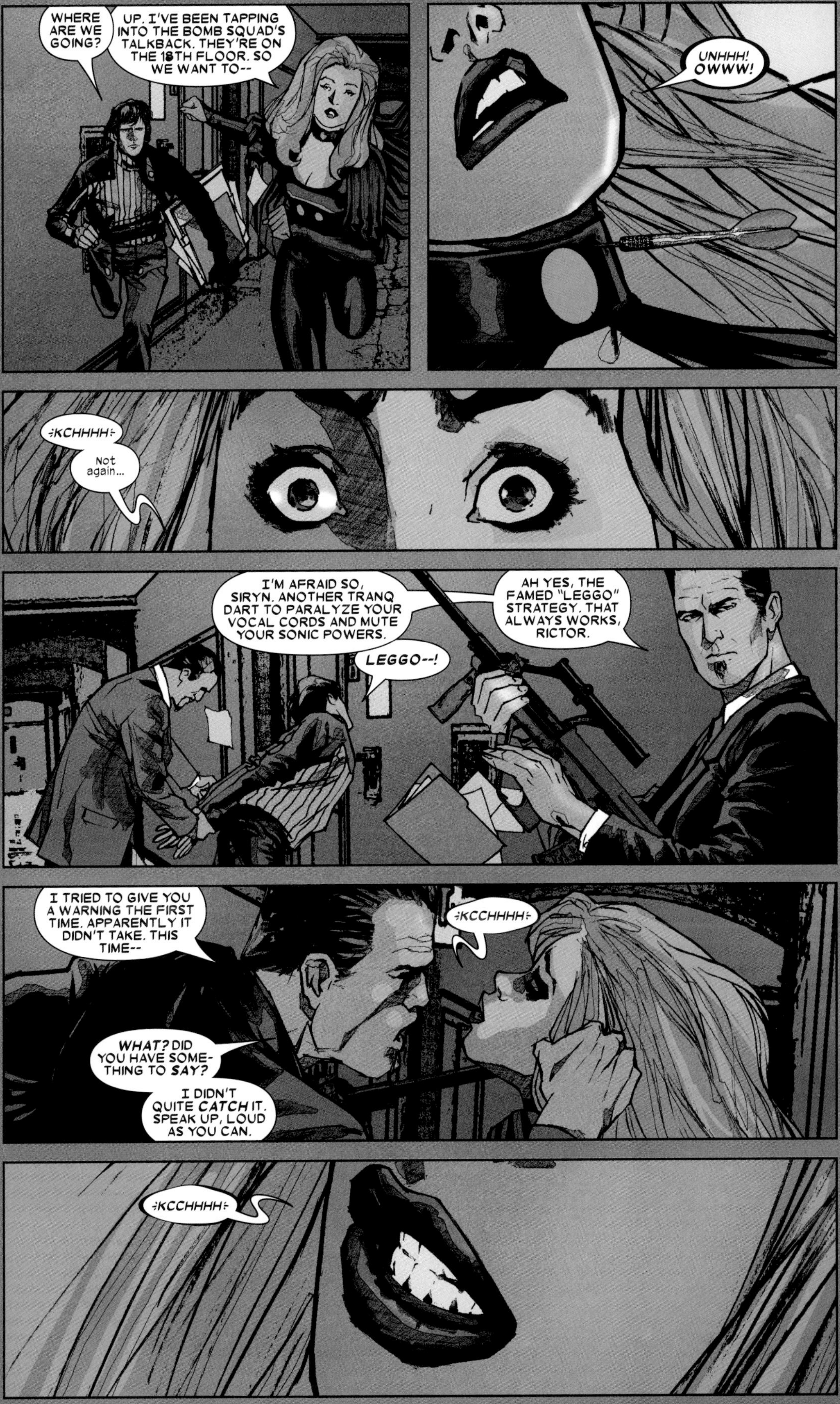
WHERE ARE WE GOING?
UP. I'VE BEEN TAPPING INTO THE BOMB SQUAD'S TALKBACK. THEY'RE ON THE 18TH FLOOR. SO WE WANT TO--
UNHHH! OWWW!
KCHHHH
Not again...
I'M AFRAID SO, SIRYN. ANOTHER TRANQ DART TO PARALYZE YOUR VOCAL CORDS AND MUTE YOUR SONIC POWERS.
LEGGO--!
AH YES, THE FAMED "LEGGO" STRATEGY. THAT ALWAYS WORKS, RICTOR.
I TRIED TO GIVE YOU A WARNING THE FIRST TIME. APPARENTLY IT DIDN'T TAKE. THIS TIME--
KCCHHHH
WHAT? DID YOU HAVE SOMETHING TO SAY?
I DIDN'T QUITE CATCH IT. SPEAK UP, LOUD AS YOU CAN.
KCCHHHH

KEVLAR... COLLAR...YOU SLIMEBAG...YOU THINK I WASN'T PREPARED THIS TIME...?

OH, N—

SHKRSSSSSSSSSSSSSSSS

UNHHHH!!

WHUMP

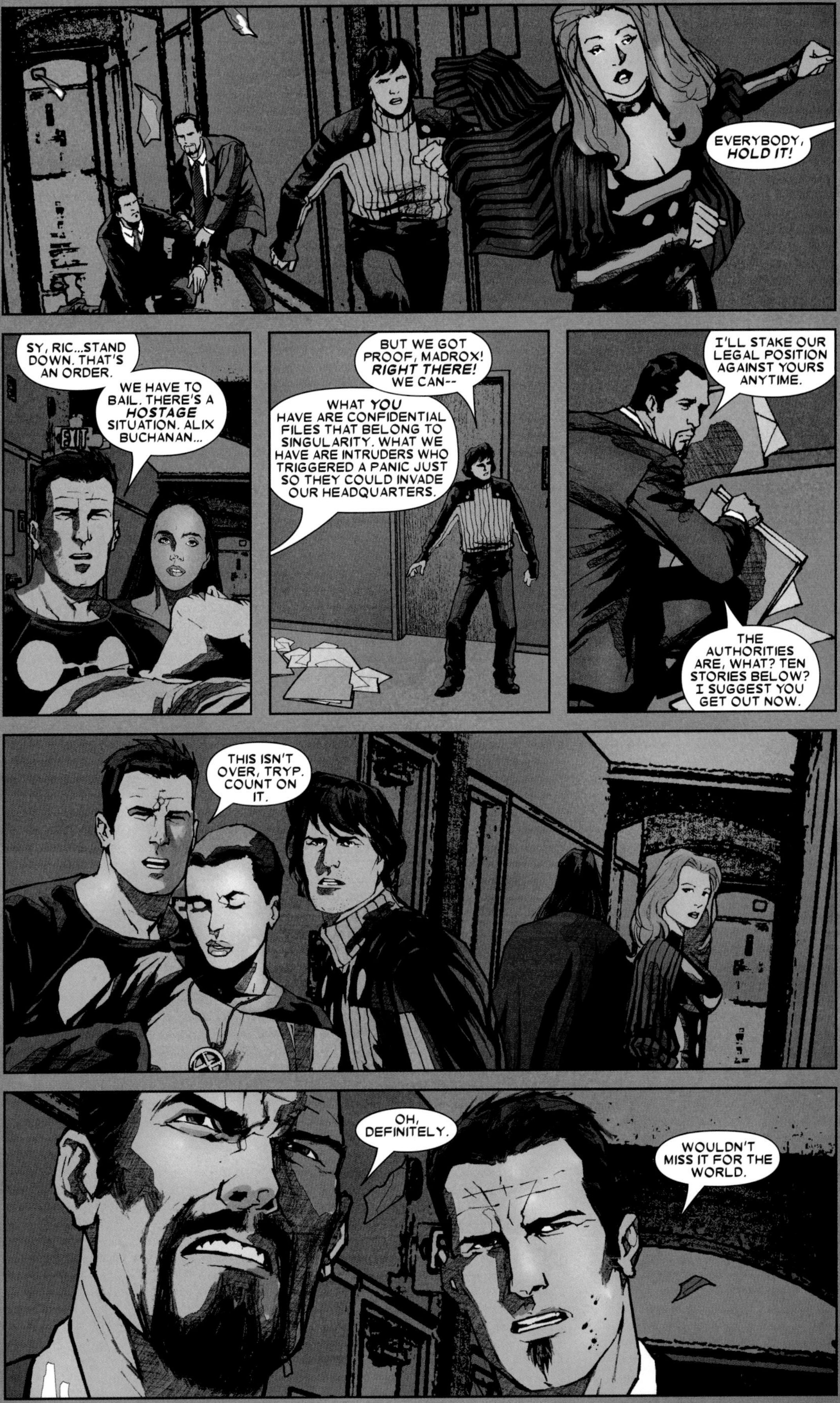
EVERYBODY, HOLD IT!
SY, RIC...STAND DOWN. THAT'S AN ORDER.
WE HAVE TO BAIL. THERE'S A HOSTAGE SITUATION. ALIX BUCHANAN...
EXIT
BUT WE GOT PROOF, MADROX! RIGHT THERE! WE CAN--
WHAT YOU HAVE ARE CONFIDENTIAL FILES THAT BELONG TO SINGULARITY. WHAT WE HAVE ARE INTRUDERS WHO TRIGGERED A PANIC JUST SO THEY COULD INVADE OUR HEADQUARTERS.
I'LL STAKE OUR LEGAL POSITION AGAINST YOURS ANYTIME.
THE AUTHORITIES ARE, WHAT? TEN STORIES BELOW? I SUGGEST YOU GET OUT NOW.
THIS ISN'T OVER, TRYP. COUNT ON IT.
OH, DEFINITELY.
WOULDN'T MISS IT FOR THE WORLD.

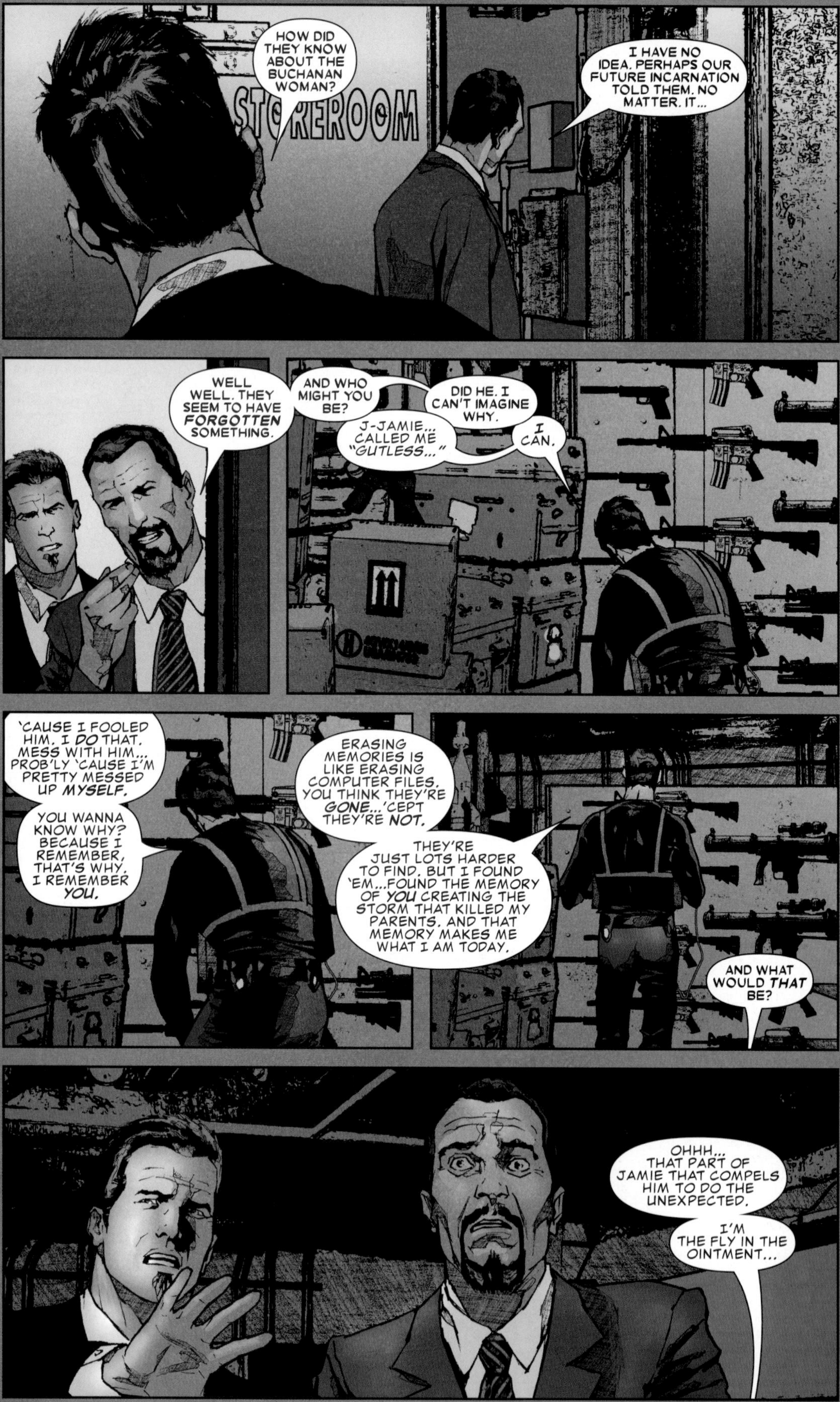
STOREROOM
HOW DID THEY KNOW ABOUT THE BUCHANAN WOMAN?
I HAVE NO IDEA. PERHAPS OUR FUTURE INCARNATION TOLD THEM. NO MATTER. IT...
WELL WELL. THEY SEEM TO HAVE *FORGOTTEN* SOMETHING.
AND WHO MIGHT YOU BE?
J-JAMIE... CALLED ME *"GUTLESS..."*
DID HE. I CAN'T IMAGINE WHY.
I CAN.
'CAUSE I FOOLED HIM. I *DO* THAT. MESS WITH HIM... PROB'LY 'CAUSE I'M PRETTY MESSED UP *MYSELF.*
YOU WANNA KNOW WHY? BECAUSE I REMEMBER, THAT'S WHY. I REMEMBER *YOU.*
ERASING MEMORIES IS LIKE ERASING COMPUTER FILES. YOU THINK THEY'RE *GONE*...'CEPT THEY'RE *NOT.*
THEY'RE JUST LOTS HARDER TO FIND. BUT I FOUND 'EM...FOUND THE MEMORY OF *YOU* CREATING THE STORM THAT KILLED MY PARENTS. AND THAT MEMORY MAKES ME WHAT I AM TODAY.
AND WHAT WOULD *THAT* BE?
OHHH... THAT PART OF JAMIE THAT COMPELS HIM TO DO THE UNEXPECTED.
I'M THE FLY IN THE OINTMENT...

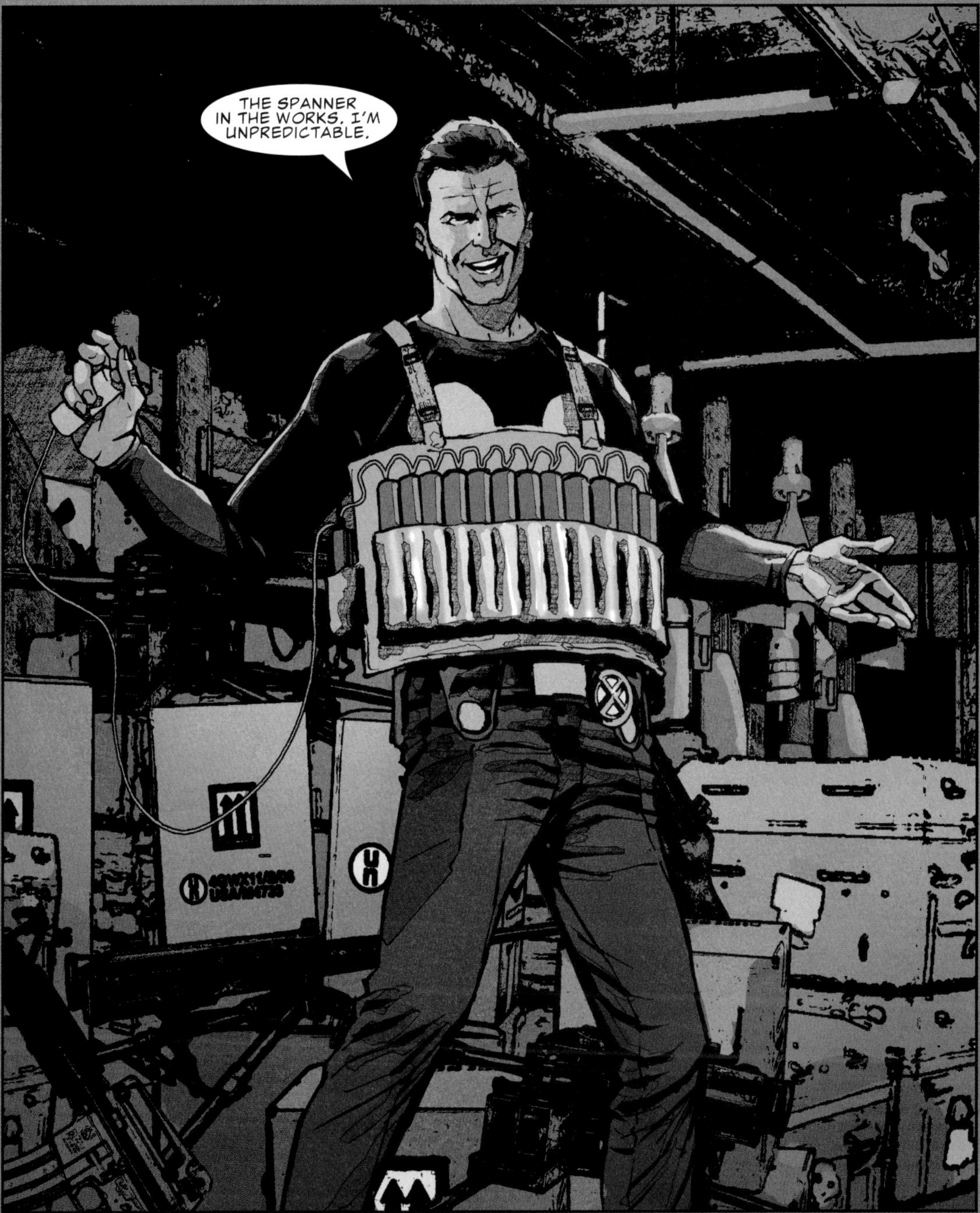
THE SPANNER IN THE WORKS. I'M UNPREDICTABLE.

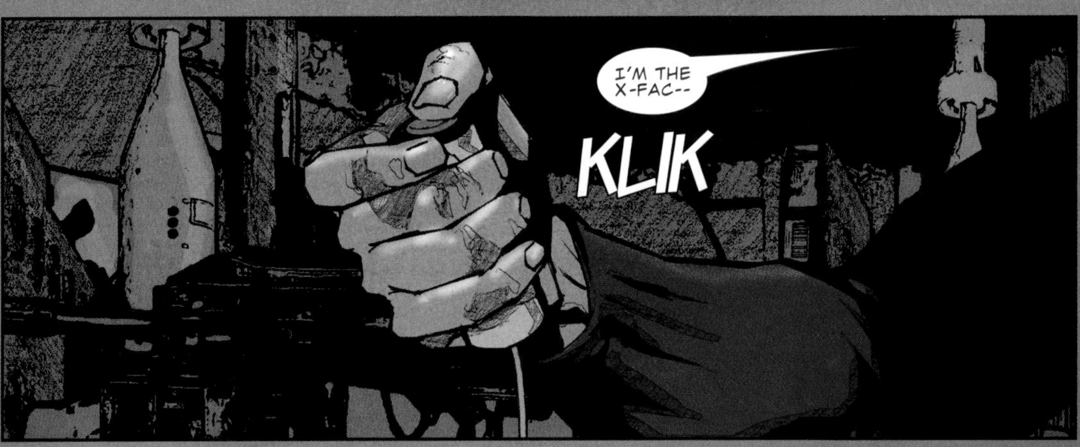
I'M THE X-FAC--
KLIK

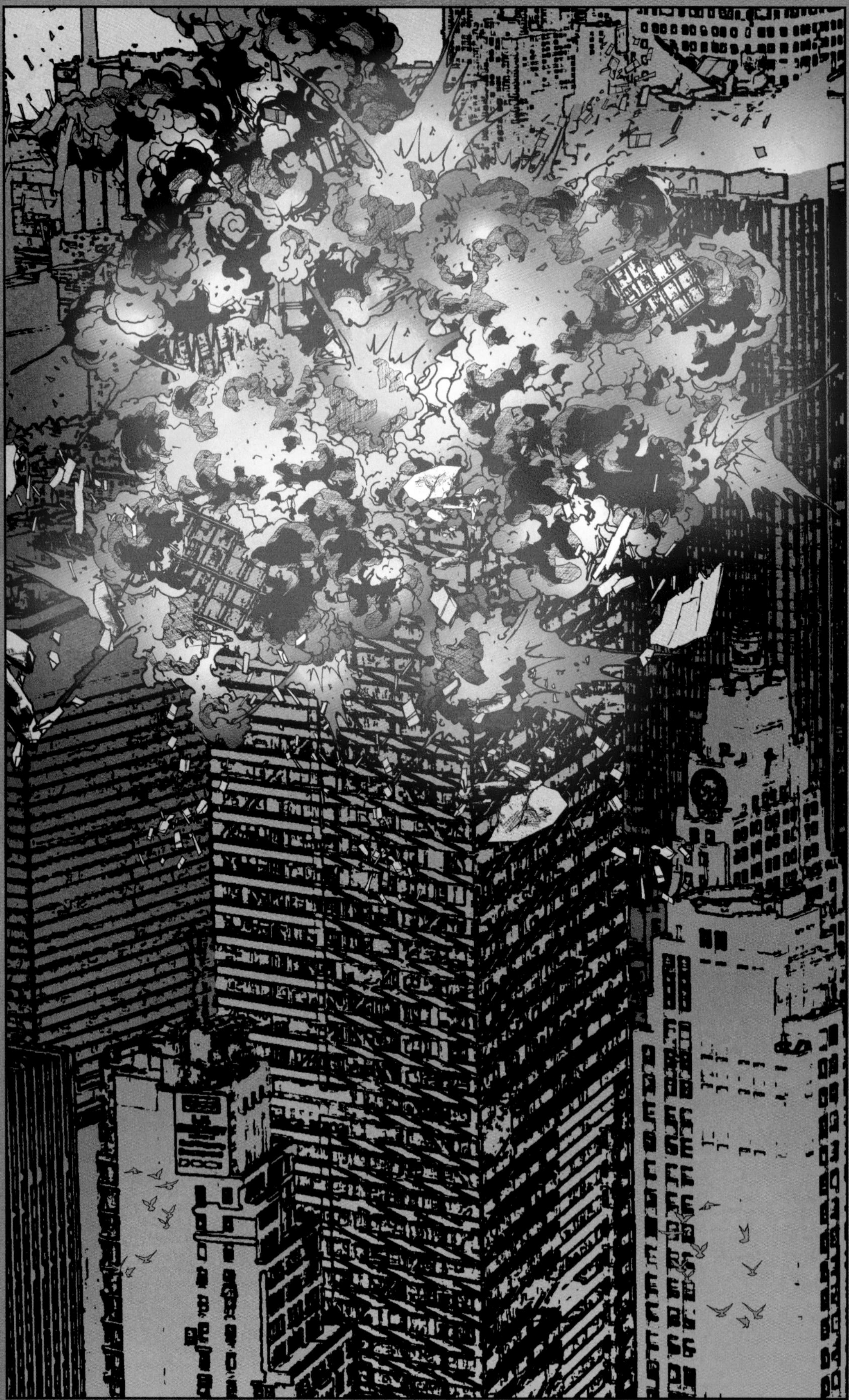

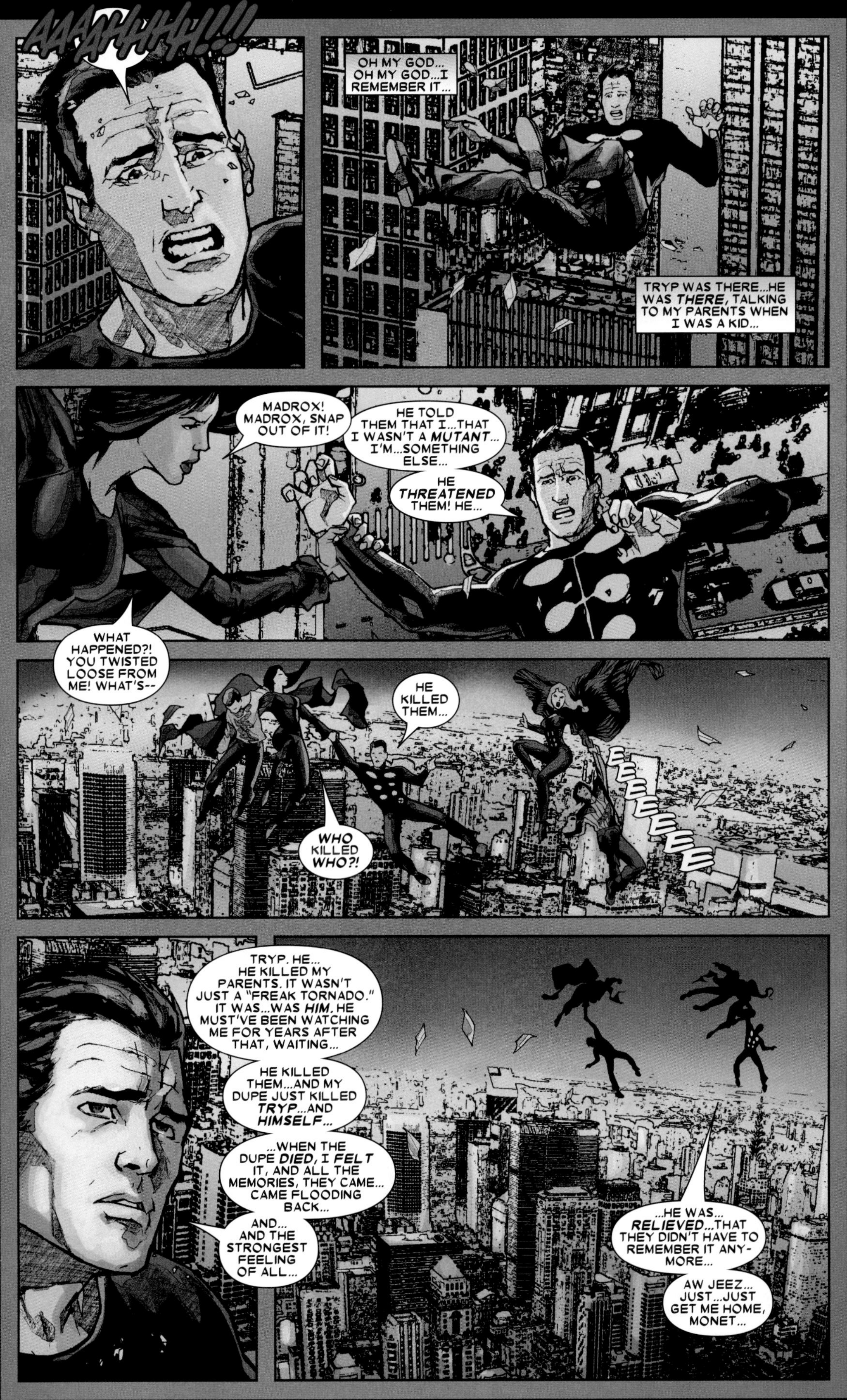
AAAAHHHHH!!!
OH MY GOD... OH MY GOD...I REMEMBER IT...
TRYP WAS THERE...HE WAS THERE, TALKING TO MY PARENTS WHEN I WAS A KID...
MADROX! MADROX, SNAP OUT OF IT!
HE TOLD THEM THAT I...THAT I WASN'T A MUTANT... I'M...SOMETHING ELSE...
HE THREATENED THEM! HE...
WHAT HAPPENED?! YOU TWISTED LOOSE FROM ME! WHAT'S--
HE KILLED THEM...
WHO KILLED WHO?!
EEEEEEE
TRYP. HE... HE KILLED MY PARENTS. IT WASN'T JUST A "FREAK TORNADO." IT WAS...WAS HIM. HE MUST'VE BEEN WATCHING ME FOR YEARS AFTER THAT, WAITING...
HE KILLED THEM...AND MY DUPE JUST KILLED TRYP...AND HIMSELF...
...WHEN THE DUPE DIED, I FELT IT, AND ALL THE MEMORIES, THEY CAME... CAME FLOODING BACK...
AND... AND THE STRONGEST FEELING OF ALL...
...HE WAS... RELIEVED...THAT THEY DIDN'T HAVE TO REMEMBER IT ANY-MORE...
AW JEEZ... JUST...JUST GET ME HOME, MONET...

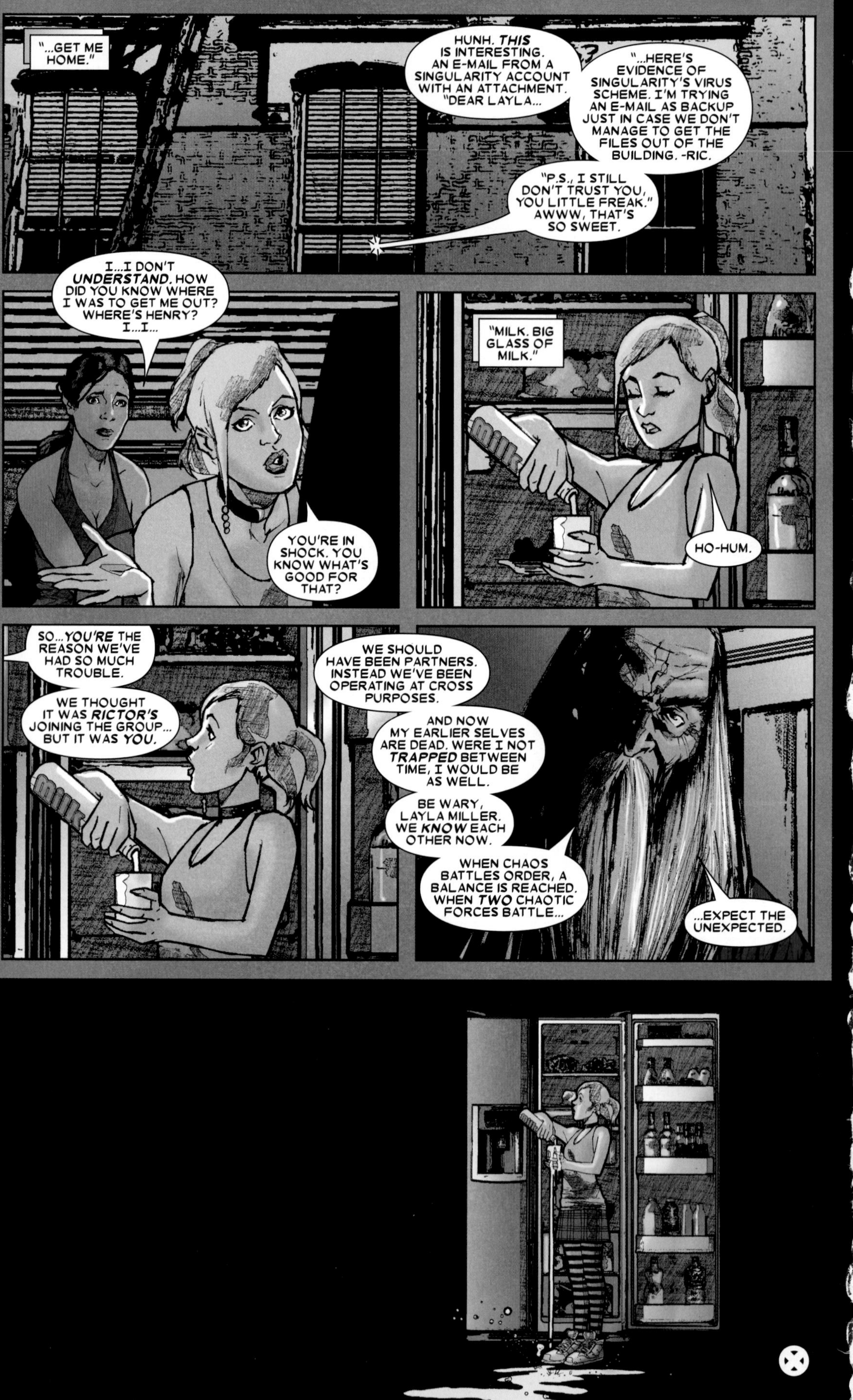
"...GET ME HOME."
HUNH. THIS IS INTERESTING. AN E-MAIL FROM A SINGULARITY ACCOUNT WITH AN ATTACHMENT. "DEAR LAYLA...
"...HERE'S EVIDENCE OF SINGULARITY'S VIRUS SCHEME. I'M TRYING AN E-MAIL AS BACKUP JUST IN CASE WE DON'T MANAGE TO GET THE FILES OUT OF THE BUILDING. -RIC.
"P.S., I STILL DON'T TRUST YOU, YOU LITTLE FREAK." AWWW, THAT'S SO SWEET.
I...I DON'T UNDERSTAND. HOW DID YOU KNOW WHERE I WAS TO GET ME OUT? WHERE'S HENRY? I...I...
YOU'RE IN SHOCK. YOU KNOW WHAT'S GOOD FOR THAT?
"MILK. BIG GLASS OF MILK."
HO-HUM.
SO...YOU'RE THE REASON WE'VE HAD SO MUCH TROUBLE.
WE THOUGHT IT WAS RICTOR'S JOINING THE GROUP... BUT IT WAS YOU.
WE SHOULD HAVE BEEN PARTNERS. INSTEAD WE'VE BEEN OPERATING AT CROSS PURPOSES.
AND NOW MY EARLIER SELVES ARE DEAD. WERE I NOT TRAPPED BETWEEN TIME, I WOULD BE AS WELL.
BE WARY, LAYLA MILLER. WE KNOW EACH OTHER NOW.
WHEN CHAOS BATTLES ORDER, A BALANCE IS REACHED. WHEN TWO CHAOTIC FORCES BATTLE...
...EXPECT THE UNEXPECTED.